"Thomas Pfizenmaier has offered a much-needed boost for the life-changing nature of love. In a broken culture, with the church as the best ray of hope, we are left with one response: lean fully into the transformational love found only in the Triune God. With dozens of historical and current companions helping him craft his message, Pf... accessible primer for the applicable gospel of l...

—STEPHEN A. MACCHIA, founder and presi...
   Leadership Transformations

"If you are concerned that the world is colder and coarser, consider this book. Thomas Pfizenmaier skillfully laces history, story, song, science, and Scripture to draw us into the continuing cosmic drama of God's love in Christ. But the reader must be ready to relinquish passivity to participate in this drama and pivot back to God's love—in short, to become Christ's disciple."

—JOSEPH BYAMUKAMA, founder and team leader, Veracity Fount Uganda

"This important work is a must-read for all of us who hold the belief that love is the cure for all pain. If you were raised in the values of Christianity, you will be moved to revisit the source of your hospitable love."

—SUSAN MACKENTY BRADY, host of *Better Understanding* podcast

"This book is a joy to read, to ponder, and to put into practice. Thomas Pfiezenmaier provides us rich insights into this cultural moment of deep confusion and divisiveness. He explores the big questions of what is true, beautiful, just, and good; what went wrong; and what is our purpose. He then exposes our need for the transcendent, emphasizing the biblical primacy of God's love. In a unique and winsome way, he calls the fearful and weary Western church to learn to love once more as disciples of Jesus."

—TASHA CHAPMAN, professor of educational ministries, Covenant Theological Seminary

"A good book keeps one's interest, stimulates reflection, inspires change. An excellent book includes these but goes further, unveiling vital truths and kindling legitimate hope. And so it is with this book. Thomas Pfizenmaier powerfully describes the necessity of genuine love, the tragic cost of love being lost, and the beautiful, restorative work of the God who loves. Providing deep insights into what it means 'to love one another,' this book inspires hope for a beautifully different world and church."

—MARK PATTERSON, president, Flourish Institute of Theology

# Whatever Became of Love?

# Whatever Became of Love?

An Invitation to Rethink Everything

THOMAS C. PFIZENMAIER

*Foreword by* KENNETH J. BARNES

RESOURCE *Publications* · Eugene, Oregon

WHATEVER BECAME OF LOVE?
An Invitation to Rethink Everything

Resource Publications
An Imprint of Wipf and Stock Publishers
199 W. 8th Ave., Suite 3
Eugene, OR 97401

www.wipfandstock.com

PAPERBACK ISBN: 978-1-6667-7509-9
HARDCOVER ISBN: 978-1-6667-7510-5
EBOOK ISBN: 978-1-6667-7511-2

Dedication

To the Next Generation of Rising Christian Leaders, Some of Whom
It has been my Privilege to Teach (You Know Who You Are ...)

Psalm 78:1–6

# Contents

PART FIVE: Tikkun Olam

# Foreword

KENNETH J. BARNES

July 1, 2016, was supposed to be a homecoming for me as I disembarked at Boston's Logan International Airport, having spent the majority of my adult life, living and working abroad. Instead, it was the beginning of a long and difficult period of disorientation and mourning, as I came to realize that the country I had left in 1993, was very different from the one to which I had returned.

On the surface, it was as though nothing had changed during my quarter-century hiatus. It was comforting to see the little New England town my family eventually settled upon, decked out in red, white and blue bunting, in anticipation of Independence Day celebrations. I reveled in the prospect of firetrucks and marching bands on parade, followed by an indulgence of clam chowder, hot-dogs and watermelon - all paid for with ever familiar "greenbacks!" It was as if the annual festivities had been planned just for my return, and I was sure that I had made the right decision to come "home." Sadly, the euphoria was short-lived, and the stark reality of what psychologists call "reverse culture–shock," bludgeoned my sensibilities and I began to feel like an alien in my own country.

Something had clearly changed, but I wasn't sure what. Was it our national politics? Perhaps, but as child of the 1960's, and 1970s, I could recall the emotional and political intensity of an era that produced race riots in the streets, deadly protests on college campuses, and the toppling of a once popular American president. It seemed to me, that our political differences are no more profound now, than they were then. Some have suggested that it is the so-called "culture wars," but this too seemed quite unlikely. As someone who has travelled the world extensively, I can attest to the fact that no pristine, homogenous, cultures exist, and that all cultures both inform, and are informed, by others. The United States, with its long history of immigration, has always been a place where people of differing beliefs and customs have found social harmony, albeit, with differing opinions on the relative merits of a "melting pot" versus a "patchwork quilt" approach.

No, I thought, it must be something else, but I wasn't sure what. Providentially, I wasn't alone in my dilemma, and I soon found myself in deep and meaningful conversations with a colleague at Gordon-Conwell Theological Seminary, who had also determined, that the problem was far more profound than political incivility, or cultural insensitivity. The problem, as he saw it, was an indisputable and palpable lack of love, not merely in society at large, but more disturbingly, in the church. His thesis sounded shocking to me, but upon further reflection, I have come to the unhappy conclusion, that he is correct. Fortunately, he's decided to do something about it. He's decided to say out-loud what most of us dare not even think, and in the process, offer a theologically sound and Christ-centered alternative to our rapidly devolving dystopia.

The colleague of course, is the author of this book, and his insights are the product of decades serving both church and academia. Viewed through the complex prism of theology, history and discipleship, the "refracted" view of both church and society suggest a culture (indeed a world), that isn't merely postmodern, or post-Christian, but "post-love;" and a world deficient in love, is ultimately unbearable.

The author's thesis is predicated on two basic, and eminently reasonable assumptions. First, is the belief that the world as we have inherited it, is fundamentally "broken." This is based, both on simple observation and the biblical metanarrative. Second is the long-held Christian view that the church, with all its flaws, and its checkered past, is still the world's "last best hope."

It is important to note that while current events and the vulgarity of our late modern culture have piqued the author's religious sensibilities, he is no romantic. He doesn't seek a return to a mythical past when loved reigned supreme and "we all just got along," as no such epoch has ever existed; nor will it on this side of Glory. On the contrary, what the author proposes is a nation and a world, where love isn't merely a mawkish emotion, relegated to greeting cards and dime store novels. He envisions instead, a place where true love, the *agape* of God is both present and available, to a world that is drifting further and further away from the thing it needs most.

To understand how we got to our pitiable state, the author takes us back to the very beginning, to the first expression of *agape* – to the creation of the universe; followed quickly by our own degeneration, and God's next great act of *agape* – our redemption. Calling upon his deep knowledge of Scripture, theology, philosophy, history, and literature, he rightfully concludes that our Enlightenment values, our scientific discoveries, and our postmodern deconstructions, are useless in our quest for meaning and purpose, for truth, justice, beauty and "wholeness," because we misunderstand the nature of our "brokenness." Our brokenness isn't merely a physical, or emotional, or psychological, or societal problem—our brokenness is a spiritual problem, because it is the byproduct of our estrangement from the God who *is* love. The divine ontology of *agape* is the key to our redemption, leading the author to conclude that we are currently in a "metanoia moment," for the church and for the world.

It is at this point, that the pastor's heart and the theologian's mind are most in sync, as he draws upon his time as the senior pastor of a large suburban church in the Midwest, and dean of a prominent Evangelical seminary. Unafraid to criticize the very institutions in which he himself was "spiritually formed," he notes that the church doesn't need better preachers, apologists, or theologians, it needs better "lovers." He has witnessed firsthand what can happen when, like the church in Ephesus (Rev. 2:1–7), we concentrate so much on doctrinal "purity" that we "lose our first love," and our "lampstand" is withdrawn. When that happens, we lose the light of Christ, the light of God's *agape*, and therefore the "light of the world."

What then are people of faith to do? Are we to sit back and watch as the church's influence continues to wane, and the world groans under the weight of unconstrained evil? Or are we to revive the ancient custom of *tikkun olam* (the repair of the world)? The author forcefully stakes his claim for the latter, beginning with a reminder that corporate renewal begins with personal revitalization, calling upon individuals and institutions to fulfill the Great Commission, by first becoming, then making true Disciples of Jesus Christ.

The author warns that such a task is not without its challenges. It will require seminaries to reimagine how they train clergy and what they actually train them for. It will require churches to regain their "first love," which is *agape* itself. It will require followers of Jesus Christ to be "salt and light" in their communities and in society at large; unafraid to speak prophetically against the "spirit of the age," while at the same time, being lovers of neighbor and lovers of God. It will require a re-centering of our culture's predilections for temporal concerns, self-aggrandizement, and decadence, with genuine concern for the "other," the common good, and transcendence. It is no easy task indeed, but one that is both necessary and worthwhile.

"Life," the author states, "is an invitation," and so too, is this book. It is an invitation to reimagine the world in which we live and the worlds that await us, both temporal and eternal. The former is unmistakably before us, the latter, less obvious, and will ultimately be decided by whatever becomes of love.

# Preface

Some days are seared into our memories forever. One of them for me was a balmy seventy–four–degree Oklahoma morning in the mid–1980s. I got up early and walked outside with a cup of coffee in hand to greet that unusually warm early spring day. By nightfall, the temperature had dropped to fourteen degrees. During the day I could feel the mercury plunge hour by hour. It was like standing in a small room where someone had turned the air conditioning on full blast—except I was standing outside. The descending arctic front drove the warm gulf air back into Texas, and we were left shivering into the night.

The world feels that way to me now, like its temperature is dropping. It feels colder, windier, darker—and stormier. It's somehow different from the world I've always known. Something has changed, something has shifted. It isn't simply that events are discouraging; we've always had that. Wars, famines, disease, and murder have populated the papers and news since I've been reading and listening, and throughout history. It's something deeper, something centrifugal pulling us apart in a world spinning faster and faster, while we're all holding on for dear life.

As I've thought about this over the last few years, I've realized that the crisis of our time is not political. It is not economic. It is not social. It is not ecological. These are only symptoms of the foundational crisis of our time.

Our crisis is a crisis of love. We in the West are immersed in a long forgetting of love. Until we're reminded of love, and converted to love, the disintegration will continue unabated. The pulling will become tearing as the strain on human relationships grows, accelerating until we're finally undone and our civilization collapses. Like Maverick's test flight passing Mach 10 at the beginning of *Top Gun Maverick*, cracks signaling our breaking apart are already visible. Perhaps collapse will be the cost of starting over and rebuilding. I hope it won't come to that, and I don't believe it's inevitable. But changing our situation will require a true spiritual awakening—a conversion to love.

The uneasiness began for me when I went to work in a theological seminary during the tumultuous election year of 2016. The students' social media postings were blowing up over the various candidates and their platforms. In the following spring, we had student elections. The student candidates were of different races and genders and also had different platforms. Again, social media incandescence resulted. I was puzzled and disturbed. The temperature among us was dropping rapidly. How could a community of men and women supposedly devoted to the Scriptures and to Christ be blown along on these arctic winds of hubris and hostility? It was incomprehensible to me at the time; now it's not. I think I'm beginning to understand how we got here.

This book is set out in five parts. In Part 1, I will explore God's invitation to love, especially as it unfolds in the story we're in. In Part 2, I will examine what authentic love looks like, beginning in the Hebrew Bible and then lasering in on Jesus as he encounters us in the New Testament. Part 3 will suggest that love, like light, is refracted into the world in a variety of ways, all worth exploring. In Part 4 we'll explore the way of return to love. What could that path look like? Finally, in Part 5, I want to talk about what a renaissance of love might look like as we take part in God's *tikkun olam*, his "repair of the world."

Let me make a couple of navigational comments that I hope will help you enjoy your read. First, I'll visit some themes more than once, viewing them from different angles so we can appreciate their nuances, connections, and impacts in different ways. So much of what I want to say is composed of interlocking elements connecting on different levels, like a three-dimensional puzzle or a Rubik's cube. Whenever one part is moved, it effects other things. So, I encourage you to work patiently at it. Take your time. Re-read and think over the things which catch your attention. I tend to believe that these are the moments when God speaks to us in our reading. I hope the effort will be worthwhile as you think freshly about love.

Second, I've invited a lot of voices into this discussion. I have several reasons for this. One is that I think you should know the people who've influenced my thinking on this subject of love. Also, I hope it will prevent parochialism. I've quoted or referred to people across the ages, from biblical writers to early church fathers, from monks in the Middle Ages to modern and postmodern figures. It's important to get out of our own historical neighborhood frequently so that our thinking doesn't become cramped and anachronistic. It's also important to realize how our own thinking has been shaped, often quite unconsciously, by those who've gone before us.

I've also tried to bring many kinds of voices into the conversation. We'll engage the thinking of journalists, scientists, philosophers, and theologians. We'll hear from literary figures, poets, sociologists, political theorists, rabbis, monks, priests, and popes. In other words, this will be fun!

Finally, I want to lay down some curiosity breadcrumbs for you to follow for any of the lines of thought I'm developing, so I've left a host of footnotes with additional comments and references for those who want to go deeper.

Let me add that I am convinced that only love has the power to save. Love is centripetal; it binds us together. Only love can offset and overpower the forces pulling us apart. Love is the warm air that beats back our cold indifference. We must learn to love all over again as we discover that not any kind of love will do. We must become Jesus-formed lovers. This won't be easy, but it must be. For this we were created, and only this kind of love can heal the wounds of the world. We—you and I—are called to a journey into a new kind of life.

And every journey begins with an invitation.

# Acknowledgements

A book is always collaborative work. Various people contribute in various ways and I would like to thank all of you for helping.

For your spiritual and emotional support (prayer and encouragement) in undertaking the work my first thanks goes to my wife Donna, who watched me disappear upstairs into my study day after day for about the last two years. Thanks for encouraging me in being supportive of the sheer amount of time this has taken.

Also, my daughters who check in periodically with "Dad, how's the book coming?" Thanks for your interest, love and support. Also, to wonderful friends who have also shown interest and given encouragement: Jeff and Denise Laveson, Gavin and Janet McGrath, John and Susan Frank, David and Deborah Hudson, John and Alice Tawresey, Reid and Elise Johnson, Mike and Karen Mizrahi. Thank you!

For those of you who have read various sections and chapters and helped refine my thinking and writing—Karen Mason, Ken Barnes, Jack Davis, Susan Brady, Gaylord Enns, Mike Pickard, Duncan Clark, Tom Duchemin, Mario White, Dave Fischer, Jim Beaver, Mike Mizrahi, Dale Naas, and Thomas Womack—who provided the initial edit for the manuscript. Thank you!

For those of you have helped me navigate the publishing world, again Ken Barnes who recommended Wipf and Stock, Thomas Womack, who gave me great resources and advice, Steve Macchia for his wise counsel, and especially my editor at Wipf and Stock, Matt Wimer.

A special thanks to Randy Baker for his faith in my work and ministry and his generous support in collaborating on many kingdom projects with me over these last fifteen years. You and Jackie are a blessing! Thank you!

Finally, as always must be said, any faults, failures, errors, mistakes, blind spots, or shortcomings in the book remain mine alone.

Eastertide
Poulsbo, WA
2023

# *Introduction:* An Invitation to Love

*The Spiritual journey is a call into the unknown.*
*Its Scriptural paradigm is the call of Abraham:*
*"Leave your faither's house, your friends, relatives, and property,*
*and come into the land that I will show you."*

—THOMAS KEATING, *INVITATION TO LOVE*

Life is an invitation—an invitation to love. In accepting that invitation, we become part of a story as broad as the universe and as deep as eternity. It's an invitation to become part of a story that's still being written. It's an invitation to leave where you are and go somewhere else, somewhere new.

When I was a high school sophomore, I was invited to become part of a story—a play, to be precise. I was cast as Tom of Warwick in *Camelot*. It wasn't much of a part, just a few lines at the end of the play. I remember vividly what it felt like to be invited to become part of the cast. Pure joy!

*Camelot*, of course, is the story of King Arthur's court and the knights of the roundtable. There's infidelity in Camelot as Sir Lancelot, the most noble of knights, and Guinevere, Arthur's queen, fall in love. Catastrophe and war ensue. Near the end of the play, the once glorious kingdom is in shambles. At the very end, in the last scene, a stowaway named Tom of Warwick is discovered by King Arthur, who interrogates him only to find in him a young boy who'd heard of the magnificent kingdom. Tom had come to Camelot to become a knight of the roundtable. But young Tom has come too late.

Arthur prohibits the lad from entering the ensuing battle, but commands Tom to return home and spend the rest of his life telling the story of the fabled kingdom, where wisdom, valor, and justice once prevailed. Listen in for a moment:

XX INTRODUCTION: AN INVITATION TO LOVE

*Arthur:* And when did you decide upon this extinct profession? Was your village once protected by knights? Did your father serve a knight? Was your mother once saved by a knight?

*Tom:* Oh, no, milord! I'd never even seen a knight until I stowed away. I only know of them…the stories people tell!

*Arthur:* From the stories people tell…you wish to become…a knight? Now tell me, what do you think you know of the Knights of the Round Table?

*Tom:* I know everything, milord. Might for right! Right for right! Justice for all! A Round Table where all knights would sit. Everything![1]

Camelot was a vision, a goal, a dream, which over time formed out of the mists of history, and in the hands of different authors and writers morphed and was shaped.

Our point here is not to search for the historical Arthur, but to understand the recurring power of the story—a noble kingdom with a noble king. In the telling, we're brought to tears by the tragedy of it all. Like all human visions, goals, and dreams, its perfection dissolved in the acids of human history. And yet the story and legend have transfixed us for centuries. Why?

I believe it's because we all long for Camelot. We long for a noble place with noble people. We long for justice, honor, courage, and fidelity to finally win out. We long for a true king who rules with strength and compassion, with justice and mercy, with truth and goodness. And the curious question is this: "Why?" Why do we long for things we've never known? We're like a blind man longing to paint a landscape, or a deaf man longing to compose music, or a woman born with no taste buds seeking to become a sommelier. It makes no sense unless there was once a time and a place when the blind man could see, and the deaf man could hear, and the tasteless woman could savor. Only when people have had a taste or a touch of something do they long for the thing itself.

Many have reminded us that thirst proves the existence of water. We all want to be invited to play a part in Camelot, but we long for the fullness of the thing, and not just its shadow.

C. S. Lewis was right when he said that all the great myths, the great stories that hold us so tenderly in the grip of astonishment and wonder, draw their power from the True Myth, the primal story of the love of God, and its fullest and final expression in the lavish life, dark death, and radiant

1. Alan Lerner and Frederick Loewe, Camelot, 52. https://www.scribd.com/doc/81524205/Camelot-Script#.

resurrection of Jesus. In Jesus, story has become history; myth has become reality.[2]

Not only is this the story we're searching for and want to find; it's the story we need to enter to discover all things, especially ourselves. In fact, we'll never truly know ourselves apart from this story. We'll be invited to live into other stories, to take up other scripts, yet we'll find that those stories of promised fresh water deliver only saline to our parched lips.

We need to be called into *this* play, to take up our part and live *this* drama into which we've been swept up just by being born. It's a drama still unfolding. From the moment we're born (and before that, really), we live in the tragicomedy of God, and we'll never find ourselves anywhere else no matter how hard we try. Because this is his story, it's inevitably our story as well.

I'm convinced that at the core of all our desires is the desire to be loved. And the corollary to that is the desire to belong. It's in belonging that we experience the true meaning of our lives, because it's in the presence of others that we know love. One can never know love alone. Love requires others. The story we're called into is, at the core, a love story—the *true* love story. This is the primal love story which funds all the others.

## THE PLOT OF OUR STORY

I once knew a man named Frank Bell. He was a member of Arcadia Presbyterian Church, where I served on staff many years ago. One day Frank told me his story. He was an officer in the Army Air Corps, fighting in the skies over Europe in the Second World War. Frank told me that one day, on mission, they were hit by enemy fire, and he was blown out of his bomber. Frank was rendered unconscious by the blast. He told me that when he came to seconds later, he was plummeting through midair. He instinctively reached for his ripcord and his parachute opened, landing him safely on the ground.

That was his story, but it would have been inconceivable to me had I not known the wider story: Frank was involved in a particular battle on a given day; this battle was one of thousands of actions taken in a worldwide war lasting six years; this war was fought over the nature and direction of a civilization. Frank's story was carefully situated in, and connected to, many other stories.

The story of our lives is not only webbed within the matrix of the world we live in, but it's also embedded in the flow of history going back to

2. Lewis, *Weight of Glory*, 119.

the beginning of all things. In fact, the script tells us that our story began before there were "beginnings."

In the most wonderful way, we're not only invited into an ongoing drama, but also privileged to know its author. We might say that the author is also the producer and director of the story. Indeed, it's the author who places his script in our hands, and personally invites us to play our part in his story.

The author is God, and the script is the history he's writing of humanity—of *his* people in particular. In that story we discover who we are, because there we discover love.

# PART ONE

The Story We're In

# 1

# Creation

The story we're invited into has been unfolding for a very long time. It's a story in four acts. Like all enchanting stories, this one begins with a once-upon-a-time statement: "In the beginning God created the heavens and the earth." It's what might be called a nested statement, because it assumes something. It assumes we know who God is. And this is part of the enchantment. Like the appearance of Strider wreathed in pipe-smoke at the Inn of the Prancing Pony in J. R. R. Tolkien's *Lord of the Rings*, we wonder with the hobbits, "Who is that? Why is he here? What does he want?" In one sense, the Bible is simply the story of the answers to those questions. But as we quickly learn in *The Lord of Rings*, the strands of Aragorn's destiny and that of the hobbits will become bound together like DNA helixing to produce a new form of life. The same is true in the story that's ours because it was already his.

As I said at the outset, we're invited into this story. Knowing the plot line—and where we make our appearance—is key to understanding our part. We enter late, in the final act. We need to do some catching up to know what has already been revealed in the first three acts before we come on stage. Only then can we understand the meaning, purpose, and destiny of our lives.

## IS ANYBODY THERE?

The script begins by telling us that its author is eternal, living outside of space-time. The Creator lives in harmonious community within himself as three perfect persons who share one common and perfect nature. This is a divine community of utter love and service. It's a community intent on reflecting its glory into the created universe. This is the Holy Trinity.

God is also a being of enormous power—so powerful that he created all that is. God spoke forth not *out of* nothing, but *into* nothing. Based upon what we learn and detect through telescope as well as microscope, this Author-Creator possesses not only vast power, but infinite intelligence. In fact, one of the most intelligent human beings ever to look through a telescope wrote, "This most beautiful system of the sun, planets, and comets, could proceed only from the counsel and dominion of an intelligent and powerful Being."[1] That was Isaac Newton, and his telescope could see practically nothing compared to the astonishing images we now see through the recently deployed James Webb Space Telescope.

As the script unfurls, we discover that the Creator is not only infinite and intelligent but also a *personal* being who's the source of all personhood. He's a God of unique being, creativity, and love. Indeed, his whole purpose in creating was to open a space in which his love could become fully realized. This God, the script says, created the earth and all life upon it as a reflection of his glory and an arena for his love. At the center of that love, God created his own unique image–bearing creatures—who were to bear that glory and reflect it into the world, building a world of love intended for communion with God.

So, if we ask *why* God created all things, the simple answer is: So that he might love them.

Love by its nature is expansive, always reaching beyond itself to create and bestow good. Nature was created to be love's playground, the place where the internal love among the Father and the Son and the Holy Spirit might become externalized, having room to run, to overflow like a great fountain watering everything in its path and bringing life wherever it goes.

## THE WHY BEHIND THE HOW

In meditating on the meaning of creation, psychologist David Benner writes, "The creation story is seriously misunderstood when it is read as science. Instead, it should be understood as a love poem."[2] I think Benner is right. To read the creation merely as science is like examining a love letter for its grammar and syntax; it's to miss the essential point.

---

1. Newton, *Principia Mathematica*, 544.
2. Benner, *Surrender to Love*, 24.

Why would we think of creation as a love letter? First, the creation supports the beloved (us). Love protects and provides for its beloved, and the creation is extraordinarily fine-tuned to protect and provide for us. As NASA astronomer John O'Keefe writes,

> We are, by astronomical standards, a pampered, cosseted, cherished group of creatures . . . If the universe had not been made with the most exacting precision, we could never have come into existence. It is my view that these circumstances indicate the universe was created for man to live in.[3]

Arno Penzias, a Nobel Prize winner in physics, agrees:

> Astronomy leads us to a unique event, a universe which was created out of nothing, one with the very delicate balance needed to provide exactly the conditions required to permit life, and one which has an underlying (one might say "supernatural") plan.[4]

You can tell a lot about how much someone loves another by the lengths they'll go to demonstrate that love. A few years ago, when we were living in St. Louis, my oldest daughter called me on the phone on my sixtieth birthday. She said she was down at my favorite neighborhood bar and grill with two of her friends, whom I knew. They wanted me to come down so they could buy me a glass of wine to celebrate. Normally I don't have to be asked twice (especially if someone else is buying), but I really didn't want to go. I was tired and just wanted to settle in for the evening. But she bullied and guilt-tripped me (as only an oldest daughter can do) until I caved in. I went to meet them.

When I walked in, a strange thing happened. Standing just inside the door was my college roommate, who lives in Seattle. Then another friend appeared, a fellow pastor living in Oregon. Then friends from Oklahoma and Kansas emerged from the darkness. As it turned out, a whole pile of people had come into town to help me celebrate. My daughter had surreptitiously contacted all of them months before to enlist them in the conspiracy, having sworn them to silence. She'd found accommodations for all of them with our friends in town.

The next day, my friend John and the others made an exquisite birthday dinner for us—beef Wellington with a duxelles mushroom reduction stuffing. John used to own his own restaurant, and let's just say he knows his way around the kitchen. (Speaking of planning, he even packed his own set

---

3. Heeren, *Show Me God: What the Message from Space is Telling Us about God*, 200.
4. Margenau and Varghese, *Cosmos, Bios, and Theos*, 83.

of chef's knives for this trip.) Great appetizers, phenomenal entrée, wonderful desserts, and beautiful wines—it was a night to remember.

Here's my point. My daughters (with great leadership from the oldest) planned a complex and elaborate three-day event around my birthday. They planned all the details, and they planned well in advance. And the planning paid off. So why did they do this? I didn't have to ask. I'm one of those lucky dads who knows his kids love him. Remember, you can tell a lot about how much someone loves you by the lengths they'll go to demonstrate that love. All the planning and preparation on my family's part (not to mention my friends) told me all I needed to know.

My point in regaling you with this story is not simply to embellish my fatherly reputation, but to turn our minds toward God's preparation for the party he has thrown, is throwing, and will continue to throw for *us*. There's a reason that the central image for the kingdom of God in the Bible is a lavish feast. God's preparations for that feast were laid in the creation, but it was planned from all eternity. The plans were unimaginably complex and happened over an immense period of time. The only motivation the script gives us as to *why* it all unfolded is the love of God.

## CHANCES ARE …

God's love for us does nothing but deepen the further we go in the story. We'll certainly focus on this when we talk about Christ's work for our redemption in act three of our drama, but we would miss something essential if we started there. The creation *itself* is a supreme act of love, and the more we gaze into the wonders of its science, the more astonishingly extravagant the love appears. Consider for a moment the implications of just these five scientific realities—and they're just a small sampling.

1. *The extreme fine-tuning of the universe.* Astro-physicist Hugh Ross identified thirty-two characteristics of our universe, and seventy-five for our solar system, which had to be precisely fine-tuned for me to be sitting here typing this. Any slight adjustment to any of them—and poof, no me, and no you. Ross estimates that the probability for randomly attaining the necessary parameters for life support on the earth are $10^{-69}$. To help you wrap your head around that number, Ross writes, "Much less than one chance in one hundred billion trillion trillion trillion exists that even one such planet [like earth] would occur anywhere in the universe."[5] As a result, our universe has been called a Goldilocks universe.

---

5. Ross, "Big Bang Model Refined by Fire," in Dembski, *Mere Creation*, 371.

2. *The perfect balance of four fundamental forces (gravity, electro-magnetic, strong nuclear, and weak nuclear) holding our universe together.* Without this balancing, we wouldn't have a universe. Physicist Paul Davies has said, "The seemingly miraculous concurrence of numerical values that nature has assigned to her fundamental constants must remain the most compelling evidence for an element of cosmic design."[6]

3. *The unique relationship between sunlight and water that allows for sustainable life.* Michael Denton has written, "Water, in one of the most staggeringly fortuitous coincidences in all of nature, lets through only the right light in an infinitesimally tiny region of the [electromagnetic] spectrum."[7]

4. *Single cell complexity.* What we once thought of as a simple basic unit, the cell, has been revealed to be phenomenally complex. In 1978, Cambridge zoologist W. H. Thorpe said that "even the most elementary type of cell constitutes a 'mechanism' unimaginably more complex than any machine yet thought up, let alone constructed, by man."[8]

5. *DNA information complexity.* To say that our DNA is information-laden is the understatement of the year. According to Harvard's Wyss Institute, "It is estimated that 1 gram of DNA can hold up to ~215 petabytes (1 petabyte = 1 million gigabytes) of information, although this number fluctuates as different research teams break new grounds in testing the upper storage limit of DNA." If you don't know what a petabyte is, don't feel badly; I didn't either. But apparently it's a monstrous amount of information.[9] Bill Gates has said, "DNA is like a computer program but far, far more advanced than any software ever created."[10]

## THE GAME IS AFOOT!

Sir Francis Bacon, generally credited as the father of the modern scientific method, wrote a book in 1605 called, *The Advancement of Learning.* Quoting a verse from King Solomon's Proverbs, then taking his word as the marching orders for natural philosophers (scientists) of his time, Bacon

6. Davies, *God and the New Physics*, 189.

7. Denton, *The Wonder of Water*, 113. Cited by Metaxas, *Is Atheism Dead?*, 80.

8. Metaxas, *Is Atheism Dead?*, 94; quoted by Denton in *Evolution: A Theory in Crisis.*

9. Hysolli, "A DNA synthesis and decoding strategy tailored for storing and retrieving digital information," August 6, 2019; https://wyss.harvard.edu/news/save-it-in-dna/#:~:text=It%20is%20estimated%20that%201,upper%20storage%20limit%20of%20DNA.

10. Gates, "DNA like computer software," from *The Road Ahead*, https://www.goodreads.com/quotes/336336-dna-is-like-a-computer-program-but-far-far-more.

helps us understand how people on the cusp of the scientific revolution in England saw their work:

> "The glory of God is to conceal a thing, but the glory of the king is to find it out" (Proverbs 25:2) as if, according to the innocent play of children, the Divine Majesty took delight to hide his works, to the end to have them found out; and as if kings could not obtain a greater honor than to be God's play–fellows in that game.[11]

So, the father of the modern scientific method saw science as a game we play with God. Amazing! This was a scintillating game of hide and seek. Bacon thought God had embedded his secrets in the creation and tasked "the king" to find them out—not unlike children on an Easter egg hunt joyfully going about their business of discovery. In Bacon's time, of course, the king didn't do the heavy lifting; he outsourced it to his natural philosophers (scientists) of the Royal Society.

What we want to hold onto from Bacon is the sense of interpersonal joy concerning the creation. Here is God planning a treasure hunt for us, and the more treasure we discover, the more we have yet to discover. As one of those who explored creation through science, Bacon reminds us that science is not some endless series of dreary laboratory experiments to discover impersonal (dead) natural laws, but instead a magnificent journey into the mind and heart of God.

When we attempt to cordon science off from the theological reflection that comes with it, we impoverish both science and theology. They're meant to be mutually reflective, which is why they were understood as two volumes (nature and Scripture) to be read together as the work of one author. This was certainly Isaac Newton's approach, and the standard approach of all believers who came before him. Newton wrote that "from the appearances of things," discourse about God "does certainly belong to Natural Philosophy."[12]

For Newton and the generations preceding him, scientific investigation was a natural by–product of theological reflection. It was a way to know God better. Scientific investigation was a form of worship for them. And it was pure joy!

11. Boorstin, *Discoverers*, ix.

12. Newton, *Principia Mathematica*, 546. It is interesting to note that Newton included these words at the end of the book in the second edition of the General Scholium, when he was in his seventies—and by that time had written an estimated 2.2MM works on Scripture, theology, and church history which were never published. For more information, see "Introduction to the Texts" at *The Newton Project* website: https://www.newtonproject.ox.ac.uk/texts/introduction.

Coming back to what we find in the results of those investigations, when we look out over the landscape of our planet and the starscape of our universe, we see an extravagant preparation for our existence, as well as an extraordinary biosphere to ensure its continuance. Someone went to an awful lot of trouble to throw this creation party for us. But that's what love does.

When God looked out over all his creation—galaxies, stars, planets—the script says that his response was to call it "good!" Thus, at the end of act one, things are off to a good start. But before we leave, let's take a moment to consider one essential theme rooted here, which will follow on through the whole drama. It's the theme of vocation, the vocation given to God's image-bearing creatures to expand his love in a unique way, across his unique creation.

## WHAT ARE WE DOING HERE ANYWAY?

The garden of Eden wasn't intended to be some kind of Disneyworld, or some form of permanent vacation. Rather, it was the arena in which all humankind was meant to exercise their vocation, their calling. That calling is given to them by their Creator in the opening scenes of act one in the book of Genesis, right after they're created in God's image. God tells Adam and Eve that he's putting them in charge of his creation. They're placed in the garden specifically to "work it and take care of it."[13] They're to multiply and have dominion over all of God's good creation.

Several things are noteworthy here. First, God is commanding Adam and Eve to manage what he has already created. They're now stewards of the creation's gifts, gifts which are grounded in God's love. Second, Adam and Eve have a cultural mandate to share in building God's kingdom in God's world. It's only after Adam and Eve are called into their proper vocation as image–bearers that God looks out over the whole of creation and pronounces it not only good, but "very good."

It is very good because this arrangement fully and perfectly reflects God's glory—his dignity, his gravitas—across all that is. It's also very good because it reflects the divine ordering of right relationship between God and humanity; they're now covenant partners in promoting the growth of creation to the glory of God under the protective canopy of his love and blessing.[14]

13. Genesis 2:15.
14. Many theologians call this first covenant the 'Adamic' covenant.

What we find at the end of Genesis 1 is that humanity has discovered its purpose in God's command to be fruitful and multiply and exercise dominion over the world God has made for them. As they fulfill that mandate, God's blessing (a form of strong love) flows over the whole earth. Adam and Eve are to faithfully partner with God in the development of this world. It's not a call to independent exploitation of the creation; it's a call to responsible and loving oversight. Just as the creation came into being out of love, so it must be maintained and developed in love.

This broad vocation will require work by the image-bearer. Work isn't something alien to the human condition, to be avoided or shunned. Work is at the core of human identity. This is not some sort of Protestant work ethic, or American obsession, or even a "Christian" principle. The call to work stands at the core of God's call to human beings as image–bearers. They work because he works. Work is not a supernumerary randomly tacked on to human vocation. Rather, it lies at its heart. Work as a creative act is a core competency for all image-bearers in the original ordering of creation.

I was walking home from lunch in town today along the bay by which I live. It was a clear, cold day, and the contrast among the blue water, the emerald forest, and white snowcapped mountains was crisp and beautiful. As I walked along, I passed a car with a license plate that read ILOV2CRE8, and I thought, "So does God. You got that from him. This is what you and I were made for."

In our drama, work will soon degenerate into toil, but we shouldn't lose sight of the fact that work is initially written deep into the script. Not only is our vocation—our calling—a part of the plan, but the work we do lies at the heart of human identity, dignity, and flourishing. We're created in the image of a Creator, and so creativity—which lies at the core of all true work—is at the center of our vocation. Our Creator created creatures to join him in creating. Our creative work is a primary expression of our dominion mandate from the Creator. It's also a primary expression of how we love. We become "co-creators" with him through how we express love through our work. This is an important theme we'll return to later.

To quickly recap, the immense and overflowing love of the God who is Trinity has brought a universe into existence as a playing field for expressing that love. That universe, created in and for love, will be the dwelling place of the image-bearers of God—his beloved ones, who are to extend the mandate of love across the world they're given as they exercise their vocation of being fruitful and multiplying, exercising wise dominion, and becoming co-creators with God.

For the story we're in, this is the end of act one. So far, so good.

# 2

# Collapse

*At present many substitute the word "evil" for "sin," but this is a poor substitute, for the word "sin" is far more specific. It denotes a definite kind of evil, namely, a moral evil for which man is responsible and which brings him under a sentence of condemnation. The modern tendency to regard it merely as a wrong done to one's fellow–beings misses the point entirely, for such a wrong can be called sin only in so far as it is contrary to the will of God. Sin is correctly defined by Scripture as "lawlessness," 1 John 3:4. It is lack of conformity to the law of God, and as such the opposite of that love which is required by the divine law.*

—LOUIS BERKHOF, SUMMARY OF CHRISTIAN DOCTRINE

AS IN ALL COMPELLING dramas, what often starts off swimmingly takes an unforeseen and dangerous turn. Just three chapters into the script, we meet a menacing presence whose mission is to sever creation's relationship from God by turning Adam's sons and Eve's daughters against their Creator.

This malevolent presence takes his form as a snake in the grass. His goal is to disrupt the life-giving covenant relationship of blessing that was inherent in the lovingly crafted creation itself. The strategy of the presence is twofold: first to bend the truth, then to break it. In both, the goal is to seduce the creature into distrust, disgust, and finally, disobedience. We might say the threatening presence is the first theologian in the story, in the sense that he dares to speak of the Creator as if he were not in the room. On his lips God is objectified, and objectification is the enemy of love. The serpent's gambit succeeds, and the fabric of the universe is rent from bottom to top, from earth to heaven, from humanity to God.

We must ask, "How could the Creator allow this to happen?" Indeed, why not prevent it entirely by making it impossible? Why not simply program humanity for obedience? The answer lies in the relationship between love and freedom. If there's to be genuine love between the Creator and the creature, the creature must be given agency, which is the moral freedom to choose to love in return. Compelled love is no love at all.

The Creator, by design, out of a pure desire to love and be loved, gives the creature freedom to love him in return. Love and freedom are a package deal. Love without freedom is coercion; freedom without love is isolation. And so, the rogue variable of freedom is introduced into the equation, with the genuine possibility that the creature could spurn the Creator's love. This is the terrible risk the Creator takes in giving to his creature this dangerous freedom. But freedom is the necessary habitat of love.

As the story continues, both Adam and Eve exchange the truth of God's love for a lie that promised them freedom, and are subsequently trapped inside that lie. I'm reminded of the sign above the entrance to Auschwitz that read *Arbeit Mach Frei*— "Work makes you free." All who entered that camp experienced neither true work nor freedom, but only toil and death. The difference is that those who suffered and died in Auschwitz were taken violently; in the garden of Eden, humanity went willingly, even happily.

The damage was plenary and catastrophic. One of the names for Satan in the script is diabolos, the devil, which means literally to "throw through" or "to split," as when one throws a hatchet and splits a wooden shingle. The diabolos lives up to his name as he splits us from God, from ourselves, from one another, and from the creation. He's the supreme separator.[1] The man and the woman eat the fruit of the tree of the knowledge of good and evil—a decisive act with overwhelming implications. The result is that the man and woman hide from God; their new "split state" of alienation is now experienced in nakedness and shame.

## SPLIT FROM GOD

Things devolve quickly when God cries out to them, "Where are you?" This question haunts the halls of human history, but also sounds a note of hope that will not only echo throughout the script, but find its apogee in a

---

1. Foerster, "διάβολος" (diabolos), Kittel and Friedrich, *Theological Dictionary of the New Testament*, Vol. 2, 71–73.

startling appearance in act three of our drama. Much of the script itself will
be devoted to this question, and to the Creator now in search of his creature.

Fredrich Buechner tells a story about being at Christmas Eve mass at St.
Peter's in Rome when Pius XII was pope. After hours of waiting, finally the
Swiss Guard brought the pope into the basilica seated on a golden throne.
What struck Buechner most was the pontiff's face, and especially his eyes.

> I can still see his face as he was carried by me on his throne—
> that lean, ascetic face, gray-skinned, with the high-bridged beak
> of a nose, his glasses glittering in the candlelight. And as he
> passed by me, he was leaning slightly forward and peering into
> the crowd with extraordinary intensity.
>
> Through the thick lenses of his glasses his eyes were larger
> than life, and he peered into my face and into all the faces
> around me and behind me with a look so keen and so charged
> that I could not escape the feeling that he must be looking for
> someone in particular.[2]

While Buchner takes this passage in the direction of wondering if the
pope was looking for Jesus that night (as do all who come on Christmas
Eve), I've often wondered whether we might also find there the face of God
looking for humanity—not humanity in general, but for each of us in particular. "Adam, Eve, where are You? I'm looking for you."

What shall we call this ruinous state into which the lead characters
have fallen? The script calls it by an archer's term: *hamartia*. The word we
normally translate as "sin" has its root with the archer who draws his or her
bow, releases the arrow—and misses the target.[3] By the time we reach the
New Testament period, the term has developed three levels of meaning: 1)
Sin as an individual act. 2) As a determination of the nature of humanity. 3)
As a personal power.[4] The meaning has been well described by Cornelius
Plantinga:

> Sin is a religious concept, not just a moral one... Sin is a smear-
> ing of the relationship, the grieving of one's divine parent and
> benefactor, a betrayal of the partner to whom one is joined by
> a holy bond... All sin has first and finally a Godward force. Let
> us say that a sin is any act—any thought, desire, emotion, word,
> or deed—or its particular absence, that displeases God and de-
> serves blame. Let us add that the disposition to commit sins also
> displeases God and deserves blame, and let us therefore use the

2. Buechner, *Listening to Your Life*, 334.

3. Gk. ἁμαρτιά.

4. "ἁμαρτάνω," Stählin, Kittel, *Theological Dictionary of the New Testament*, Vol. 1,
295.

word sin to refer to such instances of both act and disposition. Sin is a culpable and personal affront to a personal God.[5]

The impact of sin is devastating, as it leads to spiritual death. Humanity, now in rebellion against God, becomes like a fish that has leapt out of the stream of life only to be left with gasping gills on the rocks. The human being, meant to be a temple in which God dwells, has now become *ich-abod* (in Hebrew)— "the glory has departed."

Thomas Merton describes the condition of fallen humans this way:

> For his soul and body, created to be a temple of God, cannot help but seem a haunted place after the desecration that has evicted its only rightful dweller. It is of no avail to try to exorcise the accusing silence by turning the place into a den of thieves. No amount of business prosperity and luxury can hide the abomination of desolation within us.[6]

We were intended to be God's temple, to bear his glory, and now we've become the opposite of that. The phrase "abomination of desolation" refers to the second century b.c. when a Seleucid king (Antiochus IV) invaded Jerusalem, captured the temple, and established idol worship there. Merton is making the point that after we're separated from God, split by sin, the human temple is not only emptied of the divine glory, but is now actively given over to idolatry. After the collapse, humanity—corporately and individually—becomes a temple crawling with idols.

## SPLIT FROM OURSELVES

This primal splitting from God reverberates like a sonic boom, shattering the windows of our most basic relationships. Not only is our relationship with God ruined, but the script tells us that afterward we're split from ourselves.

Here is Merton's penetrating analysis of the human psychological condition after the collapse in our second act:

> Rationalizing and excusing the lusts and ambitions of a selfish and fleshly ego, camouflaging its own defects and magnifying the sins of others, evading its countless fears, forcing itself to believe its own lies, the psyche of man struggles in a thousand ways to silence the secret voice of anxiety.

---

5. Plantinga, *It's Not the Way It's Supposed to Be*, 12–13.

6. Merton, *The New Man*, 117. For biblical foundation see Romans 5:12,18–19; 6:23; 1 Corinthians 15:22; Ephesians 2:1.

Having lost his realization of his true identity, man has exchanged the peace of innocent self-realization for the agony of
guilt-ridden self-awareness. Instead of being perfectly actual-
ized in spirit, integrated and unified in the selfless ecstasy of a
contemplation that goes out entirely to the "other," man is literally "dis-tracted"—pulled apart—by an almost infinite number
of awarenesses. He is conscious of everything trivial, remembers
everything except what is most necessary, feels everything that
he should not feel, yields to demands that he should never hear,
looks everywhere, pays attention to every creaking board and
rattling shutter in his haunted house.[7]

Having lost itself to God, humanity now becomes lost to itself. We
enter a kind of amnesia in which we live zombified lives. Acedia and en-
nui become our spiritual refuge, and slowly press the breath of life out of
us. Meaning and purpose, bestowed on us in the garden, disappear east of
Eden. Work becomes toil, peace becomes agitation, longing becomes compulsion. The schizoid self is enematized, and we live our days in spiritual
spasm, oscillating between indulgent self-love and imperious self-hatred.
To put it in *Lord of the Rings* currency, Smeagol becomes Gollum. And the
biblical warning in the garden— "You shall surely die"—becomes, paradoxically, our acquaintance with life, as we slowly degenerate under the power
of the sin ring.

The split self is an intolerant self that censors any bubbling up from the
depths of our souls.  It censors any whispers of our primordial conscious-
ness. Because of the split from self, we cannot even keep company with
ourselves. Silence and solitude are threats to the split self, which insists on
an incessant chorus of lies to maintain the charade that this false self is sovereign. Life must be lived at the surface to maintain its fiction of well-being.
No questions, no doubts, no fears may be allowed to surface. Reflection
and contemplation become odious. We disgust ourselves, accuse ourselves,
denigrate ourselves, and sometimes even kill ourselves. On the battlefield
of the divided self there are no victors, only victims; no conquerors, only
wounded and slain.

Karl Barth has summarized the split self of man under sin:

If he denies God, he denies himself. He is then something which
he cannot be in the counterpart in which he is. He chooses his
own impossibility. And every offense in which godlessness can
express itself, e.g., unbelief and idolatry, doubt, and indifference
to God, is as such, both in its theoretical and practical forms,
an offense with which man burdens, obscures, and corrupts

7. Merton, *The New Man*, 116–17.

himself. It is an attack on the continuance of his own creature-
liness: not a superficial, temporary, or endurable attack, but
a radical, central, and fatal attack on its very foundation, and
therefore its continuance. His very being as man is endangered
by every surrender to sin.[8]

Another way to think of the scope of this disastrous split in the self is
to visualize what caused the HMS *Titanic* to sink. The *Titanic* was designed
with sixteen vertical compartments separated by sealable bulkheads. If a
compartment were punctured, it could be sealed off without endangering
the rest of the ship. The *Titanic's* architects had planned for as many of four
of the compartments to be compromised at one time while allowing the
ship to stay afloat. In their 'WISP' (what if scenario planning), they never
envisioned the possibility of six of the sixteen compartments being simultaneously breached—which is what happened on the night of April 15, 1912.

Until 1997, the theory was that the ship sailed next to an iceberg off
Newfoundland, whose underwater edge tore a 300-foot gash below the water line. When photos finally became available, it became clear that there
were six individual shorter slits not much wider than a human hand. But
the aggregate effect was catastrophic because each of the slits compromised
a separate compartment.

If we think of ourselves as having different compartments or faculties,
we discover that our collapse in sin has affected the totality of our humanity.
Our faculties (compartments) are our minds, hearts, wills, and bodies. The
script, and those who've commented on it, detail the devastating impact of
the fall on our humanity. Like the *Titanic*, we're *completely* compromised,
and the result is that we too are sunk.[9]

As a result of the collapse and fall, *our minds* become clouded and
confused. We rationalize evil, we're blinded to our prejudices, we overlook
evidence that troubles us, and most dangerously, we reject faith as incom-
patible with reason, rather than its rightful and faithful partner and guide.[10]

8. Barth, *Church Dogmatics*, 3/2, 136.

9. Reformed theologians refer to this as 'total depravity' not meaning there is nothing good in us, but that all of the key elements (faculties) of our humanity are compromised by the fall/collapse. As for the body, the whole notion that salvation is based
*within* the incarnation of God points to the need for a new human body and is effected
in the resurrected body of Jesus which is beyond all forms of corruption.

10. For examples of the splitting mind see Romans 8:5–8; Genesis 6:5; 1 Corinthians 1:21; Ephesians 4:17. It is worth remembering here St. Anselm's statement: "I
believe that I might understand." Or C. S. Lewis's comment, "I believe in Christianity
as I believe that the Sun has risen, not only because I see it, but because by it I see
everything else." Lewis, *Weight of Glory*, 140.

As a result of the collapse and fall, *our hearts* become darkened, and our affections misaligned. Here our passions become disordered, our loves confused, and we wreak havoc on the world by becoming idolators whose hearts have surrendered to the voracious appetites of lesser gods.[11]

As a result of the collapse and fall, *our wills* become twisted and we seek domination through power and become curved in upon ourselves.[12] The apogee of this trending is self-coronation. Here we're reminded of the ranting delusions of Nietzsche as he celebrates the supposed death of God and the subsequent apotheosis of man.

> Before God! But now this god has died. You higher men, this god was your greatest danger. It is only since he lies in his tomb that you have been resurrected. Only now the great noon comes; only now the higher man becomes—lord.[13]

Finally, as a result of the collapse and fall, *our bodies*, intended for eternal life, become subject to decay. This is manifested in pain, sickness, disease, suffering, aging, and finally death.

The plot of the script reveals that we're split from the Creator and split from ourselves with devastating results. But then the impact grows worse; we descend deeper in the fall.

## SPLIT FROM OTHERS

The contagion of separation, the splitting that began vertically in our relationship with our Creator, now mutates internally within our divided selves and begets a secondary mutation, a lateral splintering between and among us and others. The love between Adam and Eve becomes poisoned with self-justification and ego protection as they begin to blame one another for snatching and eating the fruit. In this moment we discover the seed of all marital and all human discord—a primal splitting at the very core of human relationship.

This splitting permeates the pages of the script and overflows into all human history, where people now pit themselves against one another in denial of their common humanity, seeking one another's ruin and destruction.

11. For examples of the splitting heart see Romans 1:24–27; 1 Timothy 6:10; 2 Timothy 3:4; Amos 2:4–8; 5:7–15; Revelation 13:1–7.

12. For examples of the splitting will see John 8:34; Romans 7:14–24; Ephesians 2:1–3; 2 Peter 2:19. Martin Luther made this saying famous—*Homo incurvatus in se*—but its roots go back to Augustine, and the phrase has been a theological staple in the stable of descriptions of humanity after the fall.

13. Nietzsche, *Thus Spoke Zarathustra*, in *The Portable Nietzsche*, 398.

The little scene between Cain and Abel becomes projected upon the big screen of the nations. The budding cynicism of "Am I my brother's keeper?" finds full bloom in all disavowal of our connectedness as human beings. This question becomes the seedbed of all isms, the creation of all "Samaritans," the identification and reification of all enemies. Alienation and exclusion suddenly replace access and embrace. The creative impulse of love is replaced by the destructive compulsions of apathy or hate.

## SPLIT FROM CREATION

Finally, this catastrophic tsunami of splitting, this work of the diabolos, swamps even the creation itself. No longer a steward of the good gift of the Creator's work, humankind—in its newfound Nietzschean "god-ness"—treats nature not as a glorious reflection of Supernature, to be loved and cared for, but as a commodity to be seized and exploited. The goal becomes personal gain rather than communal well-being and blessing. Here heaven and earth are torn from each other's arms. This rejection of an enchanted, sacralized nature for a disenchanted commodified one, is a direct result of the rejection in the garden of Eden (itself a place of enchantment) of the primal relationship between God and humanity.

The alienation between humanity and creation means that work becomes toil, that life ends in death, and that nature, now in its brooding alienation, becomes a threat to be feared and conquered rather than a gift to be received and stewarded. Nature can no longer fulfill its purpose of nurturing humanity because humanity has abandoned its vocation of nurturing nature. Both humanity and nature east of Eden are now embraced in a long dying. Both are slowly collapsing upon one another, exhausted.

East of Eden, entropy reigns. Like cargo in a ship's hold, the destinies of humanity and nature are first sealed together in the creation. Now they begin to sink together in the collapse.[14]

---

14. This intertwined relationship between humanity and nature is, I think, one of Paul's most penetrating insights. It brings us back again to the centrality of the incarnation of Christ in which God aligns himself with the healing of both humanity and nature. If the two are to be healed in the incarnation, death, and resurrection of Jesus, the two wounds must be treated together. See Romans 8:19–25.

# 3

# Redemption

*I cannot bear the monotonous sound of the dark sea gnawing at the shore.*
*Behind the depressing silence of this sea, the silence of God...*
*the feeling that while men raise their voices in anguish*
*God remains with folded arms, silent.*

—SHUSAKU ENDO, *SILENCE*

At this point, the Creator's Camelot is a smoldering ruin. The diabolos, the Splitter, appears to have run the table, conquering the kingdom.

But as the script unfurls, we begin to see hints of a mounting counter-offensive. A new community is formed and given the mission to set up an advance camp deep inside enemy lines. The Creator is behind it all.

The strategy is to establish a counterculture to the one currently reigning under the Splitter. This will be a culture of life meant to oppose the Splitter's culture of death. God himself will lead the movement, which is intended to be a blessing to all the nations, all the peoples of the earth, and to the creation itself. It will be a mission wreathed in gore and glory. The script tells tales of heroes and villains, successes and failures, the starts and the stops of this band of believers, decade upon decade, century upon century.

The plot builds, and the script is seeded with secrets and intimations. Patriarchs and prophets, judges and kings, wise men and fools, saints and sinners, women and men take up their scripts, play their parts, and recite their lines. Some speak in staggering soliloquy; others, in desperation, resourcefully improvise. All recede from view, generation upon generation, into the mists of history. And yet the story continues. The mission expands in starts and fits as battles are engaged. Some are won, some are lost.

All the while, the bright light of promise is cast across the dark canyons through which all humanity wanders. It becomes tempting to believe that all that wander are indeed lost. After centuries of silence, in which many had given up hope, a wild man appears in the desert and says that the story is about to reach its climax—a story many had forgotten they were part of. The central battle is about to be engaged. God's warrior is coming; he's just over the ridge of history. God himself is coming to undo the Splitter's work. Prepare yourselves by preparing for him!

Then the Redeemer appears, first in a feeding trough, later in the water. God speaks the words of Israel's coronation psalm over him: "This is my beloved Son…" With those, he adds the servant words recorded by the prophet Isaiah: "…in whom I am well pleased." The stitching together of these two passages from the early script will orient and guide the whole path of redemption in the later one.[1]

Here, with the coming of Jesus, we arrive at the very center of the drama. Here we encounter love dressed in human flesh.

If God is the central concern of Christian belief, then love is the central concern of the Christian life. If we're to love well, we want to understand how Jesus incarnated the love of God. We cannot separate Jesus's redemption from love, for the simple reason that God's love is the motivation behind Jesus's redemption. To be sure, act three of the story is the ground zero of biblical history—indeed, of all of human history. Here, in the coming of Jesus, we see love in its most vivid, disturbing, unnerving, and hopeful clarity.

In Jesus's birth, life, death, and resurrection, we see the full revelation of the love of God. I said earlier that the Holy Trinity is a community of perfect love, and we see—actually *see*—that love personified now in Jesus of Nazareth. Love is *the* reason for redemption, for the incarnation, life, death, and resurrection of Christ. He had no other motivation, because God had no other motivation, and Jesus *is* God.

Let's explore the basic content of act three, which concerns our redemption, or in a wider sense, the salvation accomplished for us in Christ. Concerning the scope and scale of Christ's salvation and our ability to fully investigate it, Athanasius warns us from the fourth century:

> In a word, the achievements of the Savior, resulting from His becoming man, are of such kind and number, that if one should

---

1. Psalm 2:7 and Isaiah 42:1.

wish to enumerate them, he may be compared to men who gaze at the expanse of the sea and wish to count its waves.[2]

Athanasius wasn't wrong. I'll try to access the key items here using the rich imagery of the New Testament itself in thinking about the scope of our salvation. Within this stunning achievement, the true depth of the love of God is revealed.


## A NEW HUMANITY

It's clear from the script that the point of departure for thinking about what happens to our status before God—our salvation—begins with the incarnation. So often Protestants run straight to the cross and resurrection when talking about salvation, but I've learned to appreciate the fuller framework of the Eastern Orthodox tradition—beginning with the incarnation, and ending with the ascension. This is not to minimize the centrality of the cross and resurrection, but only to set them in a wider and richer matrix of meaning.

After all, Paul speaks of Christ as the second Adam, a kind of reboot for the human race.[3] Christ is the New Man who replaces the old. He is the one without sin,[4] who as Israel's Messiah-King recapitulates Israel's desert history and turns it from a history of disobedience to obedience. The forty-year Exodus is backdrop for the forty-day temptation. Jesus's history is not detached from ours. Our history in Adam becomes Israel's history in Abraham, and Israel's history in Abraham becomes Jesus's history in the incarnation. He is "the firstborn of many brethren," and one day "we shall be like him."[5] In other words, in the incarnation, our destiny is tied to his.

Speaking of the incarnation, Thomas Merton writes,

> Humanity, which was one image of God in Adam, or, if you prefer, one single "mirror" of the divine nature, was shattered into millions of fragments by that original sin which alienated each man from God, from other men and from himself. But the broken mirror becomes once again a perfectly united image of God in the union of those who are one in Christ.[6]

2. Athanasius, *De Incarnatione Verbi Dei*, sect. 54, *Nicene and Post-Nicene Fathers*, Vol. IV, 65.

3. 1 Corinthians 15:45–49.

4. On the sinlessness of Jesus, see John 8:46; 2 Corinthians 5:2; Hebrews 4:15; 7:26; 1 Peter 3:18; 2:22; 1 John 3:5.

5. Romans 8:29; 1 John 3:2.

6. Merton, *New Man*, 149.

In the incarnation of Jesus, God and Man are fully joined, which means that the resources of God's deity—for example, eternal life and true holiness—now become available to us in Christ. As the Scottish theologian T. F. Torrance puts it, God gives himself to humanity "in such a way as to assume human nature and existence into oneness with himself. He condescends to enter our human nature and so elevates it into union with his own divine nature."[7]

We might say that from the incarnation forward, God and humanity are infused together in Jesus Christ in such a way that they can never be separated. Like an iron poker long in a blazing fire, the iron and the flame, while substantially distinguishable, become visibly indistinguishable, red–hot in appearance. Thus, the incarnation itself is the initial step in our salvation. When God becomes man, not only is the *destiny* of humanity changed, but human *nature* itself is decisively altered and renewed.

The New Testament writers use a splendid palette of vivid metaphors to talk about the meaning of our salvation in Christ as it is worked out in the history of Jesus. Let's briefly review some of the key ones.

## LANGUAGE OF THE MARKETPLACE—REDEMPTION

One of the ways the writers try to communicate what has happened is by using the economic term "redemption," which has a rich meaning in Israel's history. The "redeemer" was a kinsman who bought a fellow family member out of slavery or servitude if he'd had to sell himself into such a state. Likewise, the redeemer would take up his dead relative's wife and provide her with children as a way of keeping his brother's memory alive and his land inheritance intact—thereby ensuring her future well–being. Boaz is a key example of this in the book of Ruth.

Related to this is the term "ransom," which was the price paid to redeem the one enslaved, thus purchasing his freedom. This is the background of Jesus's statement, "For even the Son of Man did not come to be served, but to serve, and to give his life as a ransom for many."[8]

The script is clear on two key thoughts here. First, that God's people require redemption. In fact, the idea of redemption is tied early on to blood sacrifice in the exodus events where the blood of a lamb, slathered across the

7. Torrance, *Incarnation*, 45. Torrance later writes, "One thing should be abundantly clear, that if Jesus Christ did not assume our fallen flesh, our fallen humanity, then our fallen humanity is untouched by his work—for 'the unassumed is the unredeemed,' as Gregory Nazianzen put it." 62.

8. Mark 10:45.

door posts and lintels of Israelite houses, signals the angel of death to pass over those houses where it was so applied.

As the prophets and psalms make clear, God and God alone is Israel's redeemer. There is only one God and only one redeemer. Man does not hold the power of redemption; only God holds it. The psalmist wrote,

> No one can redeem the life of another
> or give to God a ransom for them—
> the ransom for a life is costly,
> no payment is ever enough—
> so that they should live on forever
> and not see decay.[9]

Job also understood that God is our redeemer:

> I know that my redeemer lives,
> and that in the end he will stand on the earth.
> And after my skin has been destroyed,
> yet in my flesh I will see God;
> I myself will see him
> with my own eyes—I, and not another.
> How my heart yearns within me![10]

The redemption that began in Egypt continued at crisis moments throughout Israel's history. The prophets are replete with statements referring to God as Israel's redeemer, and full of promises that his redemption would come to deliver his people in a final and decisive way. Isaiah, for example, calls God "Redeemer" thirteen times.[11]

New Testament authors understood humanity as being enslaved to the powers of sin and death (the curse of the law—Galatians 3:13), and that it was Christ who, by offering himself on the cross as the Passover lamb, paid the ransom price for their freedom. He does this as their *goel*, their kinsman-redeemer. Here we circle back to the centrality of the incarnation. If only God can redeem, and the New Testament insists that redemption has been accomplished in Jesus, then Jesus must be God in the flesh. The great Redeemer has entered human history and ransomed his beloved people, just as he had promised.

And why go to these desperate measures? *For God so loved the world...*

9. Psalm 49:7–9.

10. Job 19:25–27.

11. Olson, *Zondervan NASB Exhaustive Concordance*, 903.

## LANGUAGE OF THE TEMPLE—ATONEMENT

The language of atonement is another way in which the New Testament writers describe salvation. The idea behind atonement is that sin has opened a gap between God and us. We were warned about the penalty in the garden of Eden—that if we eat the fruit of the tree of knowledge of good and evil, we would "surely die." This makes an atonement sacrifice for our sin necessary. Atonement occurs when the curse of the law (death) is not side-stepped, but carried out—upon Christ. The law cannot be ignored, it must be fulfilled. Hence Jesus' statement, "Do not think that I have come to abolish the Law or the Prophets; I have not come to abolish them but to fulfill them."[12]

At the cross, the law is not set aside; it is exhausted. Jesus exchanged his life for ours. He took on himself the penalty that belonged to us, thereby setting us free.

In the kingdom of God, the law of double jeopardy applies. Once Christ is accused in our place, suffers in our stead, and dies on our behalf, we can no longer be held guilty. The legal remedy of our death sentence has been carried out—on him. "For the life of a creature is in the blood, and I have given it to you to make atonement for yourselves on the altar; it is the blood that makes atonement for one's life.[13]

The Old Testament sacrificial system was put in place as a temporary vehicle to manage a temporary atoning structure until the "fullness of time," when sin would be dealt with decisively. This structure included a series of sacrifices to mind the gap between us and God. As a result of its temporary nature, these sacrifices had to repeated over and over.[14] With the coming of Jesus as the God-Man, as the Messiah-King and High Priest, the final sacrifice of the "lamb without blemish" was prepared. The letter to the Hebrews tells us what happened:

> For Christ did not enter a sanctuary made with human hands that was only a copy of the true one; he entered heaven itself, now to appear for us in God's presence. Nor did he enter heaven to offer himself again and again, the way the high priest enters the Most Holy Place every year with blood that is not his own. Otherwise Christ would have had to suffer many times since the creation of the world. But he has appeared once for all at the culmination of the ages to do away with sin by the sacrifice of himself.[15]

12. Matthew 5:17.
13. Leviticus 17:11.
14. Hebrews 10:1–3.
15. Hebrews 9:24–26.

Once again, if we ask *why* Jesus did this for us—why did he sacrifice himself for us?—the script echoes consistently, "In this is love, not that we loved God, but that he first loved us and sent his son to be the atoning sacrifice for our sins."[16]

## LANGUAGE OF THE COURT—JUSTIFICATION

Another image or metaphor the authors of the New Testament use to help us understand our salvation in Jesus is drawn from the legal world. The script speaks of a coming day when all of humanity will be judged before the throne of God at the end of time. God is the one who will judge all persons as either righteous or unrighteous. If one is judged righteous, it means he has no guilt. As it stands, the problem is that no person living or ever living—except one—is righteous. Paul makes this witheringly clear:

> For we have already charged that all, both Jews and Greeks, are under the power of sin, as it is written...

And here Paul goes on to offer a barrage of evidence from a variety of psalms:

> There is no one who is righteous, not even one; there is no one who has understanding, there is no one who seeks God. All have turned aside, together they have become worthless; there is no one who shows kindness, there is not even one. Their throats are opened graves; they use their tongues to deceive. The venom of vipers is under their lips. Their mouths are full of cursing and bitterness. Their feet are swift to shed blood; ruin and misery are in their paths, and the way of peace they have not known. There is no fear of God before their eyes.[17]

Paul reminds us that sin carries the death penalty, telling us that the wages of sin is death.[18] All of us without exception stand in need of a righteous surrogate who can exchange our unrighteousness for his righteousness, and then stand in the place of judgment for us. In Christ we have one: "For our sake God made him to be sin, who knew no sin, so that in him, we might become the righteousness of God."[19]

16. 1 John 4:10.
17. Romans 3:10–18.
18. Romans 6:23.
19. 2 Corinthians 5:21.

The impact of Jesus's surrogacy as the Second Adam who overturns the destruction of humanity caused by the first Adam is staggering:

> Therefore, just as one man's trespass led to condemnation for all, so one man's act of righteousness leads to justification and life for all. For just as by the one man's disobedience the many were made sinners, so by the one man's obedience the many will be made righteous.[20]

One of my favorite illustrations of God's justification given to us in Christ is that of a little boy playing baseball with his friends on an empty neighborhood lot. When he was up to bat, the boy, a good hitter, lined one over the fence of his neighbor—and through his plate glass sliding door.

The neighbor was, as it turned out, a curmudgeon of the first order, and promptly took the boy to court. The judge in his great black robe mounted the bench and heard the evidence.

To the boy: "Young man, did you hit a baseball through this man's window?"

"Yes, your honor," the boy said sheepishly.

"And sir," the judged said, turning toward the man, "how much did that door cost?"

"Your honor, I just had it installed. It cost me $1,249. Here's the receipt."

The judge examined the receipt through his reading glasses and frowned. "Son, do you have anything else to say to this man?"

"I'm sorry, sir," the boy said.

"I believe you are," said the judge. "But that won't be enough. There are real damages here, and they must be paid. Young man, you are to reimburse this man for the full cost of the door." With that, the judge slammed down his gavel.

At which point, the boy burst into tears, because his allowance was five dollars a week, and this debt would be impossible to pay. As the boy sat hopelessly sobbing in the courtroom, the judge came down from the bench, took off his robe, removed his checkbook from his shirt pocket, and wrote out a check for the full amount. He signed it, then handed over the check to the man whose window had been broken.

You see, the judge was also this boy's father.

Once again, if we ask, "But why? Why did Jesus stand in my place?"— the answer is, "God did not send his Son into the world to condemn the world, but to save the world through him."[21]

---

20. Romans 5:18–19.
21. John 3:16–17.

We've now briefly reviewed the first three acts of our drama, this story we're in—creation, collapse, and redemption. Before we get to the fourth act—restoration—let's do a deep dive into the love of Jesus Christ who so astonishingly appears as the apogee of this third act. Having looked at some of the ways the New Testament describes what has happened in the salvation of Jesus Christ, and having remembered "why" at every turn, let's explore the love of God as it's uniquely and utterly revealed in Christ.

# PART TWO

Exploring the Love of God
Revealed in Jesus Christ

# 4

# The Dynamism of the Love of God

*The soul seeks the Word, but it had been previously sought by the Word…*
*Nor do I think that when a soul has found Him will it cease from seeking.*
*For God is sought, not by the movement of the feet, but by the desires of*
*    the heart.*
*When a soul has been so blessed as to find Him, that secret desire is not*
*    extinguished,*
*but on the contrary, it is increased. Is the consummation of the joy the*
*    extinction of the desire?*
*No, rather it is as oil poured upon a flame, for desire is as it were a flame.*

—Bernard of Clairvaux

I've been suggesting that we live inside a story, and that standing at the center of the story is the Holy Trinity of the Father, Son, and Holy Spirit, a Trinity of perfect love. The story takes place within a creation purposed (and then repurposed in Christ) for love. The universe itself was created out of love as an arena for the love of God to spread among his creatures.

Those who study the universe tell us that all the evidence available points to a purposefulness in this regard. The universe is fine-tuned for human life to a point of vanishing improbability if left to chance. Like a womb expecting a child, the universe has all the necessary characteristics for life to begin and to flourish. Moreover, within this vast universe our planet contains the goldilocks physics that has produced the perfect chemistry to yield the just right biological conditions for life—human life in particular—to exist.

None of this is an accident, none of this is statistically probable. But why? Why are we here, tucked away so safely in this corner of the universe? Why, indeed, is there something rather than nothing to begin with? The script says it's so that we might know, love, and serve God. We're created to know and to be known, to love and to be loved, by the God who is love.

## THE RICHNESS OF LANGUAGE

Let me try to describe the love we're talking about when we speak of the love of God. *Love* is used in a variety of ways in our culture, and various forms of love have been observed and noted. C. S. Lewis reminds us that the Greeks had four different words for love, whereas we have one, and usually its meaning is defined (loosely) by its context.[1] For example, I may say that I love (*storge*) ice-cream or Molly, my red heeler. Or, I may say I love (*philia*) my friends. I may say that I love (*eros*) my wife. I may say that I love (*agape*) my children. Each of these bring with them a certain caste of meaning.[2]

We know that the word the apostle John uses when he speaks of God's love is the last one—*agape*. *Agape* is usually defined as "unconditional love" and illustrated by the love of a parent for a child.

Rather than understand all these as different kinds of love, I think they're connected in a particular pattern. I've come to believe that *agape*, rather than simply being one kind of love, is the fundamental love that gives rise and shape to the other three. It's the trunk which supports the other boughs of the tree of love. When they're rightly ordered, the other loves are all expressive branches of the tree of *agape*. In other words, they are organically connected. This would mean that my *storge*, my *philos*, and my *eros* would all originate in, be nourished through, and shaped by, God's *agape*. This approach elevates and purifies the other three forms of love while at the same time rightly placing the love of God (*agape*) at the center as the source and governor of the other expressions. This is how these good, but fallen loves, are redeemed.

I mentioned the cruciality of these three expressions of love being "rightly ordered," which is to say they serve the love of God. *Storge*, *philos*, and *eros* are subordinate loves, yet they're part of the goodness of the created order when they serve the purposes of that order. When this happens,

1. Lewis, *Four Loves*.
2. Gk. Στοργή, φιλία, ἔρως, ἀγάπη.

there's a rightness and a goodness to them *because* they're rightful, well-ordered expressions of the primal *agape*.

These three loves are secondary, but not second-class. They're derivative but not demoted, any more than its rays are demoted by the existence of the sun. They're rightful and good expressions. Rather than being at odds or in competition with each other, *eros*, *storge*, and *philos* each have their unique place in God's providential order. When operating within the bounds of God's *agape*, they become part of his blessing.

When we speak of the love of God, we focus on the unusual and fundamental nature of *agape* as the active ingredient that makes the other loves viable and good in their proper ordering. *Agape* is the air that inflates these loves to their proper measure and function. There is much to consider regarding how this might look as it's fleshed out in life, but here our concern is not with the others so much as with *agape* itself.

The apostle John has written that "God is love," which means that this attribute is ontological—it describes God's very essence and being as personal. *Agape* is the core of who God is. Love without personhood is like water without wetness—unimaginable.

If we begin to look for a way forward, a way to begin to see what this love looks like in action, we're immediately swept back into our drama. The key pulse that unifies the whole biblical narrative is the love of God; it's a pulse that beats from Genesis to Revelation. The reality of this pulse becomes incarnate, and therefore visible, in the heart of Jesus. Yet to understand his heart, we must situate it in the heart of God, which is revealed in the Old Testament. In other words, we must back up a bit.

## A TELLTALE HEART

If we were to perform an EKG of the heart of God in the Old Testament, what would we find? We would find that it's a telltale heart. In the Hebrew Scriptures, one of the key words (used about 240 times) to describe God's love is *hesed*, which is translated into English in various ways.[3] According to *Vine's Expository Dictionary*, it means "loving kindness, steadfast love, grace, mercy, faithfulness, goodness, devotion. It expresses the consistent, ever faithful, relentless, constantly-pursuing, lavish, extravagant, unrestrained, love of the Father."[4]

---

3. Hb. חסד

4. Vine, Unger, and White, *Vine's Complete Expository Dictionary of Old and New Testament Words*, 142.

Perhaps the best (because it's the broadest) translation of *hesed* is "covenant loyalty," which reflects how God's love comes to his people in the broadest sense as we turn the pages of the script. God willingly binds himself to his people in this striking foundational love, which migrates into the meaning of *agape* in the New Testament. There, God's Old Testament *hesed* will be revealed as *agape* love through its incarnation in Jesus. But we're getting ahead of ourselves.

In the Hebrew Scriptures of the Old Testament, we see this love of God, as we've said, in the creation. Then when humanity rebels against God, we see new dimensions of this love arise like vast continents from the sea as tectonic plates shift. The collapse—the fall of humanity in the second act of our drama—triggers a monumental response in the heart of God.

Here we discover the first dynamic revealed in God's EKG, namely that *God's heart beats strongly for his people*. Paul's observation in Romans is certainly true in the Old Testament as well: "If God is for us, who can be against us?"[5]

Rather than abandon his people to the culture of sin and death they've chosen to create, God pursues them. He is not neutral; he is *for* them. He chases them down the corridors of biblical history. God affirms his love for Israel multiple times in a series of covenants and covenant renewals with Adam, Noah, Abraham, Isaac, Jacob, Moses, and David. The fundamental promise of the covenants is simple: "I will be your God, you will be my people."

Here it's important to pause and understand the nature of biblical covenants. They are different than our agreements. They're not a contract between equals. Robert Jenson has referred to them as "a unilaterally imposed treaty."[6] Biblical covenants are modeled after the suzerainty treaties of the ancient Near East. God both gives and guarantees the covenant. It contains blessings and curses, both of which are signs of God's love for Israel. That's how seriously he loves them—that there are consequences for their actions, which will even include the destruction of the temple, the razing of Jerusalem, and their enslavement in Babylon. Michael Pickard has written, "It is important to understand that God takes the curses seriously...He takes the curses seriously because they are part of his love. What he opposes, he curses, and he opposes all that undermines human existence."[7]

5. Romans 8:31.

6. Jenson, *Theology in Outline*, 20. For an excellent overview of biblical covenants see Kline, *Structure of Biblical Authority*.

7. Pickard, *Rediscover the Bible*, 114.

Yet despite the justified imposition of the covenant curses, God's *love* for Israel is never in doubt. Just as a parent may not always be able to bless their child's behavior—and indeed, may have to impose consequences upon them for it—their unconditional love for their child's welfare remains. I always loved my kids, but I wasn't always able to bless their choices. Unconditional love doesn't mean unconditional blessing. (This seems to me to be one of the most damaging confusions in parenting today.)

We see a second dynamic when we run this EKG on the heart of God— namely that *God's heart beats continually for his people.* Over and over, we see God's people break the covenant as they slide into disobedience, idolatry, and disbelief. Reading the book of Judges, for instance, is like watching a broken washing machine repeating its cycles again and again—Israel disobeys God, God allows an oppressor to dominate them, the people cry out, God sends a deliverer, the people obey for a while, the people disobey God again—rinse, repeat.

It's not that God lets their behavior slide—he doesn't. They must deal with the consequences of their failure to follow his will and commands. But his *love* for them is never exhausted. Both blessing and curse are signs of his covenant faithfulness.

Tellingly, when God leaves Israel's temple during the Babylonian deportations, and his glory finally departs, it leaves through the eastern gate—the gate that leads to Babylon.[8] He will go with them there. Even in the punishment of exile, God has not abandoned Israel. Even after the catastrophe of exile, God remembers his covenant with Israel and eventually brings them back to the promised land. God never gives up on his people in the Bible, even when they give up on him. The story of the Bible is the long pursuit by God of his people.

Here I'm reminded of the story of a man I knew years ago. Henry owned a prosperous business in Seattle. He had a man who worked for him, and who embezzled from the company. As a committed Christian, Henry knew this was wrong, and he had the man prosecuted. The man went to prison in another part of the state. But Henry, as a committed Christian, didn't leave it at that. Throughout the man's sentence, Henry—who had a private pilot's license—would fly over once a month to visit the man in prison. Over the course of time, Henry was able to share his faith with him, and when the man left prison they became friends, and that man came to faith. In this sense, Henry emulated the heart of God.

A third dynamic revealed in God's EKG is that *his heart is always open toward his people.* God is always gracious and forgiving. He isn't neutral

8. Ezekiel 11.

toward them, or closed to them. Even though they're serial sinners and re-
petitive repenters, God never shuts them out, never refuses their repentance.

Grace and forgiveness are themes not only in the New Testament.
They're basic to the flow of the Old Testament as well. We're poorly taught
when we conclude that the Old Testament is about law and the New about
grace. God's hand is always extended in mercy and grace when his people's
tears are real.

A fourth dynamic we find in God's heart is the strength of its pulse—
*the flow of God's love is powered by the strength of his heart.* That love will end
up filling the universe and restoring all of creation.

Let's do a thought exercise. Think of the heart of God for the moment
as a pump (which hearts actually are). Think of the power of that pump to
flow God's love everywhere and forever. The pump is initially "installed" on
the earth, in the tabernacle described in the book of Exodus.

During Israel's wilderness wandering after the exodus, the tabernacle
or tent of meeting—inside which was the ark of the covenant, with the
mercy seat upon that, and a nearby altar of incense and other holy furnishings—was God's mobile home. It was to be the place where heaven and
earth kissed, and where God would meet his people. Even as the prophet
Isaiah notes that heaven is God's throne and earth his footstool, the notion
remains that the tabernacle, and subsequently the temple, is established by
God as the unique place of contact between God and Israel.[9] When the ark
of the covenant and other sacred furnishings are relocated from the portable
tent of meeting to the temple under Solomon's reign, people came from the
ends of the earth to see its glory.

God's love flows from God's presence, and his presence was uniquely
situated in the temple. But it doesn't remain there. It begins there, with his
people, but even so, his love for the whole world becomes foreshadowed in
the temple building itself.

By the time of Jesus, Herod the Great had been remodeling the second
temple for forty-six years. This was the temple built after the Babylonian exile (Solomon's temple had been destroyed by the conquering Babylonians).
With the Herodian expansion of the second temple, we begin to read of
the Court of the Gentiles for the first time. This was the most external and
largest of the temple courts, and was the place where non-Jews could come
to worship and hear rabbinic teaching.[10] The very existence of this court

9. Isaiah 66:1.

10. I've not found any evidence that there was a court of the Gentiles prior to
"Herod's Temple," which was the elaborate restoration and renovation of the temple in
the forty-six years leading up to the ministry of Jesus, and probably still under way at
the time. See John 2:12–21 and the research presented at https://biblearchaeology.org/

indicates that God has more in view than the salvation of his people Israel. This court is a reflection of the promise to Abraham that in his seed "all the nations of the earth" would be blessed.

We see the importance of this space for Jesus in John 2, when he cleanses it from those profiteering in the courtyard. Here Jesus's heart is revealed as one that beats for the Gentiles. There in the court of the Gentiles, Jesus says something dangerously shocking in declaring himself to be the very temple of God that will replace the second temple.

John has already tipped us off when he wrote, "The Word became flesh and made his dwelling among us. We have seen his glory, the glory of the one and only Son, who came from the Father, full of grace and truth."[11] The word that gets translated "dwelling" literally means "to tabernacle with,"[12] and the language of glory is standard temple language. It's clear from John's first chapter that the glory of God is shifting from a place to a person. Love is on the move. The pump has shifted from the temple to Jesus himself, who is now the source of God's love in the world.

Once again, we see the importance of the incarnation here. The tabernacle (later the temple) had always been the place where God and humanity (heaven and earth) overlapped to meet. But now they would no longer meet in a tent or building, but in a body—the person of the Word become flesh, the person of the God-Man. Thus, it is Jesus who's revealed to be Emmanuel, "God with us."

This trajectory flow from place to person continues from one person (Jesus) to many. After his ascension, Jesus's presence becomes universalized through the Holy Spirit and flows out into the world through those in whom he, the Father, and the Holy Spirit live. This is the basis upon which Paul tells us that the church has become the temple of God—God dwelling in us individually as well as corporately. Peter makes the same point when he says that believers are living stones being built up into a "spiritual house"—a euphemism for the temple.[13]

All of this is to say that the footprint of heaven is growing upon the earth. The dynamic flow of God's love is being pumped out from Jerusalem, across Judea, Samaria, and to all the peoples of the earth. Ultimately, the prophecy of Habakkuk will be fulfilled: "For the earth will be filled with the knowledge of the glory of the Lord, as the waters cover the sea."[14] Finally the

---

research/the-daniel-9-24-27-project/4364-john-2-12-21-and-herodian-chronology.

11. John 1:14.

12. Gk. ἐσκήνωσεν.

13. 1 Corinthians 6:19–20; 3:16–17; 1 Peter 2:4–5; see also John 17:20–23.

14. Habakkuk 2:14.

reality of heaven will fill the earth and ultimately the universe with God's glory, so that "God may be all in all."[15]

This is God's endgame: full restoration of his creation. We'll talk more about that in part five. For now, we want to note that God's love, the life-blood of his kingdom, is not a stagnant pool but a rushing torrent flowing straight from the heart of the Trinity, bringing life wherever it goes. This is the meaning of Israel's history and the coming of her Messiah-King.

With this background in mind, now it's time to gaze more deeply into his story.

15. 1 Corinthians 15:28.

# 5

# The Coming of the Messiah-King and His Chroniclers

*The One who wove the helix, woven now in flesh,*
*Bound fast together on the earth, God and Man enmeshed.*
*Ineffably committed, no way out, nor back.*
*It is finished; God is Man, of mercy now, no lack.*

*Echo of sage and prophet now find your voice in Him,*
*Present now for all—and none—to hear his joyful hymn.*
*Deep shadow now illumined, in flashing flesh grown bright,*
*Present now for all—and none—to see his holy light.*

*The roadless way is traveled, with tiny fetal feet.*
*She sweats and cries and thrashes, all for him to meet.*
*Seraphic eyes now shielded under pinioned wings,*
*Creation gasps upon his birth, the heavens start to sing.*
*Oh Healer of the primal wound, who wounded must become,*
*Join us here in our travail, and be of sin our sum.*

*We welcome you, we WELCOME you! Come well—Lord Jesus come,*
*For in the chasm of our souls you'll find your journey's run.*
*Oh deep long night of winter, when all is dark and drawn,*
*Arise now all creation sing, the glories of your Dawn!*

*The endless end is ending, God's kairos now has come.*
*The Son is here to save us, "It is finished," just begun…*

—TOM PFIZENMAIER "ONE NIGHT"

Now that we've looked at the love of God as portrayed in the script leading up to Jesus, let's return to the epicenter of the drama into which we're called. That epicenter is the startling personal appearance of the author in his own story. This is the dramatic moment in which all the prophetic promises find their shocking fulfillment.

The astonishing events surrounding the birth of Jesus itself makes it easy to forget the motivation behind it. With magi bearing gifts, appearances to shepherds, angelic announcements, old ones prophesying, and maniacal attempts to kill the child in his crib, it becomes easy to be distracted from the *why* by the *what*. Yet John characteristically states it with utter simplicity in his third chapter, "For God so loved the world that he gave his only-begotten son." If we ask, "*Why* did Jesus come?" the answer is the love of God. If we ask, "What's love got to do with it?" the answer is *everything!*

## ETERNAL STORY

Love had a plan that dwelt secretly in the heart of God "from the foundation of the world." That plan was to unite us all with Christ, the lamb who was to be slain, and in that uniting to make us holy and blameless,[1] thereby restoring us to our primal vocation as royal priests who help build out God's kingdom. This was the plan in the heart of the Triune God to rescue creation from the great collapse and everything associated with it. The plan is communion in the new creation.

In the incarnation, God reaffirms his covenant love for Adam, Abraham, Israel, Moses, David, and the whole world. He offers himself in love to every person in the coming of Jesus. In the coming of Christ, all the promises of God become "yes."[2] In the words of a popular worship song from "Jesus Culture," "Love has a name, love has a name—Jesus."[3] Jesus comes *in* love, *as* love, *to* love. As Jesus rises soaking wet from his baptism in the Jordan River, his Father speaks those words of coronation love over him as

---

1. See Ephesians 1:4; 1 Peter 1:19–20; Revelation 13:8.

2. 2 Corinthians 1:20.

3. Smith, Jackson, and Jackson, https://en.wikipedia.org/wiki/Love_Has_a_Name
_(Jesus_Culture_album).

Israel's Messiah-King and the world's Savior: "This is my Son, whom I love; with him I am well pleased."[4] Now the mission of Jesus begins, and it is in part a mission of becoming the "firstborn of many brethren," which is to say the firstborn of the many sons and daughters also beloved of their Father.[5]

Love is both primal and central in the ministry of Jesus. It's a centripetal love that attracts all things, pulling them together in God. As we've seen, the force of the Splitter is centrifugal—it divides, ruins, devours, and destroys. It separates people and pits them against each other. This is why the language of reconciliation is so central in the script.[6] Through the love of Christ, God has reconciled us to himself, and on this basis joyfully commands us to be reconciled to one another. Love reconciles those who are estranged. It is proactive, reaching out to the alienated ones and inviting them home. My point here is that we see the heartbeat of the love of God in Jesus's teaching and actions, in his words and works. To know Jesus is to know God, and to know God is to know love—because, as we've seen, God is love.

We see the love of God, for example, in the astonishing parable of the prodigal son. Here I want to focus on the character and action of the father; later I'll flip it, exploring the process of the son. Keep your eye on the father with me here. Recall, simply, that the wayward son remembers who he is while in the far country, and when he comes home, the father rushes out to meet him. The father had seen him from "far off," meaning that he was looking, hoping, waiting for him to return to the father's house. Remember, the father is not neutral. When the son arrives, he's fully reconciled, which is the reason for the robe, ring, and sandals. Full restoration to the sonship is his.

Then the father immediately sets out to see his sons reconciled to each other. The older brother will not come to the party because he deeply resents his younger brother. So, the father has to go out to him. Jesus is telling this parable in the presence of the Pharisees. They're represented by the older brother in the story. They do not love the sinners and outcasts that Jesus has loved and called. They resent them. And they resent Jesus for reconciling them. The Pharisees have inhaled the breath of the Splitter; their very name means "separated ones." In the words of the father pleading with the older son to come to the banquet, Jesus is pleading with the Pharisees to come and celebrate the sinners who in their repentance are turning to God: "Your brother was dead, and is alive, he was lost and is found."

Curiously, the story ends unresolved. The invitation to the older brother has been issued. But will he come to the banquet?

---

4. Matthew 3:17.

5. Romans 8:29; 1 John 3:1.

6. 2 Corinthians 5:17–20; Romans 5:11, 11:15.

It has been suggested that had a story like this really happened in a Palestinian village in Jesus's time, not only the son's behavior but the father's forgiveness and reconciliation would have shamed the villagers, and they may well have killed both the father and the son for not upholding the social norms based in alienation and punishment.[7] If this is true, then we know the Pharisees' answer to Jesus's invitation. Their answer was no, pounded home with the nails of the cross.

Beyond the story of the prodigal son, other elements of Jesus's teaching reveal to us the deep love of God for humanity. They're words of humble truth, words that power his subversion of the world order. His parables subvert the structures of shadow and death, and bring to the front of the line those who've always been at the back. The lost are found, the distant are brought near, the lonely and outcast are embraced. Jesus's teaching on the mountainside reminds the poor, the mourning, and the persecuted of a kingdom that belongs to them. He has come to take them deep into it. The insignificant ones, the children, the infirm, the unable, the dying, now have a defender and champion. Nothing is what it seems. God has come to his people, and all shall be well. The promised dawn has come upon them, the light of the world has come, and their redemption is underway.

Moreover, the works of Jesus sacramentalize the words of his teaching. The works become the outward and visible signs of the inward and invisible word being birthed into the world. Jesus' works bring to fruition the promises of God. The miracles are the warm inner lining of the coat of God's promises. In his miracles, the not yet becomes the already, and tomorrow becomes today. In his miracles, the satanic strongman is bound and the plundering of his house has begun. In the miracles of Jesus, the reign of God begins its reification in the world. All God's promises, seeded so deep in the soil of Israel's history across the centuries, now begin to sprout like mushrooms exploding overnight across a wet forest floor.

The miracle at the wedding at Cana is a sign-fulfillment of the coming of the Messianic age in which the creation will again support human life with its overwhelming bounty. This super-abundance of vine and grapes is captured in a Jewish prophecy outside the Bible, in the text known as 2 Baruch.[8] Here we see the provision of God's love for his people and all humanity.

---

7. Bailey, *Cross and the Prodigal*, 31.

8. One sees the prophecy of the abundance of the messianic age in 2 Baruch 29, which seems the clear backdrop for the miracle at Cana. Not only will the fruit of the vine be shockingly abundant (one grape producing between thirty-five and sixty gallons of wine), but "those who are hungry will enjoy themselves and they will, moreover, see marvels every day." Charlesworth, *Old Testament Pseudepigrapha*, Vol. 1, 630.

And then there are the healing miracles. Jesus understood that healing was a core competency of the Messiah and his disciples because it's a core competency of love. He healed, and healed, and healed—the blind, the lame, the deaf, the demon-possessed, the lepers. He healed the bleeding, and even the dead.

In the Gospel of John, just days before his crucifixion, Jesus raises Lazarus from his tomb. Jesus had two emotional responses to the scene of mourners at Lazarus's tomb, both of them grounded in his love for Lazarus. One, we're told, is that he was "deeply troubled."[9] The original word here[10] is used elsewhere in the ancient world to describe the snorting of a horse preparing for battle. The idea behind the word is "suppressed rage or indignation."[11] This is how love feels about death, which Paul calls "the last enemy."[12] Here, at Lazarus's tomb, Jesus prepares to do battle with death, the signature work of the Splitter.

But Jesus's raising of Lazarus is just a skirmish compared with the culmination of the battle that takes place on the killing fields of Golgotha and in its tomb of death. Here, in the death and resurrection of Jesus himself, the Splitter is decisively defeated. The strongman is fully bound, and Jesus's disciples are given the freedom to plunder the Splitter's house full of ill-gotten gain. In the cross and resurrection of Jesus, in his conquering of death through death, the liberation of all creation begins.

In addition to righteous rage, the other emotional response Jesus had to the death of Lazarus was tears. Jesus wept.

Picture that for a moment. As the mourning friends of Mary and Martha witnessed the Rabbi weeping over Lazarus, they interpreted his tears quite simply, saying, "See how he loved him."[13] They know what his tears mean. Jesus's expression of love is to heal Lazarus, to heal him from death. The love of Jesus reconciles. The love of Jesus heals.

Once again, it's love at the center, a spiritual love of great power driving the narrative forward. This is a love that does battle for the beloved. It's a strong love, a deep love, a committed love. It's also a tender love, a love that feels loss and knows pain.

Here in this little story of the death of Lazarus, we discover the contours of Jesus's love. Jesus's response to the death of his friend reveals the alpha and omega, the beginning and the end (which always includes everything

---

9. John 11:33.

10. Gk. ἐνεβριμήσατο.

11. Zerwick and Grosvenor, *Analysis of the Greek New Testament*, Vol. 1, 321.

12. 1 Corinthians 15:26.

13. John 11:36.

in between) of the limitless prodigal love of God revealed in Jesus Christ. It's no wonder that in John's opening doxology of praise to Jesus Christ in the Revelation he identifies Jesus first and foremost as "him who loves us":

> To him who loves us and has freed us from our sins by his blood, and has made us to be a kingdom and priests to serve his God and Father—to him be glory and power for ever and ever! Amen.[14]

John says that the sacrament of Jesus's love—the way it is manifested—is the shedding of his blood. Just as the Word became flesh, so now love becomes blood. Greater love has no man than this, that he should lay down his life for his friends.

In the second Adam, we become again a kingdom of priests ready to take up our ancient and primal vocation to serve the living God. We're home once again, in the Father's house. "The kingdom of this world has become the kingdom of our Lord and of his Christ, and he shall reign forever and ever."[15] The pivot begins in the incarnation—when God becomes man. It comes with his loving birth and culminates in his loving death and startling resurrection. Consequently, it's no surprise that as we turn to Jesus's chroniclers—to the pages of those who wrote about the impact of his life, death, and resurrection—we discover the primacy of love.

## THE STORY-TELLERS

Let's start with the apostle Paul. Throughout the thirteen letters from Paul in the New Testament, he speaks of Jesus's love again and again. He speaks much about our love too, but all of that is predicated on, and fueled by, the love of Christ at which he marvels. Let's listen in.

Paul tells the Romans that they're loved by God, and that God's love has been poured into their hearts by the Holy Spirit. For Paul, God's love finds its demonstration in Christ's love, and particularly the fact that it was while we were still enemies and sinners that Jesus died for us. He goes on to say that we're more than conquerors in this love. For Paul, this love of Jesus is so strong that nothing can separate us from it.[16] It's even stronger than the love which the Song of Solomon says "is as strong as death."[17] This love is

14. Revelation 1:5–6.

15. Revelation 11:15. And blessed be G. F. Handel for reminding us every year at Easter!

16. Romans 1:7; 5:8; 8:28; 8:35–39.

17. Song of Solomon 8:6.

more than a match for death. Indeed, it breaks the back of death, sentencing death to death. In the words of the preacher-poet John Donne, "Death be not proud...for death thou shalt die."[18]

This love is a form of spiritual gravity that inexorably binds us to Christ with stronger force than anything in the universe. Having laid this monumental foundation of the love of God poured out in Christ on us and for us, Paul then pivots in chapter 12 to what it will mean for the church at Rome (and the church for all time) to love one another. Our love is possible only as an extension of his love.

Following Romans, virtually all of Paul's correspondence with the church in Corinth revolves around how to live out this life of love in community. Here the second half of Romans and both Corinthian letters share their common theme, describing what love looks like on the ground.

As in Romans, Paul in Galatians first identifies the source of love in Jesus, then speaks about our love being necessarily grounded and generated by his Jesus's death on the cross. In one of the best-known passages of the Bible, Paul writes,

> I have been crucified with Christ and I no longer live, but Christ
> lives in me. The life I now live in the body, I live by faith in the
> Son of God, *who loved me and gave himself for me.*[19]

Paul squarely places love as the motivation of Christ in his work of salvation. In Ephesians, Paul returns to the theme of the love of God and its full expression in Christ:

> *In love* he predestined us for adoption to sonship through Jesus
> Christ, in accordance with his pleasure and will—to the praise
> of his glorious grace, which he has freely given us in the *One he*
> *loves.*[20]

In these words, we hear a reverberation of the Trinitarian love of God present from before the foundation of the world. It's an echo of joy as Paul says God finds pleasure in electing us in Jesus Christ, and that this gift comes to us only "in the One he loves." The language of Jesus's baptism also finds resonance here. "You are my beloved Son in whom I am well pleased." The same love and pleasure the Father has in the Son is now extended to us who belong to him.[21]

18. Donne, "Holy Sonnets" No. 10.

19. Galatians 2:20—my emphasis.

20. Ephesians 1:5–6—my emphasis.

21. Readers of the Bible sometimes misunderstand the concept of election. Simply put, it is God's predestining decision, made outside of time, within his absolute

Over and over Paul reminds the churches that they're loved by God, and that God is the very source of their love.[22]

When we move to the apostle John, the "beloved disciple," the love of God in Jesus is again exalted. For John, the love of God is lavished upon us. It is not measured, not calculated, not stingy. It's a prodigal love.[23] Because of the pouring out of Christ's life, we know what love is, what it looks like on the ground in the real world.[24] We can love only because he first loved us.[25] And not only did he first love us, but he loved us to the very end.[26]

In all of this—God's history with Israel, the meaning of the incarnation, the words and works of Jesus, and the reflections on him by the early church—the primacy of love is not only evident but paramount. The Bible is a narrative marinated in love from first to last. Its purpose is to reveal to us the heart of God, which is love, because God himself is love. We're at once both comforted and confronted by this magnificent love.

The script resembles the Camelot story, in its apparent plot line of a glorious but finally failed king and kingdom—except that here, of course, our stories part company. The story of Arthur and his knights ends in catastrophe; the story of Jesus and the twelve ends in "eucatastrophe." This is the term J. R. R. Tolkien gave to a catastrophic story with a surprise happy ending. The Bible story in general, and the Jesus story as its climax, form a narrative that brings comfort and hope, because at its heart this script is a eucatastrophe.[27]

---

freedom, to choose Jesus Christ, who is both God and Man, and in and choosing him, to choose humanity, whom Christ represents as the second Adam. It is an election of pure grace to redeem and restore humanity in and through their new representative, Jesus Christ. He is humanity's God ordained way through and out of the catastrophe we have brought upon ourselves, yielding only sin and death. From the moment of Christ's election, we can no longer discuss humanity's relationship to God on any other grounds. The election of an individual is determined simply by his or her relationship to Jesus Christ, and can no longer be considered on any other basis in natural theology or in human achievement. Christ alone is the Elect One, and our election must be "in Him," a truth definitively driven home in Ephesians 1 with Paul's relentless repetition of that refrain.

22. 1 Thessalonians 1:4, 3:12, 4:9; 2 Thessalonians 2:16, 3:5; 1 Timothy 1:14; 2 Timothy 1:7.

23. 1 John 1:31.

24. 1 John 3:16, 4:9–10.

25. 1 John 4:19.

26. John 13:1.

27. According to Wikipedia, "Tolkien calls the Incarnation of Christ the eucatastrophe of 'human history' and the Resurrection the eucatastrophe of the Incarnation"; https://en.wikipedia.org/wiki/Eucatastrophe. For primary source see, Tolkien, "The Monsters, the Critics and Other Essays," 156.

At the same time, it's a story that confronts. It thrusts a script and a story into our hands to either open, study, and enter, or to cast aside, ignore, and walk away from. This confrontation creates a crisis for anyone who reads the script. The question becomes: Is this *a* story among many, or is it *the* story? And if it's *the* story, does that make it *my* story too?

Karl Barth expressed it this way:

> To put it in the simplest way, what unites God and us men is that He does not will to be God without us, that He creates us rather to share with us and therefore with our being and life and act His own incomparable being and life and act, that He does not allow His history to be His and ours, but causes them to take place as a common history. That is the special truth which the Christian message has to proclaim at its very heart.[28]

## TIME TO SURRENDER

But the crucial issue remains outstanding. I can understand a truth and not be touched by it. I can explain it all without being changed by it. I can stand by the sea, even marvel at its beauty, and never swim in it. I can keep God's love at bay, or I can wade in and be immersed. We're called beyond observation and consideration to surrender.

I remember reading some years ago that after Lord Nelson won one of his great sea battles during the Napoleonic wars, a defeated admiral came on board Nelson's flagship. The enemy admiral walked across the deck, stretched out his hand, according to the conduct of gentlemen, and said, "Congratulations on your great victory, Admiral Nelson!" Nelson looked the man in the eye and said, "Your sword sir, *then* your hand."

Here we're talking about the knowledge of God's love versus the surrender to God's love. You can be a theologian without surrendering to God's love, but you can't be a follower of Jesus. The surrender may be pretty, or it may not. For one of the most eloquent Christians of the twentieth century it was *not* pretty; perhaps his surrender was closer to terrifying.

C. S. Lewis describes being an atheist as a young man, then slowly realizing that the citadel of his disbelief was being breached, and there was nothing he could do to stop it. His first step toward Christ was a frightful surrender to the God whose name is "I AM":

> Total surrender, the absolute leap in the dark, were demanded. The reality with which no treaty can be made was upon me. The

28. Barth, *Church Dogmatics*, 4/1, 7.

demand was not even "All or nothing." …Now the demand was simply "All."

You must picture me alone in that room in Magdalen, night after night, feeling, whenever my mind lifted even for a second from my work, the steady, unrelenting approach of Him whom I so earnestly desired not to meet. That which I greatly feared had come upon me. In the Trinity Term of 1929 I gave in, and admitted that God was God, and knelt and prayed: perhaps, that night, the most dejected and reluctant convert in all England… The Prodigal Son at least walked home on his own feet. But who can duly adore that Love which will open the high gates to a prodigal who is brought in kicking, struggling, resentful and darting his eyes in every direction for a chance of escape?… The hardness of God is kinder than the softness of men, and His compulsion is our liberation.[29]

For others, like Blaise Pascal, the surrender could be described in terms of ecstasy. Pascal was a French polymath who had a life-changing surrender to God on the night of November 23, 1654. Pascal wrote that we have a "God shaped vacuum within us." He knew something about that. The experience of the presence of God and his surrender to it was so vivid that Pascal expressed it in writing, then secretly sewed the note into his coat, which he wore for the rest of his life. He wrote:

From about half past ten at night until about half past midnight, FIRE.
GOD of Abraham, GOD of Isaac, GOD of Jacob not of the philosophers and of the learned. Certitude. Certitude. Feeling. Joy. Peace. GOD of Jesus Christ. My God and your God. Your GOD will be my God. Forgetfulness of the world and of everything, except GOD. He is only found by the ways taught in the Gospel. Grandeur of the human soul. Righteous Father, the world has not known you, but I have known you. Joy, joy, joy, tears of joy.[30]

Companionship with God begins in surrender to God. Surrender to God is our first act of worship. It's the first realization in which we say, "You are God. I am not. Thy will be done." We say it, and mean it.

Many people are content having God as an acquaintance. But their hearts remain restless. There's a true sense in which we'll always have a

29. Lewis, *Surprised by Joy*, 228–29.

30. Fusselman, "What Blaise Pascal Saw in a November Night of Fire That Inaugurated a Year of Grace," November 23, 2017; https://thefederalist.com/2017/11/23/blaise-pascal-saw-november-night-fire-inaugurated-year-grace/.

longing heart in this world, but that's different from a restless heart. The longing heart knows its lover; the restless heart is still looking.

For some of us, perhaps most, surrender becomes the recurring theme of our spiritual life. We're called to make many surrenders at multiple junctions. Functioning almost like the covenant renewal ceremonies in ancient Israel, these "re-surrenders" call for our commitment to Christ to be instantiated again and again, often at deeper and deeper levels. For the wells of living water within us to produce more, they must be drilled deeper.

I heard something of this when I heard one of Billy Graham's daughters speak of her own spiritual path at her father's funeral. At the time, I was working at a seminary where Billy Graham was a founder. At the school, we had a live feed for faculty, staff, and students to watch the funeral taking place in Charlotte, North Carolina on the grounds of the Billy Graham Library. The most touching moment for me was the testimony given by the evangelist's daughter Ruth. She said,

> After twenty-one years my marriage ended in divorce. I was devastated. I floundered. I did a lot wrong. The rug was pulled out from under me. My family thought it would be a good idea for me to move away, to get a fresh start somewhere else. And so, I decided to live near my older sister and her family and near a good church. The pastor of that church introduced me to a handsome widower, and we began to date fast and furiously. My children didn't like him, but I thought, you know, they were almost grown. They didn't know...they couldn't tell me what to do. I knew what was best for my life.
>
> My mother called me from Seattle. My father called me from Tokyo. They said, "Honey, why don't you slow down. Let us wait to get to know this man." They had never been a single parent. They had never been divorced. What did they know? So, being stubborn, willful, and sinful I married a man...on New Year's Eve, and within twenty-four hours I knew I'd made a terrible mistake. After five weeks I fled. I was afraid of him.
>
> What was I going to do? I wanted to go talk to my mother and father. It was a two-day drive. Questions swirled in my mind. What was I going to say to Daddy? What was I going to say to Mother? What was I going to say to my children? I'd been such a failure. What were they going to say to me? "We're tired of fooling with you." "We told you not to do it." "You've embarrassed us." Let me tell you. You women will understand. You don't want to embarrass your father. You really don't want to embarrass Billy Graham.

And many of you know that we live on the side of a mountain, and as I wound myself up the mountain I rounded the last bend in my father's driveway, and my father was standing there waiting for me.

As I got out of the car he wrapped his arms around me, and he said, "Welcome home." There was no shame. There was no blame. There was no condemnation, just unconditional love. And you know, my father was not God, but he showed me what God was like that day.

When we come to God with our sin, our brokenness, our failure, our pain, and our hurt, God says, "Welcome home." And that invitation is open for you. Thank you and God bless you.[31]

Our surrender can come in many shapes and sizes, but surrender we must. Sometimes it happens as a gradual awakening, like C. S. Lewis' subsequent shift from theism to Christianity:

I was driven to Whipsnade one sunny morning. When we set out, I did not believe that Jesus Christ is the Son of God, and when we reached the zoo, I did. Yet I had not exactly spent the journey in thought. Nor in great emotion. "Emotional" is perhaps the last word we can apply to some of the most important events. It was more like when a man, after long sleep, still lying motionless in bed, becomes aware that he is now awake.[32]

When it comes to encounters with Jesus, and the surrender into his love he asks of us, one size does not fit all. Nevertheless, all of them have at the core the laying down of our swords of self-defense, self-justification, and self-delusion. When we're confronted with Love, he calls out to us to trust and to follow wherever he leads us. This is the call of the God who is love in the person of his Son Jesus: "Come, follow me." The only appropriate response is to surrender to that call.

But it's not that easy really, is it? Before we wrestle with that fact, I want to take a deep dive into the Christian meaning of love. If you were wondering why I didn't touch earlier on 1 Corinthians 13 when we looked at how Paul spoke of love, it's because what he wrote there requires fuller reflection here.

31. Graham, "Funeral Service Transcript," https://memorial.billygraham.org/funeral-service-transcript/.

32. Lewis, *Surprised by Joy*, 237.

# 6

# An Anatomy of Christian Love

*What wondrous love is this, O my soul, O my soul!*
*What wondrous love is this, O my soul!*
*What wondrous love is this that caused the Lord of bliss*
*to bear the dreadful curse for my soul, for my soul,*
*to bear the dreadful curse for my soul.*

—AMERICAN FOLK HYMN

We've seen the primal love of the Holy Trinity and its expressions in the words and work of Jesus, and in a few key reflections from New Testament writers. Here I want to explore this love, to open it up and see what it's made of.

The natural place to start is the most thorough exposition of love we have in the New Testament, which is the thirteenth chapter of Paul's letter to the church at Corinth.

The setting is important. This is no philosophical, otherworldly contemplation on the virtue of love. For twelve chapters, Paul has been lovingly slugging it out with the Corinthians. He's covered church divisions (twice), his apostolic authority (twice), sexual immorality (twice), lawsuits, Christian marriage (twice), idolatry (twice), worship, spiritual gifts, and the connected nature of the body of Christ. It's crucial that we understand that Paul's teaching on love (*agape*) lands squarely in the midst of this struggling faith community. It is love for a rough-and-tumble church, and for a world much like our own, which was withering without it.

## PAUL'S ODE TO AGAPE

For Paul, love is the antidote to all the spiritual diseases raging in the church at Corinth and the world beyond it. It's a healing balm to be applied to a sick patient. The words are familiar to church people, but often read only at weddings, where they're watered down to aphorisms to ponder rather than the only way of life the living God has given us. With this in mind, let's work our way through the words and rediscover the contours of their meaning.

> If I speak in the tongues of men or of angels, but do not have love, I am only a resounding gong or a clanging cymbal. If I have the gift of prophecy and can fathom all mysteries and all knowledge, and if I have a faith that can move mountains, but do not have love, I am nothing. If I give all I possess to the poor and give over my body to hardship that I may boast, but do not have love, I gain nothing.[1]

The first section of Paul's exposition is what I like to think of as the "If" section. Paul lists five "If" phrases—all of them describing very good things. He begins with spiritual gifts he has just mentioned in the previous section (tongues and prophecy and knowledge), then widens his horizon by adding three more: faith, generosity, and martyrdom. The shocking thing is that Paul presupposes we can do all these things *without* love. Good things, very good things—but done without love. He doesn't address what other motivations might be funding these actions, leaving it to us to fill in the blanks. Selfishness? Manipulation? Virtue Signaling? Paul never says.

But the fact that we can develop a performative spirituality devoid of love ought to alarm us. It's reminiscent of Jesus saying that in the end times many would come and tell him what they had done in his name, and he'll reply, "I never knew you. Away from me, you evildoers!"[2] Apparently, the spirit within which we work out our salvation is as important (more so?) than the specific actions we take.

Ministry in the name of Jesus—even gifts exercised in the Spirit of Jesus—must be rooted in the heart of Jesus. Interiority matters. The disposition of one's heart matters. "Noisy gong," "clanging cymbal," "nothing," "does me no good." For Paul, it must be love in all we do. *Why* we do *what* we do matters.

> Love is patient and kind; love does not envy or boast; it is not arrogant or rude. It does not insist on its own way; it is not

1. 1 Corinthians 13:1–3.
2. Matthew 7:21–23.

irritable or resentful; it does not rejoice at wrongdoing, but rejoices with the truth. Love bears all things, believes all things,
hopes all things, endures all things. Love never ends.[3]

But it isn't just about motivation, or the disposition of our hearts entering into the action. It's also about *how* our actions are delivered. Paul
is saying that love has its own unique delivery system. Actions come with
an aroma. And love has its unique own signature perfume. Love is *patient.*
Love is *kind.*

Maya Angelou is credited with saying, "I've learned that people will
forget what you said, people will forget what you did, but people will never
forget how you made them feel." The fact that this wasn't original to her
doesn't detract from its truth.[4] When we're impatient and unkind, people
remember how it made them feel.

Recently I got into a political discussion with a friend, and it got a little
warm. He made a statement, then denied he said it. Rather than let it go, I
reminded him multiple times in staccato fashion what he'd said. I hurt him,
and I knew it—but it was too late. Damage done. What I said was true, but
I delivered the truth in an unloving way. He won't remember the truth of
what I said, he'll remember the pain I inflicted.

## LOVE DOES NOT ENVY, DOES NOT BOAST, IS NOT ARROGANT OR RUDE

On the other hand, love is also characterized by what it isn't. It is not envi-
ous, boastful, arrogant or rude. At the core of all four of these defects, the
ugly ring that binds them, is our choosing to place the sun of self at the center of our constellation of consideration. We start with "What about me?"
and loop all our thinking around that central obsession. Like a coiled rattle-
snake, we become wrapped around ourselves, preparing to strike any threat
that comes too close. Martin Luther was right to perceive that without the
redemption of Christ we're all *incurvatus in se* (curved in upon ourselves).
This posture is the very essence of sin. Only the "balm in Gilead," the love
of Christ, has the power to free us from this dreadful disease and heal our
humanity to the point that we can truly love others.

3. 1 Corinthians 13:4–8 (ESV).

4. The earliest evidence for an earlier source located by Quote Investigator appeared
in a 1971 collection titled "Richard Evans' Quote Book." The statement was ascribed to
Carl W. Buehner, who was a high-level official in the Church of Jesus Christ of Latter-
Day Saints. Richard L. Evans, *Richard Evans' Quote Book* (Salt Lake City: Publishers
Press, 1971), quote page 244, column 2.

## LOVE BEARS ALL THINGS

Those who follow Jesus Christ are called to bear all things. This means a lot more than passively putting up with each other's idiosyncrasies, stubbornness, carelessness, thoughtlessness—although it certainly includes doing that. And bearing means more than not remembering or registering others' faults—although it certainly includes that too. And it means more than bearing one another's burdens of loneliness, sadness, despair and grief, which we're certainly called to do because life is heavy and sometimes too heavy to carry alone.

To truly "bear *all things*" takes us even deeper. It means to bear one another's broken humanity, and to see in it a reflection of our own. It's bearing each other's imperfection, shallowness, hypocrisy, and even hatred. To bear all things is to enter into solidarity with each person as a fellow traveler on the road of life. It is, to recast D. T. Niles a bit, admitting that I too am nothing but a beggar in search of bread. At the core, I'm no better—and possibly worse, even much worse—than anyone else.

Augustine understood the necessity of this framing in our view of others:

> Let whosoever shall have been delivered from sin remember what he was. For then he beareth another man to be healed, if he shall remember that he himself was healed. Therefore let each call to mind what he was, and whether he be not still so; and he then will succor him that still is what he is no longer.[5]

And I must not only bear my fellow human being as a sinner traveling the road of life with me; I must also remember where that road leads—and bear others along for the sake of their destiny. In his book *The Weight of Glory*, C. S. Lewis wrote,

> It may be possible for each to think too much of his own potential glory hereafter; it is hardly possible for him to think too often or too deeply about that of his neighbor. The load or weight, or burden of my neighbor's glory should be laid on my back, a load so heavy that only humility can carry it.[6]

So, we bear with one another as those who are both sinners and saints. This bearing is not a natural human power—this love that can bear not merely *some* things, but *all* things. It's a divine power of a love that has come

5. Augustine, *Psalms*, XXV, 15, cited in Williams, "The Spirit and Forms of Love," 11. https://www.religion-online.org/book/the-spirit-and-the-forms-of-love/.

6. Lewis, *Weight of Glory*, 45.

into the world with Jesus. We must see the connection between his willingness to come to us in abject humanity in a sinful world, and our willingness
to go to others in the same way, bearing his love with us. He's not only our
model for this; his Spirit is the source of spiritual power that allows it to happen. His incarnation is the inbreaking not only of a new kind of love (*agape*)
in a human being, but the pouring forth of a new strength to love others.

As Christ has become the wound-bearer for us, so we enter his wound-
bearing work for others. Speaking of this connection of Jesus's bearing and
our own, Peter—Jesus's apostle—put it this way:

> To this you were called, because Christ suffered for you, leaving
> you an example, that you should follow in his steps... When
> they hurled their insults at him, he did not retaliate; when he
> suffered, he made no threats. Instead, he entrusted himself to
> him who judges justly. "He himself *bore* our sins" in his body on
> the cross, so that we might die to sins and live for righteousness;
> "by his wounds you have been healed."[7]

The upshot of all this bearing is that when people sense our solidarity with them—especially in our bearing the brokenness of their humanity,
because in it we recognize our own—they'll come to believe in Jesus. Love
bears all things. His did, and so now must ours.

## LOVE BELIEVES ALL THINGS

Paul also reminds us that *agape* love "believes all things." This is not an
encouragement to a naive credulity. The "all things" is a reference to the
plenary promises of God—that they will all, each and every one, be fulfilled.
To believe in the promise is to believe in the Promiser. Paul is encouraging
us not only to stand on the promises of God, but to stand in the presence of
the Promiser.

Sometimes when I look at the world, and I see what a shambles it still
is in so many ways, I struggle to believe that all God's promises will come to
pass. I feel like Noah listening to his mocking neighbors, or the boy Joseph
on his way to Egypt in chains, or Esther trembling as she heads for her ten
o'clock with King Ahasuerus. Or the disciples on that Saturday night. Sometimes when I look at the big picture, it doesn't look so good.

And people. When I look at myself and see so much immaturity still,
or at others and see how they choose to live, I wonder, "Can God *really*
make a new heavens and a new earth out of this mess that we've made of

---

7. 1 Peter 2:21–24 (my emphasis).

the old ones?" When I remember Thomas Merton's startling image of man as a desolate temple—where only a haunting image dwells, but no longer the living presence of God—I struggle to "believe all things." Then I reread the story of the apostle John and the bandit, told by Clement of Alexandria centuries ago.[8] It goes like this:

When the apostle John was quite elderly and had returned from his exile on the island of Patmos (where he wrote the Revelation), he met a young man whom he brought into the way of Christ and discipled him accordingly. John was called away on a long trip, and so entrusted the spiritual care of the young man to the local bishop. While John was gone, the bishop failed in his shepherding duties and the young man returned to his former life with a dangerous gang of thieves who lived up in the hills.

When John at length returned and inquired of the bishop about the young man, he was shocked to hear the bishop say, "He is dead." Upon deeper inquiry as to what had happened, the bishop told John of the young man's return to this former life, ending his account with the words, "He is dead to God."

John could have left it at that—shrugged his shoulders and walked away. He didn't. John believed all things. He believed that the presence of Christ had taken up residence in the young man, and that however confused and misguided he'd become, Christ's promise would be fulfilled in him.

So John, now very old, saddled up and rode up into the treacherous mountain pass where the young man had rejoined the thieves. The bishop had warned John not to undertake such a dangerous mission; John had ignored him. There was a young man who still belonged to God, no matter how confused.

When John arrived at the robbers' camp in the mountains, he was captured by the lookout and taken to see their captain—the very man John was looking for. When this young man saw John, he tried to run, but the old man chased him down, crying out, "Why, my son, do you flee from me, your father, unarmed, old? Son, pity me. Fear not; you still have hope of life. I will give account to Christ for you. If need be, I will willingly endure your death, as the Lord did for us. For you, I will surrender my life. Stand, believe; Christ has sent me."

The story has a happy ending, a eucatastrophe. The young man is restored to God, to himself, and to the fellowship of believers. John believed all things. He believed that "he who began a good work in you will bring it to completion in Christ Jesus." This is how it is with love. Love believes all things.

8. Clement of Alexandria, *Ante-Nicene Fathers* Vol. 2, 603ff.

## LOVE HOPES ALL THINGS

If Christianity is nothing else, it's a religion of hope. At the center of its faith stands the resurrected Christ. That same chronicler of the truth of Christ who wrote the words above also said in his first letter to the Corinthians that if Christ has not been raised from the dead, our faith is in vain; we're still in our sins, and to be pitied most of all.[9] Everything rises and falls on the resurrection of Jesus Christ from the dead.

Without the bodily resurrection of Jesus, the entire edifice of the Christian faith crumbles. But with his resurrection, that edifice stands forever. This means that if Christ has been raised, hopelessness is next to godlessness.

Over the course of my adult life, I've spent many hours considering the evidence for the historical, bodily resurrection of Jesus, and have written elsewhere about why I find it persuasive.[10] We have solid historical grounds for this hope. History—because it's *His* story—is pregnant with hope because of Jesus's resurrection.

It's not a hope that says suffering and death are an illusion; it says rather that they're impostors posing in costumes of the last word. Christian hope has its eye on the big picture, on the final things. Hope is the "eschatological vibration"[11] of the resurrection. Hope is the tsunami created by the earthquake of the resurrection that surges humanity forward into the new heavens and new earth.

Paul tells us, "So we fix our eyes not on what is seen, but on what is unseen, since what is seen is temporary, but what is unseen is eternal."[12] Christian hope is the product of a disciplined, relentless focus on the future of Jesus Christ. Hope sees what's going on in front of its face, but also the horizon beyond it.

One fall day in 1982, sixty thousand fans assembled in Badger Stadium at the University of Wisconsin for the big game. Wisconsin was playing Michigan State, and Michigan State was beating them soundly. As the game progressed and the score became more lopsided, the Wisconsin fans would occasionally, randomly, stand on their feet and cheer. This didn't make any sense, since their team was getting hammered, but time after time they stood and cheered. How could they cheer when their team was losing so

9. 1 Cor. 15:17, 19.

10. Pfizenmaier, *For My Daughters: A Father Reflects on Family, Friendship and Faith*, 209–18.

11. Martin, *Last Things*, 31.

12. 2 Corinthians 4:18.

badly? How could they cheer at moments that seemed incongruous with their outbursts of joy?

Well, it turns out that seventy miles away, the Milwaukee Brewers were beating the St. Louis Cardinals in game four of the world series. Many of the fans at Badger stadium had brought transistor radios tuned into the series. They had their attention and their hearts set on a different game that day. Where the sun of human solutions sets, the dawn of Christ's solution rises. When people sense that we live in the neighborhood of hope, they'll want to move in next door, for love hopes all things.

## LOVE ENDURES ALL THINGS

Therefore, love bears all things, believes all things and hopes all things. And love endures all things. Christian love is gritty love. It's a passion that perseveres.[13] The two New Testament words used to describe this aspect of love are generally translated "patient endurance" and "longsuffering."[14] Once again, it is the Love who is Jesus. It's the Love who battled the tempter in the desert, set his face like flint toward Jerusalem, endured his bloody scourging, wore his crown of thorns, and was nailed to his cross. It's the Love who was raised from the dead and lives forevermore.

This love, we're learning, is not a disembodied virtue, but a living presence. This love is not a one-off thing. It's the beginning of a game-on thing. The love of God is now present in Jesus of Nazareth, who is love. And through his Holy Spirit that love is disseminated but not diluted among his followers as it floods into a parched world to renew its foundations.

This love doesn't wear out, give out, or burn out. It's a love that endures because Christ endures. It's never theoretical, but always personal, because it flows from a person. It can never be stopped. It can never be defeated. It can never be exhausted because he can never be stopped, defeated, or exhausted. This love endures all things because its source is Jesus, "who for the joy set before him endured the cross, despising its shame, and sat down at the right hand of God."[15]

This love will endure because it's the nature of reality itself—because God is love. When everything else is over and gone, love remains, because God remains.

13. I owe this definition of *grit* to Angela Duckworth and her book *Grit: The Power of Passion and Perseverance*.

14. In New Testament Greek, "patient endurance" is generally ὑπομονή, while "long-suffering" is μακροθυμέω.

15. Hebrews 12:2.

*Love bears all things, believes all things, hopes all things endures all things—and so love never fails.*

You may be more familiar with the translation "love never ends," and this is of course true. But the verb here can also be translated "fails," which opens another line of thought.[16] If God is love, and God never fails in what he purposes, then his love never fails in its purposes. Just as the creation began as an act of love, so shall it finally become at its consummation. The whole biblical narrative can be read as Love finding a way, because God is love.

16. The phrase is rendered Ἡ ἀγάπη οὐδέποτε πίπτει, see Zerwick and Grosvenor, *Analysis of the Greek New Testament*, Vol. 2, 524.

# PART THREE

The Splendor of the Light
of Christ's Love

# 7

# The Violet Light of Truth

*In him was life, and the life was the light of men. The light shines in the darkness, and the darkness has not overcome it.*

—JOHN 1:4–5

An old song says that love is a many-splendored thing, and that's true—far more so than the song conveys. Love is splendid because it's refracted into multiple colors as it expresses itself in the world. The Puritan Thomas Goodwin said of God that, "all his attributes seem but to set out his love."[1]

If we think of the love of Christ as the refraction of God's love into his creation, we'll see it as both splendorous and unique. Seen as a whole, it is resplendent as its aspects blend one into another. But it's also unique as we examine each aspect of his love on its own. Throughout we're talking about *agape*, but we're also talking about how the other loves of *eros*, *storge*, and *philos* are themselves redeemed and transformed when they're grounded in *agape*. Just as light is refracted into a spectrum of colors when viewed through a prism, so God's love is refracted into a spectrum of qualities through the prism of scripture.

These next few chapters will explore just some of these refractions, beginning with the violet light of truth. My list is not intended to be exhaustive, but suggestive.

---

1. Thomas Goodwin, "Of the Gospel Holiness in the Heart and Life", *Works* 7:211, quoted in Ortlund, *Gentle and Lowly*, 141.

## WHAT IS TRUTH?

It's a commonplace these days to acknowledge that truth in our time is an endangered species, if not extinct already. We've convinced ourselves that each of us has our own truth, that we're each a law unto ourselves, and that truth claims by anyone else are nothing but power plays meant to subjugate and oppress. And, well, there is some truth to that! (pun intended). In ways both subtle and overt, this is the dominant narrative of our age. But it hasn't always been so.

Until our time, it was assumed in Western thought that capital-T Truth existed and could be discovered. Like a family arguing over preferred routes to Yosemite the night before leaving on vacation, modern philosophers (writing roughly from the seventeenth century to the end of World War I) argued over preferred routes to the truth. Some members of the philosophy family emphasized starting with the mind. Reason was the preferable path to truth because it offered two approaches: one was deductive reasoning from first principles—for example, the *Cogito ergo sum* formula from Descartes. If you could clarify certain first principles or innate ideas that were irrefutable, you could work from the top down and discover other truths by derivation.

The second way to truth by way of the mind through reason was the path of induction or empiricism. Working from the bottom up, this approach became the preferred method of modern science. Here you find truth by starting with the evidence presented to the senses in the world around us, and you work from there. Like putting together a jigsaw puzzle piece by piece, eventually the big picture of truth would emerge.

In contrast to the road of reason there were those in the family of philosophers (and artists) who preferred the route of the heart. Relying on affective sensibility (feeling) and intuition, the Romantics held that the way of the mind was untrustworthy; it was the way of the heart that led to truth.

But the one thing everyone believed—Rationalists and Romantics alike—was that truth was "out there"; it existed and could be discovered. That core belief in Truth's existence was the bedrock confidence of modern philosophy.

Coupled with that confidence (and here's where the real trouble starts) was an excessive confidence in human capacity to discover truth unaided. Whether through hubris of mind or heart, the moderns slowly abandoned any notion that the human mind or heart needed an assist, let alone correction, from the light of divine revelation to complete its picture of truth.

Modernism has been described this way:

First, modernism can be characterized by the vesting of authority in the self. Whether following the external canons of empiricism or the internal canons of rationalism and romanticism, the modernist mind accomplished the enthronement of the individual as the final arbiter of truth. This individual authority asserts itself both against corporate authority and divine revelation either in denying them altogether or in subjecting them to the individual for validation. While human autonomy is at the heart of every non–Christian thought system, modernism distinguished itself by its self-consciousness in this regard.[2]

This hubris of the sovereign self, which was seeded in the French salons of the Enlightenment, and which subsequently budded among the romantics, became the reigning historical narrative in the progressive (Whig) interpretation of history beginning in the eighteenth century. Whig history was a narrative of inevitable human progress—the curve of history was up and to the right. Progress, in the modernist reading, was inevitable, and human ingenuity alone was its driver.[3]

This narrative exploded when the most advanced country in the world led that world into the meat-grinder of the Great War. Surveying the wreckage of World War I—the foremost casualty of which was Whig history and its modernist conceits—a group of philosophers in the twentieth century turned in a new (so they thought) direction. They would come to be called postmodernists.

Postmodernism is a complex intellectual and aesthetic view of life. Many of its initial adherents were Marxists. Later, for a variety of reasons, they became disenchanted with Marxism's failed utopias. Lawrence

---

2. Michael J. Glodo, "The Bible in Stereo: New Opportunities for Biblical Interpretation in an A-Rational Age," in Dockery, *Challenge of Postmodernism*, 108.

3. Today, the Whig interpretation of history as progress is seeing a revival. Just this week there appeared in the *Wall Street Journal* a major article by noted historian Francis Fukuyama, who portrays liberalism as an arc arising from the synthesis of the scientific method, rule of law, and economic modernization. He believes that although liberalism experiences severe gyrations in its history, the trajectory of its arc is "justice." He writes: "From a long-term perspective, liberalism has seen its ups and downs but has always come back in the end... There is indeed, an arc of history, with justice as its terminus." Fukuyama, "The Long Arc of Historical Progress," *The Wall Street Journal*, Saturday/Sunday, April 30/May 1, 2022, C1-2; quotation taken from p. C2. My own view is that everything that has an arc must be propelled by some force. I do not believe history is its own force. It is simply the recording and interpretation of events. I do, however, believe that history does have an arc, and that, moreover, justice is a part of that arc. I believe God is the sovereign force who is directing that arc by his love and will. Human beings do not direct history; God does.

Cahoone, in *From Modernism to Postmodernism: An Anthology,* describes the plight of these early postmoderns:

> Marxism had provided a philosophy of history that served for a sizable segment of the secularized Western intelligentsia as a worldly religion, a particularly potent fulfillment of that great modern hope in progress, what Christopher Lasch called the "One and Only Heaven." For many irreligious intellectuals, the hope for a utopian socialist future gave badly needed significance to a life lived after the "death of god." The loss of this hope struck a sizable portion of this group much as the loss of religion had already struck traditional society: lacking a historical telos or goal, it seemed that the world had become centerless and pointless once again. Postmodernism, a wayward stepchild of Marxism, is in this sense a generation's realization that it is orphaned.[4]

One writer defined postmodernism as "a very particular way of not knowing who you are."[5] Once God is dead, and faith in the State as a proxy for God (Marxism) dies—then what? Rather than search for a new and better story (or reconsider an ancient one) within which to frame the meaning and purpose of their lives, the postmoderns declared the whole project a farce. The idea of a truth to live by (or within) was abandoned. Put another way, postmodernism was the sledgehammer taken to the stained-glass window of modern Western epistemology. The concept of truth, along with any possibility of its discovery, was shattered.

## ALL THE LIGHT WE CANNOT SEE

The postmodernist stance relative to modernist truth–claims can best be described as suspicion and denial. Postmodernists became persuaded that all truth claims were based in language, and since language was a human construct, truth must be also. For postmoderns, language was nothing more than a political–economic–social tool used by one group of people to gain power over another. This notion fit readily into their already Marxist sympathy for seeing history as class struggle. Language games were formulated for the purposes of aggregating power and enhancing utility—getting stuff done.

---

4. Cahoone, *From Modernism to Postmodernism,* Introduction, 10.

5. Elizaga, https://www.quora.com/What-is-the-difference-between-post-modernism-and-Marxism.

Truth no longer had any foundation in external realities because transcendence was disavowed. Appeals to God, Plato's forms, Aristotle's substances, or even capital-N Nature were considered invalid. There could only be subjectively based "truths," which were grounded in one's "lived experience" or "narrative." This stance implicitly required the rejection of "metanarratives," which were overarching stories claiming to be grounded in certain truth claims of either religion or history.

These metanarratives were to be "deconstructed" (unmasked) and seen for what they are—linguistic power plays used by oppressors. Postmodernism saw itself as the "Toto" philosophy, which pulled back the curtain on the Modern wizard of Oz, revealing him to be only a fearful, fretful, desperate, controlling little man (increasingly white, European, and old) trying to manipulate his own Oz. Like the wizard, all the moderns were frauds now exposed by postmodern Totos.

Metanarratives were grand stories of how the world works. Think here of the Judeo-Christian story of sin and salvation, or of Marxism's metanarrative that economic class struggle (dialectical materialism) is the defining story of human history, or of Darwinism, which became the dominant naturalistic and materialistic metanarrative. Likewise, today's Critical Race Theory (itself a stepchild of the Critical Theory of the Marxist Frankfurt School), which says that race is the defining human trait, qualifies as a metanarrative. Whereas economics was the primary category for the Marxists, now it has become race among these critical theorists. The oppressor/oppressed paradigm remains in place, but the capitalist/worker struggle is replaced by the white / people of color struggle.

For the pure postmodern, none of these metanarratives are true, because there's no such thing as Truth. For the postmodern, all metanarratives are made up human constructs. Ironically, the assertion that there's no truth is itself a truth claim, and therefore a form of metanarrative. Postmodernism itself is a worded power play. Whereas the moderns shifted the source of authority away from external sources (God, scripture, church, and the state) to the internal sources of the self (rationalism and romanticism), the postmoderns go a step further by denying the existence of truth altogether.

See how important this is. What's at stake is more than intellectual posturing. If there's no truth, no metanarrative within which we can make sense of our lives, then how can we find our bearings? How can we know who we are? How can we know what to do? As noted above, postmodernism truly is a distinct way of not knowing who you are. We're lost to ourselves, lost to each other, lost to the creation in which we find ourselves, and lost to God, whose undertaker is (supposedly) postmodernism. It's one thing to be headed on vacation to Yosemite using the wrong map; it's another thing to say there's no Yosemite.

There have been a variety of worldviews and truth-systems in human history, and what they all share in common is the assumption that a worldview or truth-system, or "frame" is needed. Every viable civilization has been grounded in a larger metaphysical belief system—its own metanarrative. The self must be sourced in something larger than the self. Put another way, a civilization composed only of self-referential selves will never survive. It will tear itself apart. The center cannot hold when there is no center.

This is why we need a viable system of truth. Without truth, we lose our access to love. As human beings we come to each other in the search for truth, the discovery of truth, and the living of truth. Without truth we don't know who to love, how to love, what to love, or even why to love. Truth is the oxygen in the furnace of love. Truth grounds, shapes, and directs love. In turn, truth is one of love's fullest expressions and one of its most beautiful refractions.

The irony of our time is that while truth becomes more central and celebrated in the hard sciences and their technological offspring, it has become utterly marginalized among our cultural elites in all other areas of human endeavor. Philosophers, psychologists, politicians, writers, film-makers, artists, and musicians tend to proceed from the point of view that either "I myself determine what is true" (modernism), or "There is no truth" (postmodernism).

The clarion call to "follow the science" presupposes that science is real—true at least in some sense. Aside from the problematic contradiction between the call to follow the science and the very nature of science itself as always tentative and incomplete modeling, we're witnessing the odd canonization of STEM education based on the assumption that truth exists, while at the same time declaring heretical the pursuit of truth in other disciplines taught down the hall in the English and philosophy classrooms.

We've been trying to live in two different realities simultaneously. We've become epistemological schizophrenics. We've adopted truth in the culture of laboratory and technology, but orphaned it (and with it ourselves) in the public square. Having exchanged our epistemological birthright for either modern or postmodern pottage, we wonder why we haven't received the blessing. As a result, we're a bumper-car culture crashing into one another while madly chasing from fad to fad, all the while plunging deeper into spiritual and moral chaos. This is the what happens when Truth and its pursuit are abandoned.

As Yoram Hazony has perceptively stated, our cultural revolution has now migrated to its second phase. After surveying the cultural carnage left from Enlightenment liberalism's celebration of the self in its adolescent rampage through the village of our historic Western commitments, we now sit upon an ash heap of our own making:

> Now an entirely different kind of decay is ascendant: a growing lassitude and despair; a true decadence in which no praise is to be gained from moving in any direction. And so meaningful movement ceases, and all that is left is the monotonous parade of sensations induced by alcohol, drugs, and flickering screens.[6]

We're living in the time when Nietzsche's Madman has become this generation's Superman, and at the center of this is the rejection of truth, the rejection of *agape* love, the rejection of life, and the rejection of ourselves. Truth has become putty in our hands. We try to shape and form it to serve our own purpose, and in so doing it slips through our fingers, leaving us not only with empty hands but messy ones. God had warned us in the beginning not to take truth-making into our own hands lest we surely die. And dying we are. But it is a dying by choice.

The roots of postmodernism go back a hundred years or so. It has been at the core of our public university education system for the last two generations. Its reach has been intentional, systemic, and thorough. One of the great proponents of postmodernism in education is Robert Nash, and he sums it up as well as anyone:

> Postmodern conceptions of truth...entail a particular set of dispositions—what I call "postmodern virtues"—and I contend these are a necessary precursor to the development of the democratic dispositions I discussed earlier.[7]

For Nash and other postmodern educators, the classical and theological virtues of prudence, justice, fortitude, temperance, faith, hope, and love (which were the foundation for training citizens of Western civilization), must now be cast off and replaced:

> Most postmodern writing assumes the absence of a common moral standard by which to evaluate competing moral vocabularies, traditions, and frameworks (incommensurability). It also assumes that no authority can ever determine, or settle in advance, what ought to be the "final" word on truth or morality (indeterminacy).[8]

---

6. Hazony, *Conservatism*, 168.

7. Nash, *Answering the Virtuecrats*, 176.

8. Nash, *Answering the Virtuecrats*, 176.

For Nash and the postmoderns, classical virtues are set in the scales of postmodernism and found wanting:

> [Classical] virtues are anachronistic, because they are depen-
> dent on an obsolete conception of human nature; reactionary,
> because they buttress the sociopolitical status quo; unintel-
> ligible, because definitions of virtues and right actions tend to
> be circular; irrelevant, even arbitrary, because there is today
> no universal moral standard to evaluate their worth; impracti-
> cal, because too many virtues are in conflict with each other;
> egotistic, because they divert moral attention to the self rather
> than to others; and, ultimately, fatalistic and deterministic,
> because, as Aristotle believed, virtues are too closely linked to
> chance (*fortuna* L.)—to wealth, family background, training,
> and intelligence.[9]

For Nash, postmodernism has its own set of virtues that must be imposed to ensure "democratic dispositions." If we ask what these virtues might be, Nash has the answer.

> Among these [postmodern] virtues are sensitivity to the post-
> modern realities of incommensurability, determinacy, and
> non-foundationalism; dialectical awareness; empathy; herme-
> neutical sensitivity; openness to alterity ("otherness"); respect
> for plurality; a sense of irony and humor; a commitment to
> civility; a capacity for fairness and charity; compassion in the
> presence of suffering, with an antipathy toward violence; and
> humility in the face of shifting and elusive conceptions of reality,
> goodness, and truth.[10]

To summarize, the postmodern education that has been gathering steam since the sixties has its own truth: *There is no truth.* It has its own morality: *There are no fixed moral standards.* And it would impose its own set of virtues grounded in postmodernism. Since these standards are "nec-essary for democratic dispositions," we should be wondering what the role of the State will be in enforcing these new virtues—and silencing or cancel-ing competitors.

Nash, writing in 1997, recognized that postmodern educators had their work cut out for them, but their dedication as zealous missionaries of postmodernism was clear.

---

9. Nash, *Answering the Virtuecrats*, 15.
10. Nash, *Answering the Virtuecrats*, 11.

Teaching these virtues presents a formidable challenge, because students must learn a whole new way of thinking about morality, truth, and communication.[11]

Recent statistics on how Americans see truth makes it clear that postmoderns have triumphed. They have swept the pedagogical field. According to Pew Research, 33 percent of adult Americans believe there are clear standards for right and wrong, while 64 percent believe that right or wrong depends on the situation.[12] Only 15 percent of those eighteen to twenty-nine years old believe there are clear standards of right and wrong.

## WHO IS TRUTH?

Jesus taught that the truth would set us free. But how can we experience freedom if we don't believe in truth—and so never desire, pursue, and live it?

Truth matters. It always has. In the script we often see truth metaphorized as light.[13] Jesus describes himself as the "light of the world."[14] So we read, "The light shines in the darkness, and the darkness has not overcome it."[15] Then one day the Light of the world is standing before a Roman governor having an instructive conversation about truth.

Perhaps Pontius Pilate stands as the precursor of a postmodern humanity as he presides at the trial of Jesus. Pilate asks Jesus if he is a king, and Jesus responds, "For this reason I was born and have come into the world, to testify to the truth. Everyone who belongs to the truth listens to my voice." Pilate then poses his cynical question: "What is truth?" For both Pilate and the postmodern, you don't have to belong to the truth if you don't believe in truth in the first place. But doesn't he? Doesn't Pilate believe in truth? The truth is that everyone believes in truth. We can't operate without it even as we deny it.

Pilate lives in the world of Roman realpolitik where power and efficiency override every other consideration. Power and efficiency are his truth. Caesar decides what's true for Rome and what's true for Pilate. Caesar

11. Nash, *Answering the Virtuecrats*, 176.

12. "Belief in absolute standards for right and wrong," Pew Research Center Religious Landscape study; https://www.pewresearch.org/religion/religious-landscape-study/belief-in-absolute-standards-for-right-and-wrong/.

13. Psalm 43:3, for example.

14. John 8:12.

15. John 1:5.

is his truth. Pilate has chosen his king and his god, because in Rome "Caesar is Lord."

Mark's Gospel was written to the Romans, and one of Mark's themes is that Jesus is the Son of God. Interestingly, this was one of the titles of Tiberius Caesar, Pilate's boss. Tiberius's father, Augustus, had been proclaimed divine. When he died, Tiberius saw a comet shoot overhead and announced his father's apotheosis. So if Augustus is God, that makes Tiberius the son of God—and he minted the coins to prove it, with his image stamped on them next to the Latin words TI CAESAR DIVI AVG F AVGVTVS ("Tiberius Caesar Augustus, son of divine Augustus").[16] So now we have Pilate, who works for the self-proclaimed son of God (Tiberius), standing in front of Jesus, who was declared the Son of God by the voice from heaven at his baptism. If Jesus is the true king, then he's the true Son of God—and Caesar isn't. Which man is truth? Is Jesus Lord and the Son of God—or is it the Roman Emperor?

Jesus knows that neither Pilate nor Caesar has their own truth apart from God's truth. Jesus loves Pilate enough to tell him so. When Pilate asserts his authority as governor under Caesar to have Jesus put to death, Jesus tells him, "You would have no authority over me if it were not given to you from above."[17] Jesus doesn't even mention the emperor. There *is* truth, and that truth is the person standing in front of Pontius Pilate. He and the Father are one. As the incarnation of the truth, he will adjudicate all contingent truth claims.

Jesus had already told the disciples, "I am the way and the truth, and the life; no one comes to the Father except through me."[18] This is the ultimate truth claim and must be accounted either true or false. Jesus is not making this claim in its postmodern rendering of "I am my truth and you are your truth." The use of "I am" here is a use of the divine name of God as revealed in the Old Testament.[19] This is axiomatic in John's Gospel and its many "I am" sayings. This is an absolute claim to be the bearer of absolute truth, not a relative claim made by a subjective bearer. Here Jesus reveals the fundamental structure of all reality. *Light, life, truth*—together they manifest the love of God who is Jesus.

Truth, as it turns out, is a person—specifically the God who reveals himself in Jesus Christ. This is the startling promise and announcement of

16. Image of Tiberius coin, "Aureus (Coin) Portraying Emperor Tiberius," Art Institute of Chicago; https://www.artic.edu/artworks/5602/aureus-coin-portraying-emperor-tiberius.

17. John 19:11.

18. John 14:6.

19. Exodus 3:13–14.

the gospel. And our lives must answer back to this appearance of the truth who is God in history. We'll live a life of either resonance or dissonance with the truth. Henceforth we can live the truth or live a lie.

Two lies die in the presence of Jesus. One says, "I am my own truth" (the modern lie). The other says there is no truth (the postmodern lie). There's no truth apart from Jesus, who is the walking Torah, the Word of God incarnate. He himself is the very truth of God.

## THE TWO WAYS

"There are two ways, one of life and one of death, and there is a great difference between the two ways."[20] So says that bit of ancient Christian wisdom called the *Didache*. G. K. Chesterton's Father Brown says, "What we all dread most is a maze with no center."[21] That's not a bad definition of postmodernism. By cutting us off from transcendent sources, they've left us in darkness, not light, and with death, not life; we're lost but not found. In his book *The Singer*, Calvin Miller says, "The world is poor because her fortune is buried in the sky and all her treasure maps are of the earth."[22] This is the legacy of both the moderns and postmoderns because each in its own way have cut us off from transcendent sources. But as anyone who's ever been lost in a maze knows, the best way out is up. Once we're lifted above the maze, we can see our way out.

There's a deeper and more fundamental truth upon which science and all other forms of truth and knowledge depend. It's the truth of God, embedded in his creation and revealed in his word. Ironically, this belief was initially one of the pillars of the scientific method. God's truth comes from above. Human truths come and go, morph and change; they're by nature contingent. But the truth of God, who is Christ, stands forever. And in the visage of truth, we discover the face of love.

Truth is one of the refractions of love in a broken world. To the degree that we can reorient ourselves around the truth of God as manifested in Jesus—to that extent we can begin to remember whose we are and who we are, and find our way home.

The maze has a center, and we have reached it. Now we must return home by way of the truth who is Jesus.

20. "The Didache, or Teaching of the Twelve Apostles," *Apostolic Fathers*, Vol. 1, 309.

21. Chesterton, *The Complete Father Brown*, 235.

22. Miller, *Singer Trilogy*, *Finale*, 335.

# 8

# The Blue Light of Goodness

*Love is nothing but ardent desire for the good.*
—WILLIAM OF SAINT-THIERRY

What is goodness? Goodness is the glory, the moral halo of truth. This is why love desires it, because goodness *belongs* to truth. This is much like a young husband desiring the glory of his wife because they're in truth "one flesh." Goodness, like truth, is a refraction of the love of God as it's shed abroad into the world. *Good* is what God declares it to be. This is true because he's not only the source of all goodness, but also the bestower of it. Remember, as we saw earlier, when God looked over the creation he had just made in Genesis, he declares it to be "good," and then "very good."

When William of Saint-Thierry speaks of "ardent desire,"[1] he's talking about the faculty of our will. He's talking about what we want. And what we want must mirror what God wants; our affections should be aligned with his. Love is not a lukewarm desire, nor is it disinterested analytical curiosity. Love is an ardent spiritual desire for what God has ordained as good. But herein lies the problem.

We read in Genesis 3 that God had given his good creation to Adam and Eve to steward. Moreover, he'd said they could eat from all the trees in the garden except for the tree of the knowledge of good and evil.

---

1. William of St. Thierry, "The Nature and Dignity of Love," in Bernard of Clairvaux, *The Love of God*, 65.

Biblical scholars tell us that what's intended here in the word "knowledge" has to do with naming things. Human beings, as the sacramental image-bearers of God, belong to him. They don't belong to themselves. They're lords over creation *but not* over themselves. As such, they're given the privilege of naming the animals and other created things, but not good and evil. Only God can know how humans are to express his image, and what ways of living express that image clearly, and what ways do not.

Joyce Little renders the meaning of this passage in Genesis:

> The command God gives them can be translated as "Do not claim the ability to name or to define what is good and evil for yourselves, because you do not know enough about me to know what you are supposed to do to be my image in the world. Only I know how I can properly be imaged, and therefore only I can tell you what is good and evil for you."[2]

Accordingly, human beings are prohibited from deciding what is good and what is evil—how to image the character of God into the world. Joseph Ratzinger (Pope Benedict XVI) states this positively:

> Living out the Ten Commandments means living out our own resemblance to God, responding to the truth of our nature and thus doing good. To say it again another way: Living out the Ten Commandments means living out the divinity of man, and exactly that is freedom: the fusing of our being with the Divine Being and the resulting harmony of all with all.[3]

As we abandoned God's instructions for his self-imaging through us, as we abandoned the true author and giver of life, we were left only with the pursuit of ourselves. A corollary of this was our need to substitute our own thoughts on what the image of God should look like in us. In making this move, we began to play God, naming good and evil, right and wrong, for ourselves.

The result of this reorientation from God to ourselves was, and remains, catastrophic. The prophet Isaiah summed it up this way, "Woe to those who call evil good and good evil, who put darkness for light and light for darkness, who put bitter for sweet and sweet for bitter! Woe to those who are wise in their own eyes and clever in their own sight. "[4] The term "woe" is the Hebrew word *oi*. This was the lament chanted by mourners at the funeral of a dead person in ancient Israel. Our own culture writhes,

2. Little, "Naming Good and Evil," *First Things* (May 1992), 7.

3. Ratzinger, *Truth and Tolerance*, 254.

4. Isaiah 5:20–21.

twisting and turning, hoist on our postmodern petard, with little agreement concerning what's good and evil. What was once an *awe*-filled culture has become an *oi*-filled one.

It's easy now to see why we can't agree on the good. Our deep confusion here is the by-product of our usurpation of God's right to name good and evil. Moral goodness is derivative. It is derived from the truth, who is God. Once we lose (or ignore) that truth, we can no longer discern the good that relies upon it. The truth and the good are intrinsically connected. Whether their determination lies with God or with us becomes a matter of personal and cultural life and death.

One of the clear manifestations of this moral confusion is the shift in what Charles Taylor calls constitutive goods. Taylor defines these as whatever a culture comes to deem as "some action, or motive or style of life which is seen as qualitatively superior. 'Good' is used here in a highly general sense, designating anything considered valuable, worthy, admirable of whatever kind or category."[5]

Apart from general agreement around justice and benevolence, the notion of what is good is undergoing a rapid transformation. More important is the question of what "funds" these and other goods. Taylor says, "The issue is what sources can support our far-reaching moral commitments to benevolence and justice."[6]

Here modernity began to sever us from transcendent sources of moral funding. And, as we've seen, this only accelerated in postmodernity. Our situation resembles trying to support life on earth without the external "funding" of the energy of the sun. Science tells us that without the continuing presence of the sun, life on earth would have been stillborn. Confidence in the transcendent sources of God, revelation, and metaphysics has been replaced by confidence in human sources (sociology, psychology, materialist philosophy, and science). At issue is not simply what *constitutes* our goods, but how we can determine, agree upon, and build a culture upon them. This is the pressing question of our time.

For Taylor (and for me), something is good when our love for that thing "moves us to good action. The constitutive good is a moral source... that is, it is a something the love of which empowers us to do and be good."[7] Note the intrinsic connection among knowing the good, loving the good, and doing the good (moral action).

5. Taylor, *Sources of the Self*, 92.

6. Taylor, *Sources of the Self*, 515.

7. Taylor, *Sources of the Self*, 93.

Taylor, like William of Saint-Thierry, sees that our love for the good recognizes by a kind of spiritual sonar a creature's goodness signature. Having "pinged" that goodness in its object, love homes in on it and pursues it through good action. Taylor finds the center for the existence and origin of the good, for the love of the good, and for movement in and toward good action in the Genesis decree that the creation is "very good." This goodness is bequeathed, embedded, and declared as such by God, and is the glory of his truth. According to Taylor,

> The original Christian notion of agape is of a love that God has for humans which is connected with their goodness as creatures... Human beings participate through grace in this love. There is a divine affirmation of the creature, which is captured in the repeated phrase in Genesis 1 about each state of the creation: "and God saw that it was good." Agape is inseparable from such a "seeing–good."[8]

Now, the question is this: Can we truly and clearly recognize what is good apart from the love of God, specifically apart from what God lovingly *declares* to be good? We need to know both what love is and what good is—to make the connection so that the love of God passing through us can reestablish itself in the world, with the result that God may once again look upon his creation and behold it as "very good."

This is where the poverty of postmodernity becomes supremely evident. As we've just noted in the last chapter, postmodernism has created a new moral vocabulary of virtue using terms like incommensurability, determinacy, non-foundationalism, dialectical awareness, hermeneutical sensitivity, alterity, etc.—none of which qualify as virtues because they're not constitutive goods. These terms are not virtues, but simply epistemological vistas for postmodern tourists. Indeed, as we have seen, for Nash reality, goodness, and truth are "shifting and elusive conceptions." The upshot of this is that we're again left in Chesterton's "maze with no center." When it comes to goodness, the postmoderns have left us in same place as they did with truth. And that place is nowhere. Having denied the validity of appeal to transcendent sources in the search for constitutive goods, none can finally be found among the immanent leftovers either. We're twice orphaned from our transcendent sources—once by postmodernity's notions of truth, and now again by its notions of goodness. Postmodernism condemns us to wander, lost and confused, unable to find a way out.

Again, if we want to get out of the maze we need to look up—to transcendent sources.

8. Taylor, *Sources of the Self*, 516.

As we've seen, modernism was deeply hubristic. It placed human beings at the center of reality, and thereby warped reality itself. The progressivism of the late nineteenth and early twentieth century, built on enlightenment arrogance and romantic narcissism, birthed two world wars and the inhuman political ideologies of fascism and communism. The lesson to be absorbed here is that when humanity is placed at the center, humanity suffers the most.

## THE BANALITY OF EVIL?

I remember reading Hannah Arendt's work on totalitarianism in college and being very impressed with her understanding of its processes. But her observations on the nature of evil puzzle me.

> Good can be radical; evil can never be radical, it can only be extreme, for it possesses neither depth nor any demonic dimension, yet—and this is its horror—it can spread like a fungus over the surface of the earth and lay waste the entire world. Evil comes from a failure to think.[9]

As far as I know, Arendt did not avail herself of transcendent sources for defining the good. Therefore, it's not surprising to me that she so weakly portrayed evil. Her most famous phrase came from her writing about the trial of Adolph Eichmann, in which she coined the phrase "the banality of evil." Whether she was a kind of proto-postmodern is not for me to say, but I'll observe from her that where one lacks a robust and transcendent notion of the good, one is likely to have an impotent, immanent notion of evil. This is evidenced by her disavowing any reality to a spiritual source of evil (it possesses no demonic dimension). Without a moral language anchored in transcendent realities, "evil" can only be flattened to mean "bad."

Similar is Arendt's opinion that evil "comes from a failure to think." This statement is evidence of a robust rationalism of a distinctly Enlightenment flavor. The assumption that we can think our way out of evil, that evil is thus within our control, seems to me naive in the extreme. It brings a pocketknife to a gun fight.

I mention Arendt's view only because it's typical of the way so many of our cultural influencers think about evil today. Daniel Henninger, in the context of Vladimir Putin's invasion of Ukraine, made this point, saying that rather than being able to confront evil as evil, we now only confront it as "issues." Henninger calls this failing our tendency toward the "issuefication of

9. Arendt, *Eichmann in Jerusalem*.

morality."[10] Rather than evils to be confronted and defeated, we have issues to be bureaucratically sorted and debated—endlessly.

If our notions of the good are fuzzy, confused, and decoupled from a transcendent moral order of love and truth, our notions of evil will be too. To describe the horrors of Nazi Germany in aesthetic terms (banality) rather than moral terms (evil) is "like serving whiskey in a teacup." Stalin is reported to have said: "The death of one man is a tragedy, the death of a million is a statistic."[11] I'm also mindful of the press's apoplectic response to Ronald Reagan calling the Soviet Union an "evil empire" in 1983.

Today's newspaper described the murder of Olha Sukhenko and her family. She was the mayor of Motyzhyn, Ukraine. Six weeks after the Russians invaded Ukraine, Ms. Sukhenko's body was found in a shallow grave, shot in the back of the head with her hands tied behind her. The bodies of her husband and son were found with her. Some of what's happening is being classified as war crimes by Human Rights Watch.[12] Ukrainian President Zelensky subsequently spoke to the United Nations, telling them of many more civilians being tortured or killed in the city of Bucha. He added that civilians were "crushed by tanks for fun," as well as "raped and killed in front of their own children."[13] Is *banality* the right description for this?

As we've lost a sense of the reality of goodness, we've lost our sense of the reality of evil. When God declared his creation "very good," it stood to reason that anything trying to destroy it was evil. Such was the work of the serpent in the Genesis account, and later Satan (the accuser) and the devil (Splitter). Martin Luther wryly observed, "God keeps the devil on a long leash." When we evict God, his goodness goes with him.[14] Evil becomes unleashed and uncontrolled because it goes unnamed.

The first line of defense against evil is a vocabulary that can clearly articulate its presence. Postmodernism leaves us defenseless in this regard.

10. Henninger, "The Devil Resurfaces in Ukraine," *Wall Street Journal* (April 14, 2022), A-13.

11. Others have attributed this comment to the German journalist, satirist, and pacifist Kurt Tucholsky.

12. Human Rights Watch, https://www.hrw.org/news/2022/04/03/ukraine-apparent-war-crimes-russia-controlled-areas.

13. William Mauldin and Yuliya Chernova, "Ukraine's Zelensky Calls for Removing Russia From U.N. Security Council After Alleged War Crimes: Ukrainian president says newly discovered atrocities could be worse than those in Bucha." *Wall Street Journal*, (April 6, 2022), 1.
        https://www.wsj.com/articles/ukraines-zelensky-to-address-u-n-with-claims-of-alleged-russian-war-crimes-11649155565?mod=Searchresults_pos11&page=.

14. I recognize that there remains goodness in the created order by God's common grace. Yet Eden is but a shadow of its former self.

President Zelensky of the Ukraine told the United Nations Security Council that it must either expel Russia from its midst or dissolve itself. Whether you agree with him or not, he possesses a moral clarity concerning good and evil that many schooled in Western academia have too long considered passé.

If we're to pursue goodness, we must believe that it *is*. And to believe that it is, means grounding it beyond itself in the God who decides what is good and what is evil. When declaring ourselves the authors of truth and falsehood in the garden, we unwittingly committed the unforced error of doing the same with good and evil. Morality is always tied to truth. Having untethered ourselves from the transcendent, we're now helpless in the face of evil.

Our only cure is to rethink (*metanoia*) everything from the ground up—and especially from the top down. Only then can our goodness, and that of the world we inhabit, be rehabilitated and reestablished.

# 9

# The Green Light of Justice

*Do not let your heart become troubled*
*by the sad spectacle of human injustice.*
*Even this has its value in the face of all else.*
*And it is from this that one day you will see*
*the justice of God rising with unfailing triumph.*

—PIO OF PIETRELCINA

A third refraction of the spectrum of God's love into the world is his justice. In his book *Broken Signposts*, N. T. Wright says this: "God's light will expose evil deeds done in darkness. Justice is a manifestation of God's love."[1] We live in a time that is deeply thirsty for justice. We hear cries for racial justice, gender justice, ecological justice, economic justice, or political justice. People on every side are clamoring for justice. But as with truth and goodness, justice has become whatever we say it is. When that's the case, all we seem to be able to do is scream at each other.

Human beings have been writing laws for millennia. Some have approximated God's justice better than others, but none have truly inhabited it. God defines what justice is, not human beings. Not the Supreme Court, not Congress, not the President of the United States, not the International Court of Justice at the Hague, not Plato, and not Aristotle. They may decide what our *laws* are and even reflect on notions of justice, but they're not the authors of justice any more than the moon is the author of the sun. Human

1. Wright, *Broken Signposts*, 15.

81

beings write laws, but only God can define justice. God's justice is deeper than human approximations of justice (laws), just as God's truth is deeper than human truth, and God's goodness is deeper than human goodness. The best human beings can do with our lawmaking is to try hard to approximate God's justice.

The difference between God and humans concerning justice lies in the reality of God's essential righteousness. The script says that God, in his character, is righteous. This simply means that God always is, determines, and does what is right. Righteousness is one of God's central attributes. His justice is an outflowing or manifestation in history of his righteousness. Like truth and goodness, righteousness and justice are also inseparable.

When asking "What is justice?" we must come to understand that the answer is given in the Scriptures, and given in a multitude of ways. Justice is seen in stories, it is declared in laws, it is rehabilitated by prophets, it is taught in proverbs, it is explicated in teaching. It's through the close study of the Bible that we begin to see the full measure of God's justice applied across time and in diverse situations. As we grow in Christ, our own righteousness develops, and we begin to perceive God's justice more clearly.

God's justice must be understood against the basic storyline of the Bible. As we've seen that arc includes creation, collapse, redemption, and restoration. It's through the warp and woof of this story line that we see God's justice revealed and applied.

In the creation for example, we discover the baseline for justice in God speaking all things into being, crowning humanity in his own image, and declaring it all "very good." This judgment on God's part (itself a declaration of his justice) lays down the basic foundations of justice for human equality, dignity, and value.

Moving forward in the biblical narrative, any attempt to undermine God's justice proves itself unjust. This is precisely what happens in the fall and the ensuing collapse of justice. Human structures of superiority, power, and greed result not only in personal acts of injustice, but in the formation of societal structures and systems that institutionalized those acts of injustice. The illustrations of this in the Bible and throughout history are legion. They range from the seizing of Naboth's vineyard by Ahab and Jezebel to the Jim Crow laws of America's south.[2] Underneath them all is the relentless commitment to imitate Cain, who'd just murdered his brother Abel. Remember how God appears on the scene in Genesis to ask Cain where

2. 1 Kings 21.

his brother is, and Cain cynically responds, "Am I my brother's keeper?"[3] If there's one phrase that captures the heart of the unjust, this is it.

Then Jesus comes onto the scene, and we find in him that God's link between righteousness and justice holds. Jesus' justice flows from his righteousness. The redemption of God's justice centers in Jesus as the Righteous One. In his perfect righteousness, Christ alone is able to confront and exhaust injustice, not by resisting, but by absorbing its onslaught at the cross— by overpowering its evil with his goodness.

The same must be true for us. We must replicate the link between God's righteousness and his justice as mirrored in Christ. First, we must be made righteous by being in Christ. This is no self-righteousness. As has been well said, "The only thing we contributed to our salvation was the sin that made it necessary." [4] Our righteousness is a change in state brought about through the spiritual alchemy of atonement in which the lead of our unrighteousness (sin) is turned into the gold of his righteousness. Through the death of Jesus, we are *made* righteous. It's an imputed righteousness. Jesus turns the polluted water of our unrighteousness into the pure wine of his righteousness. "God made him who had no sin to be sin for us, so that in him we might become the righteousness of God.[5] In Christ's death, God changes our status and nature, as we're made to share in his righteousness. In so doing he sacrificed himself, as God, in his son, for us. *For God so loved the world…*

It has been said that "God saved you *for* himself, God saved you *by* himself, God saved you *from* himself."[6] The great Reformed theologian Karl Barth put it this way:

> The wrath of God which we had merited, by which we must have been annihilated and would long since have been annihilated, was now in our place borne and suffered as though it had smitten us and yet in such a way that it did not smite us and can no more smite us… He who on the cross took upon Himself and suffered the wrath of God was no other than God's own Son, and therefore the eternal God himself in the unity with human nature which he freely accepted in His transcendent mercy.[7]

3. Genesis 4:9.

4. The origin of this saying is disputed—some think Phillip Melanchthon, others Jonathan Edwards. I believe I also read it in one of the early Puritans years ago.

5. 2 Corinthians 5:21.

6. Attributed to a tweet by Paul Washer on January 18, 2019; https://twitter.com/paulwasher/status/1086231884139499525?lang=en.

7. Barth, *Church Dogmatics*, 2/1, 397.

Only in—and from—this new state of righteousness acquired for us at the cross can we even begin to see justice clearly and practice it well. Apart from Christ, humanity can never fully grasp, nor really fulfill, the words of Micah the prophet: "And what does the Lord require of you, but to do justice and to love mercy and to walk humbly with your God." How can we do justice or love mercy apart from walking humbly with God? We can't. We were never intended to. All the jigs in the human workshops of righteousness are bent. As a result, all forms of justice manufactured from those jigs are faulty.

Our God-infused righteousness (the result of our vertical forgiveness) informs and fuels our horizontal practice of justice. It's one of the tasks of Christ followers (those made righteous in him) to know the heart of God for justice in the Scriptures and to use that knowledge, as best we can in a broken world, to carry that justice into all spheres of human life. Like forgiveness, the pursuit of justice isn't optional for Christians; it's a core competency of discipleship—of loving like Jesus loves.

The final act in the narrative of Scripture is the restoration. Justice, which is a refraction of God's love, is one aspect of the restorative work of the church until Jesus returns. And justice in both its ends and means must align with love and serve as one of its expressions. Martin Luther King Jr. said, "Darkness cannot drive out darkness; only light can do that. Hate cannot drive out hate; only love can do that."[8] Any attempt to bring about social justice through anger and violence is doomed to fail. The letter of James reminds us, "The anger of man does not produce the righteousness of God."[9] The Bible is clear that final judgment and vengeance are not ours to deliver. Although our righteousness should be growing, we do not yet see the whole of things. The final determination of matters must be left to God.

Here it's useful to address the flip side of God's justice, which is his wrath. God's wrath in a fallen world is an expression of his love. It's his spiritual exercise to preserve, protect, and provide for what he created and loves. God's wrath is always good news for his creation, but not experienced as such for those who would thwart his will and harm his creation or creatures. God will not stand by and watch his creation be destroyed—he will intervene. God's wrath is his protective action over his creation. It's an expression of his love, which blocks from harm, protects from evil, and rightly punishes those opposed to the good ordering of his creation.

Concerning God's wrath, the New Testament commentator C. E. B. Cranfield has written this:

8. Martin Luther King Jr., https://christiananimalethics.com/martin-luther-king-jr-quotes/?gclid=CjwKCAiAsYyRBhACEiwAkJFKoprSbpvXBvyTUiSAQrZ6m qjIUUr6EbX_TeuDYwGGL9fi6WfjcaVn-xoCHpYQAvD_BwE.

9. James 1:20 (ESV).

In seeking the measure of help which human analogies can afford, we must look not to the lower, irrational kind of human anger, but to the higher kind, the indignation against injustice, cruelty, and corruption, which is an essential element of goodness and love in a world in which moral evil is present; and, secondly, that even the very highest and purest human wrath can at best afford but a distorted and twisted reflection of the wrath of God, since the wrath of men (our Lord alone excepted) is always more or less compromised by the presence of sin in the one who is wroth, whereas the wrath of God is the wrath of Him who is perfectly loving, perfectly good.[10]

Think of it this way. Let's say you're diagnosed with serious cancer. How do you want the doctor to treat it? I have a friend who was confronted with this dilemma recently after his diagnosis of prostate cancer. His decision? No half measures; destroy the cancer. The prostate was removed, and follow-up treatment commenced. Today he's cancer free. There are evils and injustices that cannot be allowed to metastasize.

Take another example. When the allies arrived at the gates of Auschwitz, how do you think the German guards perceived their appearance? How do you think the starving prisoners perceived it? Depending on where you stand, God's justice can look like good news or bad news. But from the perspective of his kingdom and its coming, God's justice and judgment are always good news, because they're always grounded in and infused with his righteousness. His wrath is a manifestation of his justice, which itself is a manifestation of his righteousness, which is a refraction of the light of his love.

Much of the progressive theology today would have us do away with God's wrath and anything related to it, including the atonement for sin Jesus offered on the cross. But this is a very shallow reading of the love of God, one that boils down to niceness. Many years ago, H. Richard Niebuhr aptly characterized this modern theology: "A God without wrath brought men without sin into a kingdom without judgment through ministrations of a Christ without a cross."[11]

At its core, justice among human beings is helping people to flourish as God intends. We may argue over the specifics of what this looks like—and I believe the script can help us here by showing us stories and principles of justice. But God's justice, as an expression of his love, is always concerned

10. Cranfield, *Critical and Exegetical Commentary on the Epistle to the Romans*. Vol. 1, 109.

11. Niebuhr, *Kingdom of God in America*, 193.

with human need. Biblical justice is more than restoring something to the *status quo ante* which is how Aristotle thought of justice.

The reason for this is that the previous situation, before an injustice occurred, may itself have been unjust. The classic example here is slavery. Theoretically an "injustice" has occurred to the slave owner who suffers financial loss when his slave escapes. So "justice" demands his capture and return—restoring the situation as it was before escape. But this assumes that *slavery itself* is a just state. Which it is not. The central narrative of the Old Testament is God's delivery of his people from slavery. The freedom of the sons and daughters of God in the Old Testament becomes seed and clue to God's endgame where his kingdom comes and his will is done on earth, as it is in heaven.

Biblical justice is forward facing. It is restorative in the sense of being part of what we will talk about in Part 5, God's restoration of all things. It takes its cues from the future into which God is leading his creation. The purpose of this justice is to align society more and more with the will of God for all of his image bearing creatures.

Biblical justice is a creative justice which seeks to keep everyone at the table of life. Without trying to be exhaustive, we might identify some of those basic needs: water, food, clothing, shelter, basic health and education, along with a level of physical, mental, and emotional security. In regard to these, we *are* our brother's keeper.

In addition to the Ten Commandments, the Hebrew Scriptures treat us to some unique and creative applications of God's concern for justice. In his laws concerning the poor being able to glean the fields, the rights of sojourners and foreigners, the property repatriation of the Sabbath year and Jubilee laws, and the right of redemption, we find God protecting and providing for the most vulnerable at the margins of society in creative and proactive ways.

Jesus inhabits and incarnates the loving justice of God. He heals the marginalized (lepers, demon-possessed) brings outsiders inside (tax-gatherers, prostitutes, gentiles), and speaks truth to power by challenging leaders of corrupt institutions (Pilate, Herod, and Jerusalem's religious leadership).

Most especially Jesus *establishes* the justice of God in the world at the cross. Here God's righteous judgment over human sin is both acknowledged and carried out. In Christ, the judge and the judged are one. T. F. Torrance writes,

> The whole life and existence of Jesus was therefore an existence of the judge and the judged in one person, and because the divine judgment reached out to its ultimate repudiation of sin in

death, the whole life of Jesus on earth has death as its ultimate goal and end, for it was in death that the judged was to acquiesce fully and finally in that divine judgment. Thus the death of Jesus was an outworking of the incarnation of the judge in our humanity, but it was such an outworking of it, that it was in our human nature that the judge bore his own judgment.[12]

Therefore, all human justice must finally and fully submit and conform to God's justice as revealed in Scripture and in the ministry of Jesus, including his cross. The cross is at once God's just and final verdict against sin and his just and final verdict in favor of the sinner. In Jesus himself, God's verdict against sin stands even as its penalty is exhausted. As Paul says,

> When you were dead in your sins and in the uncircumcision of your flesh, God made you alive with Christ. He forgave us all our sins, having canceled the charge of our legal indebtedness, which stood against us and condemned us; he has taken it away, nailing it to the cross. And having disarmed the powers and authorities, he made a public spectacle of them, triumphing over them by the cross.[13]

After Jesus, all that's left on the cross is a public notice saying "Paid in full." God's justice in the world is reestablished through Christ's justification of the sinner. From now on, all justice that we work for will be cruciformed. It will involve suffering and sacrifice. That's the price of extending the boundaries of God's justice in an unjust world. That truth was echoed by Martin Luther King Jr., as a minister of the gospel who worked for racial justice: "Human progress is neither automatic nor inevitable... Every step toward the goal of justice requires sacrifice, suffering, and struggle; the tireless exertions and spiritual concern of dedicated individuals."[14] King's first teacher in this regard was Jesus of Nazareth rather than Mohandas Gandhi.

We are a long way from living in a just world. But I believe we are on our way. The Christian vocation includes advocating for God's justice to come for everyone created in his image. Our attitudes, our laws, our behavior, and our society must reflect the contours of God's divine justice. Justice is one of the main highways through which the love of God enters the world. We are called to build that highway with all who see what God has shown us.

12. Torrance, *Atonement*, 124–25.

13. Colossians 2:13–15.

14. Martin Luther King Jr.; https://christiananimalethics.com/martin-luther-king -jr-quotes/?gclid=CjwKCAjw9LSSBhBsEiwAKtfonxYSUY3PwAX_Gwm_j4Xrls QYXTrUWSlWF2WOHBXCkqIxA35-6_h6vxoCRToQAvD_BwE.

At the heart of true justice is the heart of God. And true justice is nothing other than a refraction and outflow of the love of God. Speaking of love, (caritas), and justice, Augustine said "Inchoate charity, therefore, is inchoate justice; progressing charity is progressing justice; great charity is great justice; perfect charity is perfect justice."[15]

15. Augustine, *On Nature and Grace*, LXX, 84, (Synthesis 610), in Williams, *The Spirit and the Forms of Love*, 8. https://www.religion-online.org/book/the-spirit-and-the-forms-of-love.

# 10

# The Yellow Light of Beauty

*Beauty restores man's capacity for wonder, which remakes a tired world anew. Its power derives from its source, which is both outside the subjective self and the created world.*

—MIKE KERRIGAN

In 1964, Justice Potter Stewart was trying to decide the standard for pornography in a particular Supreme Court case. Without defining it, he simply said, "I shall not today attempt further to define the kinds of material I understand to be embraced within that shorthand description and perhaps I could never succeed in intelligibly doing so. But I know it when I see it."[1]

Conversely, love is beautiful, and people also know it when they see it. In *Broken Signposts*, N. T. Wright says that we're "hardwired for beauty."[2] This morning, while I was looking out the window of my study, I could see Liberty Bay wreathed in fog halfway down the tree line. It was beautiful. Why is nature *so* pregnant with beauty?

Some parts of nature need to be beautiful for propagation purposes, I suppose, but much of it seems gratuitous, simply there for aesthetic enjoyment, like a sunset. So much of life that could be carried on by simple utilitarian means has instead been juiced with the embellishment of beauty. Where does the "golden ratio" in geometry come from, which undergirds so many objects considered "beautiful"? Were those who came to recognize

1. Quoted in Metaxas, *Is Atheism Dead?*, 102.
2. Wright, *Broken Signposts*, 92.

that precise ratio in nature intuiting correctly when they called it the "*divine* proportion?"[3] While people disagree about the actual existence of the golden ratio or divine proportion, what all cultures seem to agree on is that there's something called beauty, and they know it when they see it.

The Bible recognizes that God is "beautiful," and that he naturally pours forth beauty into the world as another refraction of his love—just as we've seen with his truth, goodness, and justice.

> One thing I ask from the Lord,
> this only do I seek:
> that I may dwell in the house of the Lord
> all the days of my life,
> to gaze on the beauty of the Lord
> and to seek him in his temple.[4]

It's surprising how often the terms "beauty" or "beautiful" are nested with "glory" and "holiness" in Scripture. *Glory* literally has the sense of weightiness, or what we earlier called *gravitas*. But why? God himself is beautiful; beauty itself is where God's glory is revealed in the creation.[5] It's his fingerprint, pressed into the natural world. It's also interesting to note that this word group is found frequently in the events following the exodus, as the tabernacle, along with the vestments for Aaron and his sons, are prescribed by God:[6]

> "Then bring near to you Aaron your brother, and his sons with him, from among the people of Israel, to serve me as priests—Aaron and Aaron's sons, Nadab and Abihu, Eleazar and Ithamar. And you shall make *holy* garments for Aaron your brother, for *glory and for beauty*. You shall speak to all the skillful, whom I have filled with a spirit of skill, that they make Aaron's garments to consecrate him for my priesthood . . . For Aaron's sons you shall make tunics, and you shall make sashes for them. And you shall make hats for them, *for glory and beauty*. So you shall put them on Aaron your brother and on his sons with him. You shall

3. Many doubt that the golden ratio actually correlates to beauty in nature and architecture. What is of more interest to me is the reality that all cultures seem to have a *concept* of beauty—that there is such a thing—even though what it consists of may vary among them.

4. Psalm 27:4.

5. Psalm 90:17; Psalm 97:4; Isaiah 28:5.

6. See for example Exodus 28:2; 28:40; 1 Chronicles 16:29; 2 Chronicles 20:21; Psalm 96:9; Isaiah 64:11; Luke 21:5.

*anoint them, consecrate them, and sanctify them*, that they may minister to Me as priests.[7]

As noted earlier, the tabernacle was God's house, his mobile home, the place where he met with the people of Israel. It was the special place where heaven and earth, God and humanity, overlapped and touched in a unique way. In that portable tabernacle, he met with the Israelites for forty years in the desert, leading them to the promised land.

Only much later did King David secure a site for the temple in Jerusalem. This was intended by David to be God's permanent residence among his people. David secured the massive funding, and his son Solomon built the temple. The temple was beautiful. Structures resemble the tastes of those who inhabit them, and Israel's temple was considered one of the most beautiful buildings in the ancient world. We learn from the books of 1 Kings and 2 Chronicles that no expense was spared in the building of Solomon's temple. Some accounted it one of the wonders of the ancient world. Everything in it, from the stone to the furnishings, from the architecture to the priestly vestments, was made of the highest quality and by the finest craftsmen. It was truly a staggeringly beautiful house of God. The house was meant to reflect the beauty of its inhabitant.

The temple went on to have a challenging history. Solomon completed it in 957 b.c. It was destroyed by the Babylonians in 586-87 b.c., rebuilt by Nehemiah in 516, and greatly expanded by Herod in the time of Christ— then survived until the Romans destroyed it in a.d. 70. It has never been rebuilt.

The point is that wherever God dwells, he brings his beauty, holiness, and glory to bear. What is true of his nature bleeds into his creation and into his dwelling place (tabernacle, temple, Jerusalem), and is true also of his people Israel, who are called beautiful as well.[8] Wherever God is, there is beauty. He is a beautiful God, and the source of all beauty. Part of our priestly vocation is to reflect God's beauty into the world. Commenting on the art, music, and craftsmanship off Solomon's temple, Michael Pickard has written, "From this we learn that beauty, as well as goodness and truth, are expressions of God's own nature, and therefore of our nature as well. God wants to fill the earth with it. So let us follow our God–given impulse to create, express, build, decorate, and perform to his glory!"[9]

7. Exodus 28:1–3, 28:40 (ESV).

8. On his people, see Lamentations 2:1–5; Ezekiel 16:14; Isaiah 4:2; Psalm 48:2. On Jerusalem, see Lamentations 2:5; Ezekiel 16:15.

9. Pickard, *Rediscover the Bible*, 218.

Most especially this is true of his Son Jesus in whom our true and intended beauty as human beings is fully revealed. We saw earlier that the apostle John's language and the teaching of Jesus himself make clear that Jesus is the new temple where God dwells. All that pertained to the beauty, glory, and holiness of God in former locations now finds its focus in him. As we have seen, John 1:14 says that Jesus "tabernacled" among us, and that "we beheld his glory." *Glory* is temple language. All that we've said about the beauty of God finds its perfection in the Son of God.

But that's not all. The script also tells us that the Church, the body of Christ in which he dwells, is also a temple. In fact, we're told that our own individual bodies are temples in which God dwells, and that together we're a corporate temple in which God abides.[10]

It's telling that when we get to the last pages of the Bible and meet the magnificent description of the New Jerusalem, we're expressly told that it contains no temple. What was always provisional as a symbol of the presence of God has now been finally eclipsed by the reality:

> I did not see a temple in the city, because the Lord God Almighty and the Lamb are its temple. The city does not need the sun or the moon to shine on it, for the glory of God gives it light, and the Lamb is its lamp. The nations will walk by its light, and the kings of the earth will bring their splendor into it. On no day will its gates ever be shut, for there will be no night there. The glory and honor of the nations will be brought into it.[11]

The language here is indicative of the nature of the "new heavens and new earth" as the place of perfect beauty, glory, and holiness, where God dwells with his people forever. Finally, all of creation has become the temple of God—the place where God dwells. The vision of Habakkuk we saw earlier has become reality: "For the earth will be filled with the knowledge of the glory of the Lord as the waters cover the sea." This is the "new creation" and the "restoration of all things" of which Jesus spoke.

This vision of the goal, of the end of the story, is meant to inform us in how to live in the meantime. For now, part of the work of love is the restoration of beauty, both within people and within culture.

---

10. Compare 1 Corinthians 6:19 with 1 Corinthians 3:16.

11. Revelation 21:22–26.

## BROKEN BEAUTY

N. T. Wright in *Broken Signposts* describes the celebration in the world of art in recent decades of ugliness and life's dark side. This was a response to the end of the progressive fantasies of a godless humanity steeped in its own version of grandeur and glory. This was the sobering warning by postmoderns—and one worth heeding—that Whig progressivism with its rosy view of human nature had been a lie all along. This nineteenth century vision was gassed in the trenches of the Great War and swallowed whole in the ugliness that humanity created apart from God. This was only compounded afterward; less than a generation later, when war erupted in Europe again, like a cancer that had only been in remission. Thus the "beauty" of humanity under totalitarian control was on display for all to see in the manmade temples of the ghetto, gulag, and gas chamber.

One of my daughters was a Peace Corps volunteer in Kazakhstan after college. Kazakhstan is a former republic of the Soviet Union. My daughter used to say that her Kazakh friends, when they would see an old and ugly gray building built under the communists, would say, "That's so Soviet." Atheism, by itself, creates ugliness, not beauty. It's a double whammy. Because atheism chooses to live without God, it lives without beauty.

Beauty draws its life from transcendent sources. Even where atheism tries to build something beautiful—and it must try, because atheists still bear the image of God—they're cheating. They're betraying their atheism by funding their work from other sources—transcendental sources. Here's an example.

Alain de Botton is an atheist. In London's *Guardian*, he proposed in 2012 that atheists in London should build their own temples. But notice how he frames the question and the task: "Why should religious people have the most beautiful buildings in the land?… It's time atheists had their own versions of the great churches and cathedrals."[12] His baseline reference for what is beautiful is Christian architecture, and he concedes that the most beautiful buildings (churches and cathedrals) have been inspired by Christianity, and particularly by Christian worship.

I agree with him. A number of years ago I walked into King's College Chapel at Cambridge University in England. I wasn't prepared for what I experienced there. I was bowled over by the extraordinary beauty of that place. The eighty-foot fan-vaulted ceilings with the long, graceful arches were stunning. The stained-glass windows with light pouring in were lit up

12. Rose, "Alain de Botton's 'Temples for Atheists' Have a Foundational Flaw," *Guardian* (January 26, 2012). https://www.theguardian.com/artanddesign/2012/jan/26/alain-de-botton-temple-atheists.

like fire. The intricate flow to the symmetries in the wood carving of the chancel were elegant. When it came time to leave, I literally couldn't stand up. It was as if I'd been duct taped to my chair by the sheer beauty of the place.

Beauty is just one more arena where atheism wants the benefits of Christianity without its Christ. Atheism is always parasitic, and its richest host has always been the Judeo-Christian tradition with its myriad of cultural gifts. Atheists want the cultural benefits of Christianity without the rigorous transformative cult of worship that creates them. If you look at some of the models for Botton's temples—with their heavy, thick concrete structures, and their obsession with hard angular geometric shapes—they look…well, so Soviet. That's what temples look like without the beautiful God.

Back to the postmodern response to the shattering experience of two world wars. Rather than trying to rebuild beauty from the ruins of civilization, these artists and writers entered into despair and nihilism. Wright quotes the German Marxist and critical theorist of the Frankfurt school, Theodore Adorno, who said that "one cannot write poetry after Auschwitz."[13]

This response was consistent with the materialist worldview that had kicked God out of the world he'd made. Thomas Merton reminded us that as individuals without God we become the abomination of desolation, the empty temples that the Hebrew Bible calls *ich-abod*— "the glory has departed." But it isn't just individuals who experience this; it's nations and cultures. When you tear Western culture from the fabric of the Judeo-Christian cult (worship), the result is *ich-abod*. All that's left is to sit upon the dung heap and weep, clothed in the sackcloth and ashes of anxiety, depression, despair, and suicide.[14]

Here man comes to the end of himself. And his art, rather than turning to the light, gives itself evermore to the ugly, disgusting, and dark. In the postmodern and contemporary periods, artwork celebrating bodily mutilation, urination and feces, and sexual violence and perversion became common to the point of the *truly* banal.[15] These works of art should be seen

13. Wright, *Broken Signposts*, 93.

14. See, for example, recent studies which indicate that nearly sixty percent of young girls struggle with persistent sadness and one out of three have "seriously considered attempting suicide." Azeen Ghorayshi and Roni Caryn Rabin *"Teen Girls Report Record Levels of Sadness, C.D.C. Finds." N.Y. Times.* 2-13-2023.
https://www.nytimes.com/2023/02/13/health/teen-girls-sadness-suicide-violence.html.

15. The works of Andres Serrano ("Piss Christ") and Robert Mapplethorpe's lurid portraying of 'fisting' and naked children in his portraits may be considered examples of this.

sympathetically as a cry for help, a cry for hope. If, as we've seen, postmodernism is "a very particular way of not knowing who you are," then much of its art became a shocking cultural self-portrait. Much of post-modern and contemporary art is Merton's shattered mirror.

## THE ROLE OF BEAUTY

Having explored the origins and purpose of beauty as rooted in God, let's talk about how we should relate to beauty. External beauty resonates in the spiritual heart. Describing our spiritual heart, David Benner writes:

> The spiritual heart I am referring to has very little to do with personal affectivity and absolutely nothing to do with gushing sentimentality or soft headedness... Within the wisdom tradition, the heart is the fullness of the mind. It is not, therefore, something that can be reduced to emotions, and rather than being the source of human evil, it is understood as a way of accessing wisdom... The heart has a bigger perspective than the mind. It can see further than the mind because it draws its data from all levels of reality—including but never limited to the mind. The heart is our spiritual center because it is the seat of imagination and intuition. It is the heart that dreams and through our deepest desires leads us forward. Unlike ego, the heart doesn't perceive by differentiation but by means of its inherent resonance with the wholeness, alignment, oneness, harmony, proportion, and beauty. There should be no surprise therefore that it is the heart that has long been recognized in spiritual teaching as the core of our being.[16]

Beauty pings the heart. This is a universal phenomenon, because it's God's beauty stimulating our response capacity, which he placed within us as part of the divine image. As deep calls to deep, so beauty speaks to beauty. This heart-felt resonance to beauty is part of what it means for us to be created in the image of God. It's also what allows us to create beauty.

The trick with beauty is that it's intended to be something of a sacramental inkling that leads us from the beautiful creature to a more beautiful Creator. When we fail to take that final step, we end up in idolatry. We miss the mark, which is exactly what the New Testament word for sin means. This missing of the mark is what creates the disordered passion that Augustine warns us against:

16. Benner, *Desiring God's Will*, 112–13.

A delight to my eyes are beautiful and varied forms, glowing and
pleasant colors. May these get no hold upon my soul; may God
hold it! "He has made these sights and they are very good" (Gen.
1:31). But he is my good, not these.[17]

Christians should be great promoters of beauty—and we often have
been. The best music, literature, art, and architecture of the West and Byzan-
tine East bear witness to this. Christians have always had a strong tendency
toward aestheticism—toward the creation of the beautiful.

I confess that beauty has always had an intoxicating effect on me. In
nature, for sure. One of the reasons I wanted to move to our present location
is that I wanted to live in "Colorado by the Sea"—which is my nickname
(and shameless marketing device to get friends and family to consider relo-
cating here) for the Pacific Northwest. The raw beauty of the sea, mountains,
and forests all in one place feels to me like a divinely drawn tableau. And
I'm noticing extraordinary kinds of flowers here I never remember seeing
before. This sensual banquet feeds my soul and makes me feel more alive (in
the truest sense), which is to say, closer to God.

I've also been attracted to a beauty lodged in quality as well. I love
to see something well made, where craftsmanship is evident. A Harris
Tweed jacket, a Craftsman bungalow, or a Leonetti cabernet, it doesn't matter. Whether it's a beautifully written novel (Amor Towles's *A Gentleman
in Moscow* comes to mind) or a beautifully prepared meal—think *Babette's
Feast*—I find myself enamored by beauty.

I remember many years ago going down to Baja, Mexico. I was staying
in a little place nestled in a community called Las Gaviotas, by the Pacific
Ocean. There were lovely condominiums stretched along a walkway above
the sea. I remember one condo in particular; along the outside stairway
leading up to it were tiles inscribed with the words "La Pintura de Dios es
El Mundo": "The world is God's painting." The beauty of God leaks into my
soul through the beauty of his world. I believe he did it on purpose.

And women. I'm attracted to beautiful women, I confess it. I love to
embarrass my wife Donna by repeatedly telling the story of how seeing her
for the first time affected me. I thought she was the most beautiful woman
I'd ever seen. Some say that beauty is only skin deep. Not at all true. In her
case, there were layers of beauty of soul as well. Like the grain of fine wood,
true beauty always runs deep.

17. Augustine, *Confessions*, 209.

## BEAUTY LOST AND FOUND

Like the slipping away of truth, goodness, and justice that we've seen so far, we're also losing our grounding of beauty in God. When we detach beauty, especially human beauty, from transcendent sources, it becomes quickly degraded and commodified. This is reflected in our growing acceptance of pornography and the degrading of human sexuality in general. The loss of our understanding of the meaning and purpose of beauty has resulted in splitting people's bodies from their souls. It is disintegrating in the extreme.

There's a reason people call out "Oh God, oh God" in porn films when they're having sex. That cry bears unwitting witness to a deep truth. Sexual union with another person is the closest analog in human experience to union with God. The problem isn't that porn is addictive (it can be). The problem isn't that porn is shameful (although it has that effect). The problem isn't that porn is degrading (although it becomes that).

The problem with porn and all other illicit sexual activity is that it's one of the highest forms of idolatry, and therefore more spiritually dangerous. It creates a serious dislocation of the soul. Porn is anti-beauty masquerading as beauty, because its sexual portrayal has been prised away from its biblical foundations in love and marriage. The advent of virtual sex will take us further afield. As C. S. Lewis warned concerning human sexual relationships and marriage, a fire is beautiful inside the fireplace, it provides warmth and light. But outside of one, it will burn your house down.

This became clear to me years ago when a friend of my daughter's suggested I read a new book called *Blue Like Jazz*, by Donald Miller. I read it while I was on a train traveling around England in 2006. Miller talks about the first time as a teenager he saw a naked woman, in a porn magazine. Here's how he describes that experience with his friends.

> We found a portal, it seemed, into a world of magic and wonder, where creatures exist in the purest form of beauty. I say we found a portal, but it was something more than that; it was as if we were being led through a portal because I sensed in my chest, in the pace of my heart, that I was having an adventure. I felt the way a robber might feel when he draws a gun inside a bank…
>
> We were not speaking, only turning the pages, addressing the miraculous forms, the beauty that has not been matched in all mountains and rivers. I felt that I was being shown a secret, a secret that everybody in the world had always known and had kept from me.[18]

18. Miller, *Blue Like Jazz*, 7.

Plato himself couldn't have written a better description of the effect of first experiencing the nakedness of a person, the miraculous *form* of the opposite sex. I thought it was one of the most honest paragraphs I'd ever read. The human form *is* beautiful.

The problem with porn is that it takes that beautiful form of sacred creation, engages it in the most sacred act (sexual union), then desecrates the sacred by stealing it from the covenant context (the fireplace) of marriage. When we watch pornography, we participate in that desecration. I'm reminded of N. T. Wright's analogy of an instrument maker watching his prize violin being used as a tennis racket.[19] We feed this pouncing beast of inordinate lust by believing the primal lie about who we are. We are no longer a temple of God, but simply bodily instruments to be exploited for pleasure and profit. It is a radical debasing of our humanity.

The problem with porn is not that it's too sexual, but that it isn't sexual enough. C. S. Lewis's words apply:

> We are half-hearted creatures, fooling about with drink and sex and ambition when infinite joy is offered us. Like an ignorant child who wants to go on making mud pies in a slum because he cannot imagine what is meant by the offer of a holiday at the sea. We are far too easily pleased.[20]

Indeed, porn doesn't understand the purpose of human sexuality at all. Pornography reduces human beings to a caricature of their true identity, and it reduces human sexuality to a hollow, empty, and sad affair. There's a reason why the walkway at my daughters' alma mater between the men's and women's dorms—frequently trod on a Saturday or Sunday morning in the clothes one had on the night before—was called "the walk of shame." Sadly, most colleges have one.

In contrast to the pornographic degrading of the beautiful, there's a fictional account of Jesus having an interaction with a prostitute in Kahlil Gibran's book *Jesus of Nazareth*. The book is a series of fictional stories about Jesus told through the eyes of those who knew him (people in the Gospels). One of them is Mary Magdalene. Gibran wrote when the Roman Catholic Church still thought that Mary Magdalene was the prostitute named in John's Gospel—they've since realized better. Nonetheless, the story *as fiction* has meaning and power, creating a striking contrast between how the porn industry views women and men, and how Jesus (and therefore God) views them.

---

19. Wright, *Day the Revolution Began*, 132.

20. Lewis, *Weight of Glory*, 26.

In Gibran's story, Jesus comes wandering into Mary's garden, and she tries to seduce him. She senses something special about him and wants to be near him. She tries, delicately, to tempt him to come inside. Mary says, recording her experience years later,

> And I said, "I beg you to come into my house." And it was all that was sod in me, and all that was sky in me calling unto Him.
>
> Then He looked at me, and the noontide of His eyes was upon me, and He said, "You have many lovers, and yet I alone love you. Other men love themselves in your nearness. I love you in your self. Other men see a beauty in you that shall fade away sooner than their own years. But I see in you a beauty that shall not fade away... I alone love the unseen in you."
>
> Then He stood up and looked at me even as the seasons might look down upon the field, and He smiled. And He said again: "All men love you for themselves. I love you for yourself." And then He walked away.[21]

I read this passage to my seminary students in class one day, to make a wider point. One of them, a beautiful young woman, had tears silently streaming down her face. I never learned why; I felt that to ask would have been to intrude on holy ground where God was bringing her healing. Perhaps this was the first time she understood how *God* sees women.

## EYE OF THE BEHOLDER

If every human being is created in the image of God, and God is beautiful, then we're called to look beyond the ugliness that each of us sometimes manifests, and see the inner beauty we possess. In the final analysis, we're beautiful because God says we are. Martin Luther put it this way: "Rather than seeking its own good, the love of God flows forth and bestows good. Therefore sinners are attractive because they are loved; they are not loved because they are attractive."[22]

Dostoyevsky wrote, "To love someone means to see him as God intended him."[23] This is one of the hardest things of all. It means, on the one hand, to give up the roles of auditor, attorney, physician, engineer, and manager of the lives of others. Each of those roles carries an assumption that we

21. Gibran, *Jesus the Son of Man*, 14–15.

22. Luther, "The Heidelberg Disputation," sect. 28 in Lull, *Martin Luther's Basic Theological Writings*, 48.

23. Dostoyevsky, in Wellman, "Top 25 Christian Quotes about Love." https://www.christianquotes.info/top-quotes/top-25-christian-quotes-about-love/.

have the measure of the other person. We know where their balance sheet falls short, we know their guilt, we can diagnose their disease, we alone hold the key to fixing them. We believe that we see people as they truly are. This is a dangerous delusion.

Speaking of how we view "the least of Jesus' brethren," Hans Urs von Balthasar has written,

> If Christ has borne the least one and taken away his guilt, then I have to see him through my faith in love, as he looks in the eyes of my Father in heaven; this image alone is true, and the one that I have, which seems so clear to me, is false.[24]

The second hard thing, after laying aside this delusion that we really know others, is to accept as real *God's* view of that person. Only God has access to a person's true heart. Only God knows the person's deep history. Only God knows what the full flower of his beautiful image within another person should look like.

And whatever the inner realities of another person, we must remember that they're beloved of God, no matter what. Whether they believe they're enemies of God (and like it that way), whether they believe there is no God, or whether they believe they're beyond divine reach and help—they are beloved of God.

We're called to join God in searching for the lost, watching for their return over the horizon, believing that God desires good for them. This preferential option for the beautiful in others must be our primal response to all the good, the bad, and the ugly we see in others and ourselves. First, because it's God's response to us. And if to us, then to them as well.

If we ask what God intends each human being to be, the answer is to become bearers of his glory—those whom, having become partakers of the divine nature, have become not gods but holy ones, in whom the Holy Trinity has taken up lodging. People *are* beautiful, because they're loved by a beautiful God who has made them in his image.

---

24. von Balthasar, *Love Alone Is Credible*, 114.

# 11

# The Orange Light of Responsibility

*Today's church wants to be raptured from responsibility.*

—LEONARD RAVENHILL

The more I think about what mature love (*agape*) looks like, the more I think it's a responsible love. One of my daughters once had a fender bender in her high school parking lot. I asked her who was going to pay for it. She sheepishly hung her head and said, "It was my fault." I heartily agreed with her! Then I asked, "Whose *responsibility* is it?" She looked at me quizzically and said, "Mine."

Thus burst forth the teachable moment. I explained to her that, as a legal adult and the registered owner of the vehicle, *I* was responsible to make good on the damages to the car she hit. Even though it was her fault, it was *not* her responsibility.

Such is the case in our relationship with God. He created everything, including us. When we chose the path of sin, we crashed the good creation God had lovingly made. We alone were and are at fault in this. But while we're at fault, God remains responsible for what he has created. And that's really good news for us. God could have said, "Tough luck, you've chosen the death I warned you about, see ya!" But *agape* love is responsible love. As we've seen, this kind of love "never ends." Love takes responsibility for what belongs to it. Responsibility is one of the refractions of *agape* love.

Like my guilty daughter, Christians know we've done real damage. In fact, we're guilty of irreparable damage beyond any possibility of our own restitution and repair. But we also know that God, in Christ, has come to pay the price for the damage we've done. He has executed both justice and mercy by taking upon himself the responsibility of us all.

From the beginning, God—as Lord of creation—has exercised responsibility for his creation's well-being. We were called to have a share in that responsibility as God's people—as royal priests and holy citizens of God's kingdom. But when we dropped the ball, God picked it up. He saved what he created from utter destruction because everything that happens, happens on his watch.

This is not some sloppy enabling or needy codependence. Rather it's the clear recognition that love will not oversee the destruction of the beloved. Love will step in and save when life itself is at stake.

In an extraordinary passage in his magnum opus *Church Dogmatics*, Karl Barth meditated upon the responsibility Jesus undertook at the beginning of his ministry when he was baptized among many in the Jordan River,

> The seriousness with which others, frightened before God and setting their hope in Him alone, confessed their sins, is infinitely surpassed here by the divine earnestness with which this One, when faced by the sins of all others, their confusions and corruptions, their big and little acts of ungodliness, did not let these sins be theirs, did not regard, bewail or judge them from a distance with tacit or open accusation, did not simply characterize them as sins by His own otherness, but as the Son of His Father, elected and ordained from all eternity to be the Brother of these fatal brethren, caused them to be His own sins, confessed them as such, and therewith confessed that He was baptized in prospect of God's kingdom, judgment and forgiveness.
>
> No one who came to the Jordan was as laden and afflicted as He. No one was as needy. No one was so utterly human, because so wholly fellow-human. No one confessed his sins so sincerely, so truly as his own, without side-glances at others. He stands alone in this, He who was elected and ordained from all eternity to partake of the sin of all in His own person, to bear its shame and curse in the place of all, *to be the man responsible for all*, and as such, wholly theirs, to live and act and suffer. This is what Jesus began to do when He had Himself baptized by John with all the others. This was the opening of His history as the salvation history of all the others.[1] (my emphasis).

If you need to go back and read that over a couple of times (like I did), I'll wait.

1. Barth, *Church Dogmatics*, 4/4, 59.

The script teaches that its central actor was without sin. So how is it that Barth can speak of Jesus this way? The answer is that beginning with the incarnation, moving through his baptism, and culminating on the cross, Jesus willingly and freely took our sin upon himself, the righteous for the unrighteous—as we just saw. He trades places with us so that Paul could write, "God made him who had no sin to be sin for us, so that in him we might become the righteousness of God."[2] This is no surface acquaintance, no playacting. This is the innocent stepping in for the condemned at the last minute and trading his life for another's. This is the Creator of the universe taking responsibility for what was never his fault, out of love. Remember, Jesus said, "Greater love has no one than this: to lay down one's life for one's friends."[3] This is the love which is stronger than death.

One of the hallmarks of a disciple of Jesus is his or her willingness to take responsibility. Jesus's responsibility as the Savior of the world was God's responsibility. Ours is to continue the work of rebuilding what has begun in Christ. Love is an exercise of profound responsibility for the world in which we live, and for those who are placed in the orbit of our care.

In his book *Wind, Sand, and Stars,* Antoine de St. Exupery tells the story of his friend and fellow pioneer mail pilot Guillaumet. They and other men were flying routes together over the Andes Mountains in Argentina when Guillaumet went missing. He was presumed dead after five days. But in fact, he'd been able to land his plane near a lake in a winter snowstorm. He spent those days and nights trying to walk out to safety while nearly freezing to death in the fierce winter snow. His greatest temptation was simply to sleep, which would have been his last.

Interestingly, as Guillaumet later shared with St. Exupery his grim story of what happened in the mountains, he said this:

> After two or three or four days of tramping, all you think about is sleep. I would long for it; but I would say to myself, "If my wife still believes I am alive, she must believe that I am on my feet. The boys all think I am on my feet. They have faith in me. And I am a skunk if I don't go on."

As he plodded on, tearing off pieces of his shoes to relieve the swelling of his feet, he remembered his wife again. "I thought of my wife. She would be penniless if she couldn't collect the insurance." Guillaumet realized that if he were declared missing instead of dead, the company insurance would not, by law, pay his wife the policy death benefit for four years, at which time

2. 2 Corinthians 5:21.

3. John 15:13.

he could be declared legally dead. This thought kept him going, and he was eventually found and rescued.

In reflecting on Guillaumet's noble character, it wasn't his courage that St. Exupery celebrated.

> Guillaumet's courage is in the main the product of his honesty. But even this is not his fundamental quality. His moral greatness consists in his sense of responsibility... To be a man is, precisely, to be responsible. It is to feel shame at the sight of what seems to be unmerited misery. It is to take pride in a victory won by one's comrades. It is to feel, when setting one's stone, that one is contributing to the building of the world.[4]

Responsibility then—yes. But responsible to whom? For what? And why? Responsibility assumes obligations and obligations assume values. Values in turn assume constitutive goods, and constitutive goods, as we saw above, assume truth. So my question is: Has the very notion of responsibility become an artifact of a world gone by? And if not, can this deeply human sensibility, this persistent and personal feeling that we're responsible beings, put our feet back on the path to God?

Because either we're playing at responsibility, like children making vows at a pretend wedding, or we really are responsible, and will be held responsible. Not in the ultimate sense of the fate of the world, but in the derivative sense of our original garden of Eden mandate which has now been restored to us in Christ. If, however, responsibility is *not* a response to a transcendent reality of truth to which constitutive goods are pegged, then to insist on it is only a postmodern power play. In which case, why not just head for the savanna with Timon and Pumbaa? Why be responsible at all?

Many in our world are making just that choice. Many of them are men. But is it the right choice?

## HAKUNA MATATA

As a father of three daughters, I watched endless cartoons and movies. One of my all-time favorites is Disney's 1994 animated film *The Lion King*. It's a coming-of-age story about responsibility.

As you may recall, the movie's beginning has Simba (the title character) playing with friends Timon and Pumbaa in the African savanna. But soon we realize the dark backstory of how Simba got there. His father Mufasa was killed by his evil uncle Scar, who has taken over the kingdom and

---

4. Saint-Exupery, *Wind, Sand, and Stars*, 30–39; quote taken from 39.

ruled it with an iron fist. Scar has ruined the kingdom and the lives of its citizens. Scar tried to have Simba killed, but he was saved and whisked away to the savanna for safety when he was just a cub.

Some years later, a young lioness named Nala finds Simba and tells him he's the king and must return to retake his father's kingdom from his evil uncle. Simba's response is "Hakuna matata," which is Swahili (and "lion" apparently) for "No worries." Simba has been living a carefree life with his buddies and no responsibilities. But things are about to change. When Simba asks Nala why he should worry about his father's kingdom, she says, "Because it's your responsibility."

Simba's crisis deepens when he meets the monkey-sage Rafiki, who's something of a priestly figure in the story. Rafiki had poured the ceremonial water from the gourd over Simba's head when he was born (think baptism). They run into each other one day in the savanna, and Simba, startled by Rafiki's appearance, asks him, "Who are you?" To which Rafiki responds, "The question is, who are *you*?" Then he adds, "I know who you are; you are Mufasa's boy."

Our crisis culminates in Simba's vision of his father, Mufasa. Simba goes to a pool of water, looks down in it to drink, and sees his father's face. Then he hears his father's voice: "Simba, you have forgotten who you are. You are more than you have become—you must take your place in the circle of life." Simba is inspired to return to his kingdom and his responsibility.

The core question, however, at the center of Simba's life is not that of responsibility. Rather, it is the question of identity. Responsibility flows from identity. We must *do* who we *are*. If we don't know who we are, we don't know what to do, or what our responsibilities in life are. Rafiki's question to Simba is God's question to us: "Who are *you*?" Just as Rafiki already knew the answer— "You are Mufasa's boy"—so does God: "You are my beloved son/daughter."

If there's a God who is responsible for the universe, who calls us to share in that responsibility in penultimate ways, then we're dignified, glorified actually, by the weight of those responsibilities. Indeed, the more responsibility, the more glory—because the word "glory," remember, means "weightiness." As we bear the weight of our responsibilities our glory is revealed.

The script says that the responsible God has called his sons and daughters to share in responsibility. We're not *foundationally* responsible (only the Creator can bear that load), but we're *filially* responsible, as members of his family, for the secondary roles that are ours to carry out. Just as the Pevensie children in the Narnia books do not bear the weight of Aslan's role to die on the great stone table, they do indeed bear their weight and grow in responsibility as sons of Adam and daughters of Eve to help Aslan plunder the palace of the White Witch. (Incidently, that theme of maturing responsibility may be one way of understanding the Narnia series itself.)

## OUR GOD-GIVEN RESPONSIBILITIES

If one refraction of God's love is his responsibility as Creator, Redeemer, and Sustainer of all that is, what do our responsibilities look like?

The first is to be his image-bearers. This is to realize our fundamental identity as those who bear the impress of the divine character. There's a strong denial of this reality today, as seen most clearly in those schools of Darwinian naturalism that are atheistic. For them, we're nothing special— just the current expression of the ever-mutating gene pool, nothing more. Indeed, Richard Dawkins has stated that we're just genetic placeholders, temporary phenotypes, whose only purpose is to be a way station for the evolving human genotype.

> Where are these facts leading us? They are leading us in the direction of a central truth about life on earth… This is that living organisms exist for the benefit of DNA, rather than the other way around… Each individual organism should be seen as a *temporary vehicle*, in which DNA messages spend a tiny fraction of their geological lifetimes.[5]

Peter Singer, a Princeton ethicist, carried Dawkins's reasoning forward in stating that we're no different from other creatures, that there's nothing qualitatively distinct about us. This is a perfectly understandable conclusion, given his naturalistic premises. But the ethical implications of this position are both congruent and appalling:

> If we compare a severely defective human infant with a nonhuman animal, a dog or a pig, for example, we will often find the nonhuman to have superior capacities, both actual and potential, for rationality, self-consciousness, communication, and anything else that can plausibly be considered morally significant.[6]

In his book *The Human Body Shop*, Andrew Kimbrell quotes one scientist saying, "I foresee growing fetuses someday for spare parts."[7]  As we

5. Dawkins, *Blind Watchmaker*, 126–27 (My emphasis).

6. Singer, *Rethinking Life and Death*, 201; originally published in *Pediatrics*, Vol. 72 (July 1983), 128–29.

7. Kimbrell, *Human Body Shop*, 49.

THE ORANGE LIGHT OF RESPONSIBILITY 107

can see, any diminishment of our humanity results in a diminishment of our responsibility. Ideologies that see human beings as simply gene hostels, or not qualitatively different from the other animals breed irresponsibility. Not only that, they open the door to a severe barbarism in how we view and treat one another.

In contrast, the script says that human beings *are* qualitatively different from all other creatures because they're created in the divine image. As such, we're to live in a glorious dignity that bears the family resemblance in character. Darwinian naturalism can never ground human dignity; it can only grind it. Once again, we're finding that cut off from transcendent sources, we're marooned on an archipelago of multiple disconnected human opinions concerning our identity. But when we're rightly grounded on the continent of the revelation of God, we know who we are—as those who bear the image of God.

Our second responsibility is to exercise what's often called the cultural mandate. As we saw earlier when God created the earth, he handed over the keys to human beings to manage it on his behalf. This is a grave responsibility. The call comes in Genesis 1:28— "God blessed them and said to them, 'Be fruitful and increase in number; fill the earth and subdue it. Rule over the fish in the sea and the birds in the sky and over every living creature that moves on the ground.'"

Here we find our twin responsibilities—to be fruitful and to rule. Human beings are to populate the earth. This is not about arithmetic, but about God's intention to extend his field of love and glory through the procreation of image-bearers. Their rule over other creatures and the earth itself is not a license for rapacity; rather, it's a legacy of responsibility to be carried out in such a way that the goodness of creation is manifested, maintained, and amplified.

This expansion of the mandate is carried out primarily through the blessing of labor. Building out God's world is at the core of our responsibility, our vocation.

Our third responsibility is to serve as a royal priesthood.[8] As children of the King of heaven and earth, we are royalty. The key here is not to focus on the symbols of our estate (thrones, scepters, and the like), but to treasure the relationship. God is our Father, and Jesus is our brother. Through the Holy Spirit we share in their dignity and glory—not accidently, but substantially—through their life within us.[9] We are "partakers of the divine nature,"

8. 1 Peter 2:9.
9. See John 14:20, 15:4, 17:10, and especially 17:20–24.

meaning that although we don't possess *deity*, which is God's alone, we do possess a derived *divinity*, the full disclosure of which remains a mystery.[10]

In terms of our priesthood, the primary thing to catch is that we stand as intermediaries between heaven and earth. As image-bearers, we represent God to the earth. As part of the creation (sons of Adam, daughters of Eve), we represent—and intercede for—the earth before God.

In ancient Israel, the priestly office involved two components that represented these twin roles. As God's representatives on the earth, priests taught the law of God to the people. Moses and Ezra are prototypes here. As representatives of the people before God, priests offered sacrifices on behalf of the world to God. Aaron and his descendants are examples of this.

Jesus, as the perfect high priest, not only taught God's law but was *in his person* God's law—the Word (Torah) become flesh. He also became the final sacrifice sufficient for all time in his death on the cross. Our high priest himself became the sacrifice passing through the temple curtain that separated us from God; he ended the temple sacrificial system by offering the pure and final sacrifice.[11]

The role of priest continues in Christ, so it continues in us. We are, to use the Reformation catch-phrase, a "priesthood of all believers." We continue Christ's work of declaring and teaching the word of God and offering prayer and spiritual sacrifices on behalf of the world. In both, we announce the gospel—that what God had purposed for humanity and the creation in the beginning has now been recast and accomplished in the Messiah-King. In him, heaven and earth now cohere in congruity. In N. T. Wright's imagery, they overlap and interlock.[12]

As we review the range of our responsibilities, we can see how they're impossible to uphold unless we're grafted into Jesus himself. Yet when that happens, our yoke becomes easy, and our burden becomes light. The residence of responsibility—first in him, then in us—is one of the deepest refractions of God's *agape* love. It is one the world so desperately needs to perceive freshly.

10. 2 Peter 1:4; 1 Corinthians 2:9.

11. For background on Jesus's priesthood, see Hebrews 4:14—10:23. Note that Jesus is not a priest according to the bloodline of Aaron, but according to Melchizedek, who possessed an "indestructible life" (Hebrews 7:16). Therefore, he is high priest "forever."

12. Wright, "Beginning to Think about the New Creation," https://www.ntwright-online.org/beginning-to-think-about-the-new-creation/.

# 12

# The Red Light of Spiritual Tolerance

*Love is the active concern for the life and the growth of that which we love.*
*Where this active concern is lacking, there is no love.*
*This element of love has been beautifully described in the book of Jonah.*

—ERICH FROMM, *THE ART OF LOVING*

Christians believe that the fundamental truth of reality finds its source in God and its expression in Christ. But most people in the world don't yet believe in Christ, and therefore not in the truth he taught. So how do I, as a Christian, love the person who doesn't see truth the way I do? Should I be silent? Should I ignore them? Should I go along to get along? Should I silence them? Condemn them? Cancel them?

Here, as in all other matters that matter, we follow the way of Jesus. So how did he who was himself the incarnation of love relate to others who didn't receive the truth that was a central expression of his love? After his ascension into heaven, how did his disciples deal with the hostility they often encountered as they shared the gospel? How does love respond to its rejection or avoidance?

This question is becoming more and more pressing if Aaron Renn is right in saying Christianity in America (and the West in general) has passed from being viewed positively (pre–1994) to neutrally (1994–2014) to negatively (since 2014). For those of us who live in pluralistic democracies, especially those that no longer hold a Judeo-Christian moral consensus on constitutive goods, this issue is becoming more pressing. How Christians relate to those who hold different worldviews will become increasingly more vital.[1]

Which leads us to Jonah.[2] Erich Fromm reminds us that Jonah was a man caught between two worlds. One was the powerful Assyrian Empire, with its capital city Nineveh, and its pantheon of gods led by Ashur, Anu, Enlil, and Enki. The other world was the tiny northern kingdom of Israel, its little capital Samaria, and its one God, Yahweh. God commands Jonah to go to Nineveh, preach his word, and call the Ninevites to forsake their idolatry and enter God's way of life so that they wouldn't be destroyed. We're told twice that God's reason for this was his pity. Jonah had a better idea: Why not just slip out of town and hop a ship going as far away from Nineveh (and God's calling) as possible? Let Nineveh go to hell in a handbasket. Call it the "Jonah option."

That effort ended badly. Jonah ended up in the belly of a great fish, from which he was vomited onto a beach to rethink his decision. He went to Nineveh and preached to the people, with a heart of stone toward them. And lo and behold, they gave up their pagan religion and turned to Israel's God! Rather than rejoice in that, Jonah sat under a little booth/shelter and pouted. If you hear echoes here of the story of the older brother in the prodigal son parable, you're not wrong. Fromm writes of Jonah, "He is a man with a strong sense of order and law, but without love."[3] In *Les Mis* language might say he is Javert, not Jean Valjean.

As Jonah's story progresses, God sets a little plant over him to provide shade from the scorching sun. Jonah rejoices in the plant, but God kills it the next day. Jonah is angry about it. And here comes the challenge from God's heart to Jonah's:

> But God said to Jonah, "Do you do well to be angry for the plant?" And he said, "Yes, I do well to be angry, angry enough to die." And the Lord said, "You pity the plant, for which you did not labor, nor did you make it grow, which came into being in a night and perished in a night. And should not I pity Nineveh, that great city, in which there are more than 120,000 persons who do not know their right hand from their left, and also much cattle?"[4]

---

1. Renn, "The Three Worlds of Evangelicalism," First Things, February 2022, 26.

2. In addition to the book of Jonah, this historical person is also mentioned in the Old Testament in 2 Kings 14:25. He lived during the reign of Jeroboam II, King of the northern Kingdom of Israel, before its defeat by the Assyrians in 722 BC.

3. Fromm, *Art of Loving*, 25.

4. Jonah 4:9–11 (ESV).

Fromm writes, "God explains to Jonah that the essence of love is to 'labor' for something and 'make something grow,' that love and labor are inseparable. One loves that for which one labors, and one labors for that which one loves."[5]

As a refraction of love, Spiritual tolerance is my active labor on behalf of another with the goal of seeing them mature in the image of God. That's "Spiritual tolerance" with a capital S. It's a very specific tolerance, the tolerance of the Holy Spirit. A *spiritual* person in the New Testament is someone inhabited by the Holy Spirit of God. Thus, tolerance for another is defined not by us, but by the Holy Spirit. This is the tolerance the Christian extends. Consequently, this tolerance, which is guided by the Holy Spirit within us, can never be divorced from the truth of the Holy Spirit-inspired word.

In Jonah's case, the truth was that Nineveh, an "exceedingly great city," was a spiritual dumpster fire. For that reason, Jonah hated Nineveh. For that reason, God loved Nineveh. God's truth didn't change; neither did God's heart. God was teaching Jonah how he felt about Nineveh, and the only way he could communicate it was for Jonah to watch the plant he loved die. God was watching Nineveh die, but rather than let it happen, he sent Jonah to intervene.

For the believing Christian, the question of Spiritual tolerance is Janus-faced. Like the Roman god with two faces, this form of love must face fellow believers on one hand, and nonbelievers on the other.

Concerning believers, the martyr-theologian Dietrich Bonhoeffer said in *Life Together*, his invaluable little book on Christian community, "Nothing can be more cruel than the tenderness that consigns another to his sin. Nothing can be more compassionate than the severe rebuke that calls a brother back from the path of sin."[6] Here the question is generally one of a loving reminder of the teaching of the Scriptures and strong encouragement to be obedient to its teaching.

The Gospels are clear that Jesus had deep disagreements with the Pharisees. He didn't like the way they understood and lived out their faith. After all, he *did* call them hypocrites and vipers. Love doesn't sugarcoat the truth. Paul called out Peter for his hypocrisy in living differently with the Gentiles than he did with the Jews. Jesus called his star pupil "Satan" when he tried to dissuade him from the path to the cross. But notice that in all these cases, it's believers in a shared faith who are calling each other to accountability. But what about those who don't share the faith? This, after all, was Jonah's situation.

5. Fromm, *Art of Loving*, 25–26.
6. Bonhoeffer, *Life Together*, 107.

We live in a world that celebrates love at every turn, but when we un-pack the loves on offer, we see fundamentally two kinds. The first is love in its unredeemed state. The second is love that has been redeemed in God. Bonhoeffer clarifies this critical distinction in contrasting what he calls hu-man love and spiritual love:

> Human love makes itself an end in itself. It creates of itself an end, and idol which it worships, to which it must subject ev-erything... Spiritual love, however, comes from Jesus Christ, it serves him alone; it knows that it has no immediate access to other persons. Jesus Christ stands between the lover and the others he loves.[7]

When I used to officiate at weddings, I occasionally spoke of the rela-tionship between husband and wife using the analogy of bricks in a wall. I wondered out loud whether they were stronger with one sitting directly on top of another or with mortar between them. I suggested that the couple think of themselves as the bricks and Christ as the mortar. With him in between us we're actually stronger. And this is true of every relationship, not just marriage.

If I've placed Christ between my friend and me, or between my enemy and me, or between a stranger and me, and I know them through him, only then will I truly know how to love them. The love of Jesus Christ becomes our bond, whether the other person knows that love or not. Jesus defines the relationship between us; they don't, and I don't. Because Jesus stands between us, we actually have a deeper intimacy, even if we have yet to realize and embrace it.

Almost none of the love songs on the market today (I have a playl-ist full of them) are about spiritual love; they're about Bonhoeffer's human love. So many of the lyrics are about feelings of possession and control and desperation and craving. I like *eros* as well as the next guy, but like a wild boar, *eros* off the leash of the *agape* of Christ's redemption rapidly tramples everything and everyone in its selfish path.

Bonhoeffer continues,

> Contrary to all my own opinions and convictions Jesus Christ will tell me what love toward the brethren really is. Therefore, spiritual love is bound solely to the Word of Jesus Christ... Human love can never understand spiritual love, for spiritual

---

7. Bonhoeffer, *Life Together*, 35.

love is from above; it is something completely strange, new, and incomprehensible to all earthly love.[8]

Whether it's *philos* (friend-love) or *eros* (sexual desire) or *storge* (affection), all these loves stand in need of the mediation and redemption offered through Christ the Word. Without the mediation of Jesus and purification of *agape* he brings through the Holy Spirit, human love becomes instrumentalized, commodified, and weaponized by the sinful self. It's just what we do—when we do it without him.

What happens when Christ comes between the "other" and me? In short, *agape* love becomes possible, and with it the redemption and restoration of the other loves. Where Spiritual love reigns, Spiritual tolerance surfaces. And again, by "Spiritual" I mean what the New Testament always means: being grounded in the Holy Spirit of God made available to us in Jesus.

And who is the most difficult person to love with Spiritual tolerance? Our enemy. Our enemies are the hardest people to love. Let's start there. If we can crack that toughest of nuts, the rest will follow. What did Jesus say about this? He commanded his followers to love (*agape*) their enemies. Here it is in the context of Jesus's Sermon on the Mount:

> But I tell you, love your enemies and pray for those who persecute you, that you may be children of your Father in heaven. He causes his sun to rise on the evil and the good, and sends rain on the righteous and the unrighteous. If you love those who love you, what reward will you get? Are not even the tax collectors doing that? And if you greet only your own people, what are you doing more than others? Do not even pagans do that? Be perfect, therefore, as your heavenly Father is perfect.[9]

This may be the most distinctively Christian and dastardly difficult imperative in the New Testament. Of all the hard sayings of Jesus, this may be the hardest. And it stands at the center of any Christian understanding of love as Spiritual tolerance.

This command is a new thing in the world. It's not even found in Judaism, although its roots lie there. Here's a reflection on a passage in Exodus from Norman M. Cohen, Rabbi emeritus of the Bet Shalom synagogue:

> The Torah tells us to be fair, just, and giving, even to our enemy.
> It does not tell us to love our enemy, nor does it tell us to hate
> him or her. The Torah recognizes reality. Loving our friend and

8. Bonhoeffer, *Life Together*, 35.
9. Matthew 5:44-48.

neighbor is easy. Loving our enemy is probably impossible, and that is why our Torah does not command such a thing. While recognizing the reality of human nature, our tradition also emphasizes our ability to do battle with the power of the yetzer hara, "evil inclination." Yes, you may hate your enemy, but do not allow that hatred to consume you, to destroy you, and to lead you to forfeit your opportunity to remain in a covenant with God.[10]

The late Rabbi Jonathan Sacks, former chief rabbi of Britain and one of the most respected Jewish leaders in the world, has written,

In speaking about enemies, the Torah is realistic rather than utopian. It does not say: "Love your enemies." Saints apart, we cannot love our enemies, and if we try to, we will eventually pay a high psychological price: we will eventually hate those who ought to be our friends. What the Torah says instead is: when your enemy is in trouble, come to his assistance. That way, part of the hatred will be dissipated. Who knows whether help given may not turn hostility to gratitude and from there to friendship. That surely is enough to refute the suggestion that Judaism contemplates, let alone advocates, hating enemies.[11]

Both Rabbis rightly stress that the Torah never teaches one to hate their enemies, but the germane thing is their acknowledgment that Judaism did not teach the love of one's enemies either. It really is something new that comes in Jesus. Rabbi Cohen says, "Judaism recognizes reality," while Rabbi Sacks says, "The Torah is realistic rather than utopian" in this regard. I agree with Rabbi Sacks when he says, "Saints apart, we cannot love our enemies." I think he's right, at least in my experience. But that's the whole point: *Christians are called to be saints.* Each of us. All of us.

To love our enemies requires more than simply not hating them. It requires more than tolerance. It's a supernatural act. Hence the need for *Spiritual* tolerance. Jesus is asking us to do something that's utterly impossible for us in the power and perspective of our fallen natures. Judaism is right to acknowledge this on behalf of all of us. That's why Jesus requires us to undergo a *metanoia,* that radical reconsideration, the "thinking again" that we learned about earlier. This isn't simply a cognitive adjustment, but

10. Cohen, "Love Your Enemy? No Way! Treat Him Fairly. Way!" *Mishpatim*, Exodus 21:1–24:18 d'var torah"; https://reformjudaism.org/love-your-enemy-no-way-treat-him-fairly-way.

11. Sacks, "The Rabbi Sacks Legacy"; https://rabbisacks.org/covenant-conversation-5769-mishpatim-helping-an-enemy/.

a reappraisal of all of reality in the light of the dawning of the kingdom of God. It's a gift of the Holy Spirit.

Part of this *metanoia* is to realize that we are not the saviors, that we don't control the responses or outcomes to the good news. To the contrary, our efforts often result in apparent failure. But Jesus calls us not to success but to faithfulness. Frederick Christian Bauerschmidt has said it this way:

> To love our enemies is to renounce the idea that we have it in our power to make history turn out right, to end all suffering, to banish all evil. To love our enemies is, in the end, to disarm ourselves of any weapons except the cross and the Spirit's gifts of faith, hope, and love.[12]

With the coming of the kingdom of God, human constructs like "reality" (Cohen) or "utopia" (Sacks) melt away like snow upon the earth in springtime. Jesus's kingdom is already manifesting itself in human history, and perhaps the strongest manifestation is in the love of one's enemies.

For Jesus, this radical love is the characteristic of one who belongs to God. Jesus tells us, "Be perfect, as your heavenly Father is perfect." For Jesus, the love of enemies is a defining mark of God's family. And here we want to avoid a moralistic reading of this text, as if Jesus were teaching some kind of perfectionism. That's not at all what this passage is about, as the context makes clear. That context points to *how* God loves. He loves indiscriminately.

God "causes his sun to rise on the evil and the good, and sends rain on the righteous and the unrighteous." Jesus is telling us, "Love like that. Love like God loves."

The Greek word for "perfect" in this verse would be better translated here as "total," or "unrestricted," or "complete,"[13] in the sense of something fully formed or developed. Jesus's point is that we're to be like God in not discriminating in our loving. To love perfectly means to love completely, to love fully as God loves, without distinction—that's the point here, as the context makes clear.

Loving in this brand-new way is a hallmark of one who belongs to Jesus, who belongs to God. This is how God is. This is how God loves. Paul puts it this way:

> But God demonstrates His own love toward us, in that while we were yet sinners, Christ died for us. Much more then, having now been justified by His blood, we shall be saved from the

12. Bauerschmidt, *Love That Is God*, 89.

13. Gk. is 'τέλειοι'. On the translation see Delling's article, "τέλειος" in Kittel and Friedrich, *Theological Dictionary of the New Testament*, Vol. 8, 73-74. See also Zerwick and Grosvenor, *Analysis of the Greek New Testament*, Vol.1, 14.

wrath of God through Him. For if while we were enemies we were reconciled to God through the death of His Son, much more, having been reconciled, we shall be saved by His life.[14]

And Jesus practiced what he preached. As we've seen, at the Passover meal on the night before His death, Jesus served Judas Iscariot communion before Judas walked out the door to betray him. He shared table fellowship with him, a sign in Judaism of deep community, knowing full well what was in Judas's heart. The very next afternoon, when Jesus was slowly dying in agony on the cross, he prayed for those who'd put him there: "Father forgive them, for they don't know what they are doing."

Facing real enemies in the faces of the segregationists, Martin Luther King Jr. wrote this:

> With every ounce of our energy we must continue to rid this nation of the incubus of segregation. But we shall not in the process relinquish our privilege and obligation to love. While abhorring segregation we shall love the segregationist. This is the only way to create the beloved community.[15]

This way of loving even our enemies can only be a supernatural gift. Indeed, it's a gift of the Holy Spirit in Jesus. It is and has always been a hallmark of the saints—of all who believe in Christ.

Which brings me back to the notion of Spiritual tolerance. If we're called to love our enemies, what about those with whom we simply disagree? There was a time when tolerance was thought to be enough. I've become convinced that tolerance, though necessary, is insufficient.

Tolerance presupposes a difference of opinion and opens a spacious place for us to agree to disagree. But our notions of human tolerance also carry with them a kind of indifference, a cold, and even arrogant aloofness. Usually, we don't care about those we merely tolerate. And that's the problem. Tolerance is often the luxury of those who control the cultural discourse. They don't fear being displaced, so they don't have to engage; they merely put up with. At the core, human tolerance is a stance that's passive, not empathic. Viewed through the teaching of Jesus, this tolerance is not enough. What is needed now is his gift of *Spiritual* tolerance, grounded in the Holy Spirit of Jesus himself.

According to Aaron Renn, evangelical Christians have offered several responses to their cultural disagreements with others. Those responses

---

14. Romans 5:8-10 (ESV).

15. Martin Luther King Jr., *Strength to Love*, 54.

range from becoming culture warriors, to being seeker sensitive, to cultural engagement.[16]

My purpose here is not to assess, let alone recommend, a strategy. Each has its own demonstrated strengths and weaknesses. I think what's needed in our time is an infusion of a spiritually tolerant love into whatever approaches we may take.

## THICK EMPATHY

Daniel Goleman has identified three different types or layers of empathy. First is cognitive empathy, which is "the ability to understand another person's perspective." Second is emotional empathy, "the ability to feel what someone else feels." Third is compassionate concern, "the ability to sense what another person needs from you."[17] Spiritual tolerance must operate at all three levels of empathy to be experienced as loving. It must be thick.

Entering another's thought world will require a temporary suspension of our own assumptions for the sake of understanding them within their own frame. Only when we work hard enough to do this will we gain access to their heart and be able to feel from the inside what they feel. And only then can we sense what they really need from us. So often it's just the assurance that we care for them, and that this care, this *love*, is not conditional. Nor is it compromised by any deep disagreements we may have.

The central thing to remember is that our engagement with others over questions of truth, goodness, justice, beauty, and responsibility can never be fruitful in an us-versus-them paradigm. Paul reminds us that "our struggle is not against flesh and blood, but against the rulers, against the authorities, against the powers of this dark world and against the spiritual forces of evil in the heavenly realms."[18] To say that our struggle is not against flesh and blood simply means that it's not against people. People are not the enemy (and even if they were, we're commanded to love them). We must remember that there exist "spiritual forces of evil in the heavenly realms," actively at work in all of our lives.

16. Renn, "The Three Worlds of Evangelicalism," *First Things*, February 1, 2022. https://www.firstthings.com/article/2022/02/the-three-worlds-of-evangelicalism.

17. Goleman, *Empathy*, Harvard Business Review Emotional Intelligence Series; https://books.google.com/books?hl=en&lr=&id=qGofDgAAQBAJ&oi=fnd&pg=PT7&dq=daniel+goleman+on+empathy&ots=zDMOunlS25&sig=eZuyD1dPeDL-iJuSAkid1JxUmoc#v=onepage&q=daniel%20goleman%20on%20empathy&f=false.

18. Ephesians 6:12.

The script says that as fallen people, we're often blinded by the god of this world.[19] This is why Jesus was able to pray for the forgiveness of those who crucified him. Because they *really* didn't know what they were doing. He was tolerant to the point of allowing them to carry out their plans. But his tolerance was Spiritual, because it came from the passionate love of the Holy Spirit fully manifest within him.

## AN EPISTEMOLOGY OF LOVE

Epistemology is a fancy word philosophers use to describe theories of knowledge—in other words, how we know what we know. So how do we come to *really* know other people? This comes only through love. I would add my voice to those who've recently been calling for the church to be converted to an "epistemology of love." This means having a default, a preferential option for seeing others with the eyes of spiritual love. Our initial approach to knowing them is always by loving them. It must become the starting point of all our relationships, not merely the endpoint of some of them.

N. T. Wright speaks of this as an important stance relative toward history. Rather than evaluate history in some pretended "anti-septic," "balanced," or "objective" manner, we should approach history with a heart of love. Such a heart tries to truly understand and sympathize with the humanness of those who lived that history before us. Historians should be lovers.

> A lover! Yes indeed: one who simultaneously enters sympathetically into the life of the beloved while honoring and celebrating the vital differences between the two of them. This is the paradox of the epistemology of love, and we see it clearly in the work of the historian as anywhere else... It is possible and necessary for the task of history to discern, to describe, and imaginatively to inhabit other minds, other worldviews, and to see how people who saw the world like that would plan, make decisions, respond to events, and so on. This is fundamental to what historians do.[20]

Wright argues elegantly and persuasively for modern and postmodern types to take a fresh look at the Gospels of Jesus with loving eyes, and not the old critical ones.

---

19. 2 Corinthians 4:4.

20. Wright, *History and Eschatology*, 97–98.

I'm suggesting that we take this idea and make it the basis of all our relationships. Here historical posture becomes personal stance. An epistemology of love would become the first and primary lens through which we know people. We would know people *through love*. An epistemology of love would see people differently, not as others to be studied or strangers to be feared, but as image-bearers to be spiritually loved by us in the way we and they are already loved by Jesus.

To borrow Paul's phrase concerning how God sees us, we would be "for them." *For* them, because we're so profoundly *like* them. If love becomes the starting place of our knowledge of other people, it will mean we've learned to love our neighbors as ourselves, because we've learned to *know* our neighbors as ourselves.

We would read the newspaper of their lives not starting with the "classifieds" of race, gender, class, neighborhood, political party, or team. We would start with the "front page" of their thirst, hunger, tears, smiles, and laughter. We would move to our differences by way of the sameness of our common humanity. We would find a way to cheer each other on in life's race, knowing that God has placed us all on Team Human. We would take up the posture of Winnie the Pooh who said, "On the outside we're different, but inside we're all the same." This is not to minimize our differences, which are real, but to deny them hegemony. Let the love of Christ alone hold hegemony over us, so that we see others as he does.[21]

## SPIRITUAL TOLERANCE ILLUSTRATED

Let me supply a personal story of what Spiritual tolerance might look like. My mother was a heavy smoker. Long after the anti-smoking campaigns commenced in the sixties, with warnings on the side of every cigarette pack—the surgeon general alerting people to the risk of cancer and emphysema—she clung to her cigarettes as if they were the crown jewels. She even received a pen in the mail inscribed with the words "Smoker's Rights Achievement Award," which she got from some organization that convinced my mother that her right to smoke was under siege.

---

21. Here I am reminded of the deep friendship of the famous preacher of the Great Awakening George Whitefield, and his publisher, the Deist Benjamin Franklin. As far as history knows, Franklin never came to believe in Christ as his savior and Lord. Nonetheless, it is clear from their correspondence that Franklin cared deeply for Whitefield, and Whitefield for him. For more see Frank Lambert, "The Religious Odd Couple: Benjamin Franklin and George Whitefield: Theologically, they were miles apart, yet they became affectionate friends." *Christianity Today*, Issue 38, 1993.

It will come as no surprise if I tell you she contracted emphysema and was subsequently diagnosed with lung cancer. She quit the day she was diagnosed, after fifty-five years of smoking. But of course, by then it was too late.

We live in a world that is inhaling a steady stream of spiritual smoke. My suggestion is that we relate to that world the way I related to my mother before she died. I simply did the best I could by trying to love her well. I tried to get her to quit. I told her the truth about the effects of her smoking. (No easy words there!) I constantly tried to remind her that a healthy lifestyle would help support her goals for the future. I asked her if she thought about the impact her smoking had on the health of those around her.

I challenged Mom to think about whether she was exercising her freedom when she smoked, or revealing her slavery. Over many years I argued, I cajoled, I pleaded, I prayed. But through it all, I stayed in relationship. I never wrote my mother off. And when she died, it broke my heart. I loved her. I spiritually tolerated her smoking and never tried to force my convictions on her, but only tried to help her see that her convictions were not serving her well. Slowly and surely, the lies she told herself about her smoking were killing her.

But here's the thing. My mother knew I loved her. There was much more to our relationship than our deep disagreement about her smoking. The basis of our love for people can never become the imperious demand that they conform to our standards, no matter how right they might be.

I didn't just tolerate Mom's smoking; I also tried to get her free of it by being spiritually tolerant. I tried to understand and address her reasoning (cognitive empathy), to feel and sympathize with her addiction (emotional empathy), and to provide real support (compassionate empathy) in dealing with the situational changes her decisions forced upon her. I flew from the West Coast to the East Coast to help her choose the nursing home where she would ultimately die.

At the same time, I didn't violate her responsibility, her agency as a human being to make that decision herself. Neither does Jesus do that with us. Jesus is tolerant, but he's also deeply and perfectly filled with the Holy Spirit. He too warns, cajoles, pleads, and prays for us. He hangs in there with us by hanging there for us, on the cross. Speaking of his disciples, the script—by way of laconic lament—simply says, "He loved them to the end."

Christians must move beyond mere tolerance to a Spiritual tolerance for others. This tolerance has the spirit of Augustine's "fierce love" (without its excesses). This must be a tolerance that speaks the truth in love, and goes beyond speaking to providing love for the other person in the form of Spiritual tolerance.

This will require the hard work of getting to know and understand others. Psychiatrist and Auschwitz survivor Victor Frankl wrote,

> Love is the only way to grasp another human being in the innermost core of his personality. No one can become fully aware of the very essence of another human being unless he loves him. By the spiritual act of love, he is enabled to see the essential traits and features in the beloved person and even more, he sees that which is potential in him, that which is not yet actual but yet to be actualized. Furthermore, by his love, the loving person enables the beloved person to actualize these potentialities. By making him aware of what he can be and of what he should become, he makes these potentialities come true.[22]

We must work at the relationships by staying engaged, recognizing the reality of spiritual warfare, and never giving up on the other person. We must, in short, love them with the same Spiritual tolerance with which Jesus has loved us. Regardless of the outcome of any disagreements we may have of truth, goodness, justice, beauty, and responsibility, we must love them like God loved Nineveh; like Jesus loved his disciples. We must love them "to the end."

22. Frankl, *Man's Search for Meaning*, 176–77.

# 13

# The White Light of Submission, Service, Suffering, and Sacrifice

*Christianity is a religion of salvation,*
*and there is nothing in the non-Christian religions*
*to compare with this message of a God who loved,*
*and came after, and died for, a world of lost sinners.*
—JOHN STOTT, *BASIC CHRISTIANITY*

As all the wavelengths of light merge together, giving us one "white" light, so all these aspects of love converge in Jesus's submission, service, and sacrifice on the cross. The refractions of truth, goodness, justice, beauty, responsibility, and Spiritual tolerance all merge in the light-giving submission, life-giving service, and love-giving sacrifice of Christ. It's through him who is the light of the world that this light is refracted into its various wavelengths. And in him, they're finally gathered and united once again.

## SUBMISSION

Whereas God lacked a faithful covenant partner in Adam, he found one in Christ. Adam and Eve refused to submit to the commandment of God not to eat from the tree of the knowledge of good and evil. As we've seen, this decision created a parallel rebellious moral universe in which human beings named their own good and evil, and led all of humanity after them into sin and death.

Jesus, as the obedient son who submitted himself to the perfect will of the father, not only kept faith with God, but did so *for Israel* and *for us*. Once again, we see Jesus's submission to the will of God in the desert temptations and the recapitulation and reversal of Israel's history. In his radical submission to the Father and utter rejection of Satan, Jesus recasts the history of all humanity and establishes it once again on the foundation of his own righteousness and joyful submission to the will of God.

This trajectory is carried all the way through to his death on the cross: "Nevertheless not my will, but your will be done."[1] In Christ we see the perfect model of human submission to the will of God, and are given access through his death and resurrection to a new life of joyful obedience in the power of the Holy Spirit.

## SERVICE

When this Spirit of obedience is lovingly massaged into our lives by Jesus, it takes the form of service to others. Augustine once asked,

> What does love look like? It has the hands to help others. It has the feet to hasten to the poor and needy. It has eyes to see misery and want. It has the ears to hear the sighs and sorrows of men. That is what love looks like. [2]

Augustine goes on to say that love can be seen. It is seen most profoundly in the incarnation of Christ, but not only there. Now, because Christ lives in those who believe in him, love is seen incarnationally through his disciples.

Christ-bearers are necessarily love-bearers. The apostle John taught us that we cannot love God without loving others and caring for their needs.[3] D. L. Moody said that the world does not understand theology or dogma, but it understands love and sympathy.

I happen to believe that both theology and dogma are important, very important. But Moody's point stands. He was talking about the importance of what we've come to call EQ (emotional intelligence). Moody is reminding us that EQ is as important as IQ (intellectual intelligence). The old saying

---

1. Luke 22:42.

2. Augustine, https://www.azquotes.com/author/663-Saint_Augustine/tag/love.

3. 1 John 4:7–12.

that they won't care how much you know until they know how much you care is simple human nature.

Jesus cared about people. His compassion was gentle rain released from the clouds of his love. The way he treated people opened the door to belief in him. In the capacious presence of his love, a tax-collector, a thirsty soul by the well, a woman host to seven demons, and a Pharisee who came at night could all take the time to reassess their lives, and begin again.

Jesus's service to others was not conditional. We've seen how he served Judas dinner the night that disciple went out and sold out his master for thirty pieces of silver. Jesus fed him the bread, the cup, and the lamb that night, which gave Judas the strength to betray his teacher. Jesus washed Peter's feet that night, knowing that he would deny him three times before dawn. Jesus washed his disciples' feet that night to teach them the way of the towel and basin. Jesus served them all that night, though he knew they would desert him.

The active presence of his service in the grace and mercy of God were so transparent in him that people came to put their trust in him over and against their national religious leaders, whom Jesus accused of using the people for their own advantage. The fact that he put the law back into its service to human flourishing rather than using it as a club to condemn people was the coming of the dawn after a long night of pious pontification. Jesus said, "For even the Son of Man did not come to be served, but to serve, and to give his life as a ransom for many."[4] And then he lived it.

I have a picture on the wall a few feet from where I'm sitting. It's the cover of *Life* magazine on March 17, 1921. It shows Humpty Dumpty sitting on a wall, eating and drinking from a silver tea service with a delightful grin on his face. The caption written on the wall beneath him reads "Easter." While the artist's intent is for us to clearly see Humpty as a symbol of Jesus and his victory, I'm convinced that it's also a symbol of the victory we all will share in him. Its symbolism points to both the last supper and the wedding supper of the lamb. The true Torah, the true light, the true bread of God, the true vine, had come to serve people by putting them back together again.

I'm Humpty Dumpty. We all are. And neither the epoxy of enlightenment, nor the duct tape of self-discovery, neither the rubber bands of relationships, nor the bailing wire of bank accounts can put us back together again. Only a love that's stronger than death can do that. As Hans Urs von Balthasar has written, "Love alone is credible."[5]

---

4. Mark 10:45.

5. von Balthasar, *Love Alone Is Credible*. This is not only the theme, but the title of his book.

The first responder of love's mission in the world is service. Love as only a thought is not credible in a suffering world. Love as only sympathy or empathy is not credible in a suffering world. In such a world, only love as concrete acts of service is credible. Perhaps the most impactful icon of this in today's culture is the Red Cross.

Acts of service to other human beings in the name of Jesus is the signature of Christianity—the cup of water, the blanket, the meal, the shelter from the winter storm. But also, a listening ear, a visit to the hospital room, a trip to the prison yard, a call, a text, or an email to our lonely neighbor. There are many ways to serve, some more visible than others, but every act of serving love performed in Jesus's name is credible. And service *in extremis* points us in the direction of sacrifice. The two are tied together; the latter is a deep form of the former.

## SALVATION THROUGH SUFFERING AND SACRIFICE

> What does this salvation mean, O Lord, from whom it comes and whose blessing is upon your people, if it is not in the gift of loving You and being loved by You. (Bernard of Clairvaux)[6]

> The cross does not contradict the dignity of the Son of God but, rather, is his image in this world, the image of self-giving love, which becomes powerless and thus becomes what is truly divine and holy. (Cardinal Joseph Ratzinger [Benedict XVI]).[7]

Few people have thought as deeply about love as Bernard of Clairvaux, the most remarkable monk of the Middle Ages. In fact, he wrote an entire book on loving God. In the striking quotation above, Bernard reminds us of the heart of the script, the golden thread of the biblical story from Genesis to Revelation. It is this: The love of God *is* our salvation. Salvation isn't separate from love; it is not something other than love; it is not before or after love. Salvation is the full and final face of love revealed on the cross of Jesus. This is Benedict XVI's point as well, with the added reminder that self-giving love is revealed as divine and holy when it comes in powerlessness.

One of the deep problems of the church today is that we've forgotten this. We've tried to separate love from salvation by grace through faith. I'll talk more about this below, because I believe that the future of the church and the effectiveness of its witness depends on recapturing this connection.

6. Bernard of Clairvaux, *Love of God*, 118.

7. Ratzinger (Benedict XVI), "On Love," in *Selected Writings*, 125.

For now, we remember that when the Bible talks about salvation, it is talking about love—specifically the sacrificial love of God for all creation. And here we must understand salvation in its widest sense. For human beings, it is not only salvation from sin and death, but carries within it the seeds of the restoration of all things—the making of all things new. When we reclaim the wide aperture of biblical salvation as it unfolds in Scripture, we understand that the love behind creation, the love behind salvation, and the love behind restoration are one in the same love.

At the center of Christianity lies the scandal of the self-sacrifice of Jesus Christ. The cross is the central symbol of Christianity and the preeminent sign of love. As the old hymn has it, "Lift high the cross, the love of Christ proclaim, to all the world, his sacred name." No other symbol of love comes close. But what is it, specifically, that the cross of Jesus teaches us about the love of God?

First, that his sacrifice was love's necessary expression. It isn't that Jesus just *happened* to die on the cross. We know from the script that this was set, from the beginning, by the "predetermined plan and foreknowledge of God."[8] The reason for this sacrifice was that Jesus was bringing the Old Testament sacrificial system to its climax and completion. Remember, once human beings had fallen, their relationship with God was broken, but temporarily mediated through the temple sacrificial system established by God through the law of Moses. At the center of this system was the necessity of blood atonement.

God had warned Adam and Eve that they would "surely die" if they ate the fruit of the tree of the knowledge of good and evil. And they did. We remember that this involved naming good and evil themselves, thereby placing themselves in the role of God. They'd staged the ultimate *coup d'état*. When human beings do this, death comes to them. Not only do they choose the way of death in this terrible decision, but they also stand under the positive judgment of God. They've made themselves God's enemies. They've compromised his creation and are therefore guilty of a capital offense. They have no excuse; they were warned about this: "You shall surely die."[9]

Over the course of the Hebrew Bible, we discovered that the temple had become the place where the sacrificial drama of Jesus was presaged in the slaughter of various animals. There could be "no forgiveness of sins without the shedding of blood."[10] But these sacrifices were a temporary arrangement and reminder of the Israelites' ongoing need (as well as our

8. Acts 2:23.
9. Genesis 2:7.
10. Compare Lev. 17:11; Heb. 9:22.

own) for the forgiveness of sin. The temple sacrifices were the preparatory season of God's love, which maintained the relationship between God and his people so they would continue to have a managed covenant relationship to him.

Only in the coming of Christ the New Man could humanity be reoriented to God, and as a result, be restored to him and to themselves. This process began in the incarnation, and flourished in Jesus's life of covenant faithfulness, publicly commencing in his baptism. As we've noted, in his forty days in the desert, Jesus was reliving Israel's forty-year history in the desert, and rewriting it from a history of disobedience to a history of obedience.[11] His desert faithfulness established the Messianic trajectory that led him all the way to the cross as its sacrificial culmination. His love, expressed in sacrifice, is our salvation.

The script says, "But when the fullness of time had come, God sent forth his Son, born of woman, born under the law, to redeem those who were under the law, so that we might receive adoption as sons."[12] As we saw earlier, this redemption Paul is talking about in Galatians means literally to be bought out of slavery to sin and death. And where and how did this redemption occur? On the cross. The cross is both the climax and the end of the sacrificial system. It's the conclusion of the third act of the great drama of salvation. And it is the final revelation of the love of God.

After Jesus was crucified, Matthew says, the veil in the temple was torn in two from top to bottom. It was the veil which separated the holy God from sinful man. Once a year the high priest would go through the veil into the presence of God and offer the sacrifice of atonement. This sacrifice had to be repeated in the temple annually. After Jesus, there is no more veil (separation) and no more temple building (place for blood sacrifice). The veil was torn from heaven's side (top) to the earth's side (bottom). This indicates that the tearing is the work of God. It is God's response to the substitutionary sacrifice of Christ on the cross for us. We may now come freely into the presence of God because we're in Christ. Jesus's atoning sacrifice has effected our "at-*one*-ment" with God. As a result, the love of God is now flooding into the world.

The temple was destroyed in a.d. 70 by the Romans and never rebuilt. Jesus had prophesied this destruction himself. The apostle John wrote, "The

---

11. A close study of the temptations in Matthew and Luke reveals the deep linkage here. If one explores Jesus's response to the devil taken from the book of Deuteronomy, and looks at the Exodus events referred to there, it becomes clear that in every instance where Israel failed in its vocation to be faithful to God, Jesus, as Israel's Messiah-King succeeded, giving God's people a new history with a refreshed Script.

12. Galatians 4:4 (ESV).

Word became flesh and tabernacled (templed) among us, and we beheld his glory." Jesus himself was the new temple, the place on the earth that God inhabited, and now we are the temple that Jesus, as God, inhabits.[13]

Jerusalem's temple had served its time and purpose. The relationship between God and humanity has been restored in Christ. No other blood sacrifice will now be needed or necessary. When Jesus on the cross said, "It is finished," he meant it. The necessary sacrifice of the cross is the key to plumbing the depths of the love of God. This is what Paul means when he writes, "God was in Christ, reconciling the world to himself."[14] Our salvation from start to finish was a Trinitarian inside job. It was the perfect act of creative sacrifice. As a result of Jesus's death and resurrection, love is re-established in the world as the foundation for the new community and the new creation.

Another thing we learn from the sacrifice of Jesus is that it was deeply *personal.* God is a personal being. Jesus was the incarnation of that personal being, and we bear that image as personal beings. The meaning of the sacrifice of Christ can never be plumbed through the lens of philosophy or the observations of history. Philosophy and history may elucidate elements concerning the events and impacts of what happened at Calvary, but they'll never pierce its essential meaning, because its meaning is personal.

Jesus' sacrifice is an act of pure love. It has to do with an exchange between persons—life for death, hope for despair, union for separation. But the exchange is not transactional, it's relational. It's true that the coming and cross of Jesus changes humanity's status before God, just as the love of the Father changed the status of the younger brother in the story of the prodigal son. But the change in status is a *consequence* of that love, not its *cause.*

Remember what Martin Luther wrote,

> The love of God does not find, but creates that which is pleasing to it. Rather than seeking its own good, the love of God flows forth and bestows good. Therefore, sinners are attractive because they are loved, they are not loved because they are attractive.[15]

Finally, we realize in the love of Jesus on the cross that his sacrifice was *costly.* It cost him his comfort, his reputation, his friends, and finally his life. It cost him everything. Love costs. Love requires costly sacrifice if it's to be

---

13. On the language of Jesus and the temple see also John 2:19–21, Matthew 12:6, Matthew 24:1–2; Rev. 21:22. On the Church as the temple see 1 Corinthians 3:16–17; 1 Peter 2:4–6.

14. 2 Corinthians 5:19 (see ESV's secondary reading).

15. Luther, "The Heidelberg Disputation," section 28, in Lull, *Martin Luther's Basic Theological Writings*, 48.

Christian love. Human love thrives on addition. Christian love thrives on subtraction because sacrifice is subtractive. It requires a giving up for the other.

This is not to say that there aren't great benefits associated with sacrifice; there are. Jim Elliot, who was martyred by and for the Auca Indians, had years before written in his journal, "He is no fool who gives what he cannot keep to gain that which he cannot lose."[16] These benefits are spiritual in nature. When we "fill up the sufferings of Christ,"[17] our union with him is deepened. When we share with others—especially with the "least of these"—we're ministering to Jesus himself. In ministering sacrificially to others, our love touches Jesus's love. In the strange alchemy of Christian sacrifice, the higher the cost the deeper the communion.

Because it is costly, Christian sacrifice requires a kind of preparation in our soul, a preparation of shedding. This preparation is both internal and external. Internally, we're called to shed our illusions about the world and our place in it. This preparation requires the shedding of the false self we've so assiduously cultivated. It requires a shedding of false frames that place humanity at the center of reality.

Our external preparation also requires a shedding, but of a different kind. It's a shedding of overweening attachments to "the world" and its "lust of the flesh, lust of the eyes, and pride of life."[18] It's a shedding of our desire to have it both ways—to be "in the world *and* of the world," to "serve God *and* mammon." It's overcoming the temptation not only to admire the emperor's clothes, but to try them on.

These two sheddings are preparatory; they have a purpose. The letter to the Hebrews encourages us:

> Therefore, since we are surrounded by such a great cloud of witnesses, let us throw off everything that hinders and the sin that so easily entangles. And let us run with perseverance the race marked out for us, fixing our eyes on Jesus, the pioneer and perfecter of faith. For the joy set before him he endured the cross, scorning its shame, and sat down at the right hand of the throne of God. Consider him who endured such opposition from sinners, so that you will not grow weary and lose heart.[19]

16. Elliot and Elliot, *Journals of Jim Elliot*, entry for October 28, 1949. Many of that indigenous tribe in Ecuador (known then as Auca, and today as the Huaorani or Waorani) became followers of Christ.

17. Colossians 1:24.

18. 1 John 2:16.

19. Hebrews 12:1–3.

The way of Jesus reminds us: first the stripping off (shedding), then the sacrifice, then the joy—in that order. My friend Jim has run five 100-mile ultra-marathons. When race day comes, there's first the stripping away off all things not related to the race, then the agony of the race itself, and finally the joy of the finish.

Christian art doesn't always do us a favor in covering Jesus with a loin-cloth on the cross. We know the Romans were not so kind. The sacrifice of the cross involved the deepest shame, the complete stripping, and most painful death imaginable. Jesus died naked on the cross, having absorbed the sin of the world so totally that Paul says he "became sin" for us.[20] This was his submission, suffering and sacrifice as the Messiah-King. Hebrews instructs us to "consider him." Think about the opposition, the shame, the suffering, and the sacrifice. But remember also "the joy set before him." And when you're in the middle of your race, remember his—and draw your strength to endure from him, through his Holy Spirit who lives within you.

To be a Christian is to take up one's cross and follow Jesus Christ wherever he may lead. And if it's Christ who leads us (and not our own fantasies about him), there will be suffering and sacrifice involved—and it will be worth all of it, because this is the way of love—to sacrifice for others. Any Christianity without sacrificial love at the center is an impostor.

The white light of God's *agape* love is refracted through truth, goodness, justice, beauty, responsibility, and Spiritual tolerance, as fully revealed in Jesus's submission, service, and suffering sacrifice. If we're to understand the meaning of Christian love, it can be seen in these ways. But it is Jesus himself in whom and through whom these things are revealed and known. He himself is the light that shines in the darkness, which the darkness cannot and will never overcome. He himself is the image of the invisible God of love through whom we can know God as love and become lovers ourselves.

20. 2 Corinthians 5:21.

# PART FOUR

Responding to God's Invitation

# 14

# Traversing the Obstacle Course

*Our question is how we moved from a condition in 1500*
*in which it was hard not to believe in God,*
*to our present situation just after 2000,*
*where this has become quite easy for many.*

—CHARLES TAYLOR, *A SECULAR AGE*

We've realized that God has a love story underway which he's still writing. It's the most ancient of stories, originating from before time began, pouring forth from the Trinitarian love of God and creating a theater called the universe for the love of God to go on display. At the center of that story is the revelation of God's "second self" in Jesus Christ.[1] He is the light who was "coming into the world." He is the flawless, sinless, incarnation of love.

In the person, words, and works of Jesus, we see the love of God come alive and active in a new way in the world. We've also seen that the coming of Christ is not intended as something to be observed or studied. Rather, he is some*one* to be engaged, to be loved, to be followed and to be obeyed, because love requires obedience as the path to joy.

But joining him in his invitation to love is not easy. It's an invitation cloaked in the fog of our confusion and sin. That's what I'd like to explore now. The fallen world is not a level playing field. The Splitter works outside and inside us to turn us away from the Divine Lover and his gracious invitation to be loved and to become lovers. We encounter obstacles at every turn.

1. Wright, *Day the Revolution Began*, 288.

## EXTERNAL WOUNDS OF PERCEPTION

### *The Autocracy of Reason*

One of the strongest currents in our culture is the de-centering of faith by a metastasizing, autocratic allegiance to reason. We inherited this from the Enlightenment movement of the eighteenth century, which was based upon the assumption that any other sources of authority besides human reason must be swept aside. This is seen most starkly in a remark from the French crypto-atheist Jean Meslier: "The last king should be strangled with the entrails of the last priest."[2]

In the Christian tradition, however, faith and reason have always been partners, each needing the other to complete our picture of reality. While reason was a gift of God and part of man's image-bearing, it too was damaged in the fall of humankind, and needs the light of faith to clarify its understanding of the world. In the eleventh century, Anselm—building on Augustine before him—bound the two together: "I do not seek to understand in order that I may believe; rather, I believe in order that I may understand."[3] For the Christian, faith without reason goes blind, and reason without faith goes mad. Both are necessary, since both are a gift of God meant to partner together in guiding us.

This autocracy of reason is usually showcased in our culture as a war between science and religion. From a Christian perspective, there never was such a war, nor could there ever be.[4] Historically, Christians have believed there are two "books," one of nature, another of Scripture. They reinforce one another because they have the same author. Sometimes, the analogy of two "lights" is used to make the same point—the light of nature and the light of revelation. Since God is the only source of true light, these two can never

---

2. Jean Meslier, 15 July 1864; "Le testament: 1 éd. Orig." (Meijer, via Google Books). The quote is often attributed to Diderot and Voltaire, who both used it in the decades prior to the French Revolution, but it is likely original, at least in written form, with Meslier. "Interestingly when the student demonstrations broke out at the Sorbonne during the political unrest of May 1968, the radical students of the Sorbonne Occupation Committee paraphrased Meslier's epigram, stating that 'humanity won't be happy till the last capitalist is hung with the guts of the last bureaucrat'"; https://en.wikipedia.org/wiki/Jean_Meslier#cite_ref-13.

3. St. Anselm, *Proslogion*, 1.

4. The so-called "warfare thesis" was promulgated by two scientists (Draper and White) in the nineteenth century. Prior to that, Christians natural philosophers (scientists), including Isaac Newton, had always understood Scripture and science as two sides of the same coin. They were meant to be read together and mutually interpret one another.

be in conflict; they are intended to be used to interpret each other, thus giving us a fuller revelation of reality itself and the will of God.

If we can reclaim reason in the light of faith, and let the two work together to lead us to God, then the script's message—that not only does this God exist, but that he loves us—becomes once again both believable and reasonable.

## Scientism

Related to the autocracy of reason, and a corollary of it, is today's totalitarian scientism. Scientism is a philosophical privileging of knowledge acquired through the senses to the exclusion of any other form of knowledge acquisition. Harvard's James Hankins has recently described scientism as "unwarranted reliance on science, or a predisposition to believe opinions that present themselves illicitly as scientific fact."[5]

Scientism is philosophy masquerading as science. Sometimes known as philosophical materialism or scientific naturalism, scientism extends science's empirical methodology to all of reality by means of an epistemological imperialism asserting something which itself can't be scientifically verified viz., that all of reality is subject to empirical verification by the senses. But that statement itself is beyond scientific verification. In short, scientism is unscientific. It's a classic example of the fallacy of assuming *a priori* what has yet to be demonstrated. Scientism is raw assertion, a totalitarian power play, and epistemological bullying. It is ideology masquerading as science.

Science itself is a humbler enterprise. Science is circumscribed by severe epistemological constraints. It can know only certain things, and those are only of nature. All valid science must be conducted within the space-time envelope and cannot *scientifically* address matters beyond it. Science, by definition, can be applied only to questions that can be proven or disproven by repeatable experimentation. Questions concerning the existence of non-material reality, the existence and nature of God, the meaning and purpose of life, and salvation all lie beyond validation by the scientific method. When scientists seek to answer such questions *as scientists*, they're

5. Hankins, "Imprudent Expertise," *First Things* (June/July 2020), 25. In addition, a number of other factors contribute to what is considered to be scientific "fact." This has become clear during the recent scientific pronouncements during the Covid-19 debates. Other contributing factors which warp scientific perspectives include dissonance, social proof, self-selection, in-group and out-group dynamics, cultural cognition, self-interest, and funding. See Trevan, "Why Scientists Got the Covid Lab Leak Wrong," *The Wall Street Journal*, Tuesday, March 7, 2023, A15.

operating beyond their brief, and have become philosophers (and poor ones at that) now masquerading as scientists.

I once had a conversation with a medical doctor friend who is not a believer. He said to me, "How can I believe? I'm a man of science. People can't walk on water; miracles are scientifically impossible. If I can't prove it, I can't believe it." So I asked him, "Do you believe in love?" He replied, "Of course!" I said, "Can you prove love exists?" He grew quiet.

None of us really believe that the material is all there is, we just pretend to. Not all of life, not all human experience can be stuffed into a test tube and distilled over a Bunsen burner. Science, like all other forms of learning, is a gift from God. I'm deeply grateful to scientists for their work. Indeed, I'm alive because of it. But scientism as a philosophy radically expands and then totalizes the boundaries of the scientific method, insisting that all of reality must submit to it. This is an illegitimate claim, which itself is unverifiable and must be resisted.

Scientism has led some thinkers to try to explain love scientifically, because it involves chemical reactions in our body. But who's to say it isn't the emotion triggering the production of serotonin, epinephrine, or dopamine, rather than the other way around? While there are certain kinds of love (*eros*) associated with bodily response, this reductionistic approach reveals the utter poverty of scientism. Try telling your wife on Valentine's day that your love for her is just biochemistry. (Good luck with that!)

Other devotees of scientism now hold that even altruism or higher forms of love are simply the product of material forces. But this whole approach is akin to a man born in a prison cell insisting that anything outside it must be made of steel and concrete.

Once we see scientism for what it is—an imposition of culturally manufactured evidentiary blinders—we're free to return to the evidence itself. No longer blinkered, we can seek what philosophers call an "inference to the best explanation" of what we find there. Does the evidence from the big bang, the fine-tuning of the universe, the almost impossibly complex nature of our own earthly habitat, and the resemblance between the ordering of the human genome and information theory suggest a loving, intelligent presence behind it all?

Historically, materialistic scientism has accused Christians of using a "God of the gaps" argument. The idea was that the gaps in our knowledge were simply attributed to the work of God. As science was closing those gaps, God would no longer be necessary as an explanation for anything. This was Laplace's view of God when he responded to Napoleon's question about why his celestial mechanics did not reference God. Laplace told his former student, "Sir, I have no need of that argument."

But as we glimpsed in Part 1, the problem for those holding the scientism position today is that the gaps are actually growing. The more we know, the more we know we don't know. The deeper we go, the more complex things look. As the evidence accumulates, where does it point? Might there be a growing perception among scientists that the "God hypothesis," in the light of new scientific discoveries of the last century, provides us with that inference to the best explanation of why the universe, our world, and we, are as we are—that Laplace was wrong after all?[6]

Beyond all this, scientism is based on a science that's out of date. Its roots are in the mechanistic view of the universe upheld by many (not all) in the early-modern science of the seventeenth and eighteenth centuries. As my former colleague Professor John Jefferson Davis has demonstrated, the later insights of James Clerk Maxwell and Albert Einstein, coupled with the revolution of quantum mechanics, point to a world that operates with much more subtlety, and along very different lines than modern science could have possibly conceived.

This is particularly true in our current understanding of energy, which has revolutionized our understanding of matter. Biblical data such as the burning bush, the transfiguration of Jesus, miracles, and his resurrection from the dead are becoming comprehensible within the framework of the new physics. Here the biblical notions of the immanence of God in creation, the indwelling of the Holy Spirit in believers, and our union with Christ are understood as ontological realities, not simply as metaphors. Davis writes,

> The newer "picture" of later modern science, which envisions the immanence of electromagnetic energy in matter, with an ontological reality equal to that of solid material objects apparent to the senses, makes it easier to recapture the Bible's imaginative vision, seeing, with the "eyes of our hearts" (Eph 1:18), the Spirit's immanence in the material world. We can indeed see that the heavens—the stars, the multitude of galaxies revealed by the Hubble Deep Field telescope—indeed are "telling the glory of God" (Ps 19:1).
>
> We need not continue to be held captive by a picture painted by Galileo and Descartes that "de-spirits" the material world. We can imagine again, perhaps in a newer and deeper way, a redeemed creation that is destined to enjoy the glorious freedom, in the Spirit, of the children of God (Rom 8:21), an earth that will be filled with the glory of God as the waters cover the sea (Hab. 2:14).

6. See for example Meyer, *Return of the God Hypothesis,* and Meyer, *Mere Creation.* Also, Metaxas, *Is Atheism Dead?*

> We can imagine the Spirit of God dwelling in the human
> body—the body imagined not as a machine or a computer—but
> as a living temple of the Spirit, connected in a real union with
> the risen Christ, a body destined from eternity to share the glory
> of the transfigured Christ (Rom 8:30).[7]

You can't believe in the love of God if you don't believe in the existence of God. Thankfully, that position is looking less and less tenable. And science itself is making it look that way. But we have to be open to where the new science is leading.

In 2004 the world's leading British philosophical atheist, Anthony Flew, announced at a widely publicized debate that he now believed in the existence of God. In his book *There Is a God,* he writes that the rest of that evening with his interlocutors, rather than being "an intense exchange of opposing views," became instead "a joint exploration of the developments in modern science that seemed to point to a higher intelligence."[8] Commenting on the complexity and subtlety of how our DNA are formulated, Flew wrote, "It is all a matter of the enormous complexity by which the results were achieved, which looked to me like the work of intelligence."[9] What makes Flew so interesting is that he is not a believing Christian, but claims that he reached this conclusion by simply following where the scientific evidence led. "In short, my discovery of the Divine has been a pilgrimage of reason and not of faith."[10]

When we, like Anthony Flew and so many others, become willing to take off the blinders of scientism and keep an open mind while reviewing the evidence, we may well reach the same conclusion. We cannot prove the existence of God, but as the evidence mounts, it seems extremely probable. If that's the case, then the probability of the love of God for us—especially when viewed against the backdrop evidence of the fine-tuning of the universe, the earth's ecosystem, and the sophistication of the human genome—follows close on. Of course, this is what the script has said all along.

---

7. Davis, "The Spirit and the Glory's Banishment from the Material World: Reimagining Divine Immanence in the Light of Later Modern Science," in *Science & Christian Belief* (Vol 32, No. 2), 36–37.

8. Anthony Flew, *There Is a God: How the World's Most Notorious Atheist Changed His Mind,* 74.

9. Flew, *There Is a God,* 75.

10. Flew, *There Is a God,* 93.

## Secularism

Secularization is another external or cultural wound to our perception. Charles Taylor, in his magisterial work *A Secular Age*, makes the case that Christianity, while carrying seeds of secularity, was not preordained to take that road. Rather, a branch of Christianity migrated first into what Taylor calls "providential deism" (focusing on the personal provision of God, particularly in providing the universe modern science was beginning to reveal), then to "the primacy of impersonal order"—focusing more on the order than its author—and finally to the notion of a "true, original natural religion."[11] Thus deism, the notion of the "clockmaker" God, became fully established.

This last step could now be taken based upon reason alone. For the deist, Nature (capital N) itself revealed the need of, and contours for morality, which could be determined by reason unaided by revelation. "Natural religion" became more and more anthropocentric, with human beings calling the shots based upon reason rather than revelation. Indeed, the biblical text itself eventually became suspected of corruption.

The so-called Jefferson's Bible is iconic of this approach. Thomas Jefferson went through the Gospels and excised all references to the supernatural—no prophecy, no miracles, no incarnation, no resurrection. For Jefferson, and many of the deists of his period, Jesus was reduced to a purely moral teacher. This of course is exactly the sort of thing C. S. Lewis denounced in his "liar, lunatic, or Lord" argument. Lewis famously pointed out that the extraordinary claims of Jesus force us to decide whether or not he is who he says he is. We can no longer seek a middle ground delimited by human reason. We can no longer say,

> "I'm ready to accept Jesus as a great moral teacher, but I don't accept his claim to be God." That is the one thing we must not say. A man who was merely a man who said the sort of things Jesus said would not be a great moral teacher. He would either be a lunatic—on the level with a man who says he's a poached egg—or else he would be the Devil of Hell. You must make your choice. Either this man was, and is, the Son of God: or else a madman or something worse. You can shut Him up for a fool, you can spit at Him and kill Him as a demon; or you can fall at His feet and call Him Lord and God. But let us not come with any patronizing nonsense about His being a great human teacher. He has not left that open to us. He did not intend to.[12]

11. Taylor, *Secular Age*, 221.
12. Lewis, *Mere Christianity*, 56.

Deism, then, became the rest stop on the way to the contemporary atheism behind our modern secularism. Taylor writes,

> The crucial feature here is the change in the understanding of God, and his relation to the world. That is, there is a drift away from orthodox Christian conceptions of God as an agent interacting with humans and intervening in human history; and toward God as architect of a universe operating by unchanging laws, which humans have to conform to or suffer the consequences… From this perspective, Deism can be seen as a half-way house on the road to contemporary atheism.[13]

With the personal God who is to be loved and obeyed escorted to the margins, thereby placing nature and human reason at the command center of moral reasoning, it became a short step to deny the existence of and need for a personal, loving God altogether.

In a nutshell, the progression was from orthodoxy to deism to atheism. The new scientific method, which began at roughly the same time, abetted this shift in turning human attention toward the seen world as opposed to the unseen world, with some in its community eventually denying the existence of the latter altogether. Today a majority of America's top scientists are either agnostics or atheists. This number is highly disproportionate to the general population. According to Elaine Ecklund's recent study from Oxford Press, *Secularity and Science,*

> The level of disbelief in God among US scientists is striking, largely because belief in God is so high among the general US population: 92 percent of the US public believes in a personal God or a higher power, compared with 36 percent of US scientists. While only 3 percent of the US public identifies as atheist, nearly 35 percent of scientists say they don't believe in God.[14]

This is even more the case in Europe, particularly in the UK and in France.[15] The French Revolution—under the sway of its father, the Enlightenment—was explicitly biased against the Christian religion and particularly Roman Catholicism. The best symbol of this turn was the enthronement

---

13. Taylor, *Secular Age,* 270.

14. Ecklund et al., *Secularity and Science: What Scientists Around the World Really Think about Religion,* 31. This may be simply an example of Trevan's "in-grouping/out-grouping" observation.

15. Ecklund, *Secularity and Science,* 54–103.

of a young actress[16] as the "Goddess Reason" on November 10, 1793, at the Cathedral of Notre Dame. According to history writer Geri Walton,

> The Cult of Reason (Culte de la Raison) was the first state sponsored atheistic religion. Bringing this civic religion to fruition was the Festival of Reason (Fête de la Raison), a celebration that would launch a dechristianization movement... The Cult of Reason was based on the principles of Enlightenment and anticlericalism. Its goal was the perfection of mankind through the attainment of Truth and Liberty and its guiding principle was to exercise reason... The opening words were given by a Prussian nobleman who was instrumental in the French Revolution named Anacharsis Clootz. He declared that the Republic would contain but "one God only, Le Peuple."

The "Cult of Reason" with its excesses was soon eclipsed by the "Cult of the Supreme Being," which established deism in France. French secularism is the stepchild of Enlightenment deism. Secularism (*läicité*)—the effectual banishment of religion from the public square and life—is still state policy in France.

The effect of this stringent secularism became evident in 2003 during discussions concerning the writing of a European Constitution, and the push from some to produce a preamble free from any references to Christianity. The proposed language was, "Conscious of its spiritual and moral heritage, the Union is founded on the indivisible, universal values of human dignity, freedom, equality and solidarity; it is based on the principles of democracy and the rule of law."[17] The Constitution was never ratified.

This secularist bias was highlighted by an Orthodox Jew named Joseph Weiler.[18] Weiler's point was that constitutions serve several functions, one of which is to remind people who they are and who they want to be. In attempting to scrub the preamble of a European Constitution of any Christian references, substituting a vague reference to its "spiritual and moral

16. The identity of the woman is uncertain, "Reports indicate it could be one of three women—mademoiselle Maillard (a danseuse de l'Opéra), Thérèse-Angélique Aubry (a figurant de l'Opera), or Sophie, "wife of the printer Mormoro." Each woman was described as being of "unparalleled beauty," and whoever impersonated the Goddess of Reason "was borne in triumph over the heads of the people to receive their worship, with all the pomp and display the promoters could invent." Geri Walton, "Festival of Reason During the French Revolution," https://www.geriwalton.com/festival-of-reason/.

17. Preamble of the European Constitution, https://fra.europa.eu/en/eu-charter/article/o-preamble#:~:text=EU%20Charter%20of%20Fundamental%20Rights,-Previous%20title&text=Conscious%20of%20its%20spiritual%20and,and%20the%20rule%20of%20law.

18. Weiler, *Christian Europe: An Exploratory Essay.*

heritage," the leaders were intentionally seeking to disavow their Christian cultural sources. Weiler, on the other hand was envisioning a Christian Europe which would be non-confessional (nondenominational):

> It is a Europe that, while celebrating the noble heritage of Enlightenment humanism, also abandons its Christophobia and neither fears nor is embarrassed by the recognition that Christianity is one of the central elements in the evolution of its unique civilization.[19]

Such "Christophobia" and embarrassment are the results of this smothering secularism that sees religion—particularly Christianity—as a threat. Reflecting upon this European trend twenty years ago, George Weigel wrote in his *The Cube and the Cathedral,*

> A thoroughly secularized world is a world without windows, doors, or skylights: a claustrophobic, ultimately suffocating world. A thoroughly secularized culture from which transcendent reference points for human thought and action have disappeared is bad for the cause of human freedom and democracy because democracy, in the final analysis, rests on the conviction that the human person possesses an inalienable dignity and value and that freedom is not mere willfulness.[20]

In this we hear echoes of Taylor's concern for the maintenance of transcendent sources as the lifeblood of Western civilization. Weigel sees Europe, which has embraced secularism more fully, as a cautionary tale for America.

This is not to say that Americans have ceased to be religious, or that orthodox Christianity is dead. Rather, American spirituality, and its expression of Christianity in general, has mutated. As the West shifted from orthodoxy to deism to atheism, a similar mutation was happening in America from orthodoxy to what sociologist Christian Smith has called moralistic therapeutic deism (MTD). Based upon his research with students (who are now adults), this new spirituality has five key components:

1. A God exists who created and ordered the world and watches over human life on earth.

2. God wants people to be good, nice, and fair to each other, as taught in the Bible and by most world religions.

---

19. Weiler, cited in Weigel, *Cube and the Cathedral: Europe, American and Politics Without God,* 66. This is Weigel's translation ofWeiler's original.

20. Weigel, *Cube and the Cathedral,* 172.

3. The central goal of life is to be happy and to feel good about oneself.

4. God doesn't need to be particularly involved in one's life except when God is needed to resolve a problem.

5. Good people go to heaven when they die.[21]

Smith has suggested that in this belief structure, God is "something like a combination Divine Butler and Cosmic Therapist: he's always on call, takes care of any problems that arise, professionally helps his people to feel better about themselves, and does not become too personally involved in the process."[22]

N. T. Wright has noted in all this a resurgence of ancient Gnosticism, with its emphasis on a secret inner knowledge lodged in the self, coupled with the escapist bent of liberating the self (soul) from the body (real life). Wright finds evidence of this neo-Gnosticism in our self-centeredness and our growing admiration for virtual reality.[23] More significantly for our purposes, Wright shows the linkage among the ancient Epicureans, the Enlightenment philosophes, and today's secularists. Speaking of the Enlightenment he writes,

> With many Christians bent on escaping the present world, leaving it to its own devices and desires, the world channeled the optimistic energy of the earlier Christian mission into "secularism," the development of the world and society as though God was either remote or nonexistent. Having banished God to a distant "heaven," earth was free to move under its own steam and in its own chosen direction. This split-level world, a modern version of the ancient philosophy called Epicureanism, is still widely assumed as the norm. The Enlightenment was, in effect, trying to get the fruits of the older Christian culture while ignoring the roots.[24]

Ross Douthat has recently referred to the sum of these secular tendencies as "Post-Protestant Gnosticism," which "descends along different lines from early American deism, transcendentalism, and various health-and-wealth enthusiasms... And it now operates in American life in roughly the

---

21. Smith, *Soul Searching*, 162–63.
22. Smith, *Soul Searching*, 165.
23. Wright, *Broken Signposts*, 64–65.
24. Wright, *Day the Revolution Began*, 360. For more background on Epicureanism's connection to the Enlightenment, Deism, and modernity see Wright, *History and Eschatology*, 7-10.

same way, with the same sort of influence, that Mainline Protestantism did a hundred years ago."[25]

However we might map and name the various tributaries of secularism, one thing is clear: We're living in a period telling ourselves a story which is decidedly different from that of the biblical God and his story. And the stories we tell ourselves have consequences.

It's important to understand that the church itself has been permeated with this view. While retaining biblical and orthodox theological language, the secular ideas of MTD have entered and mutated the church's DNA. If the biblical teaching on sexuality constrains my quest for freedom, expression, and happiness, then it deserves to be ridiculed and jettisoned. If what the Bible teaches about the value and dignity of human life becomes professionally or personally inconvenient, then it must be ignored. If the Bible seeks to curtail (let alone name) some excess in my life as sinful, it must be reinterpreted to teach health and wealth as the goals of the Christian life. Or more recently, if my biological sex is at odds with my internal sense of self (gender), then I must be free to "identify" in the way I choose, and not be restricted by my genetic coding.[26]

Beyond these problems, secularism has produced a dark economics of the commodification of people, making them mere human capital. This is accelerated by secularism's loneliness producing hyper-individualism. We've become people who "bowl alone," to borrow Robert Putnam's memorable phrase. Technology has been a mixed blessing here, allowing people across wide distances to connect, but also reinforcing a lack of incarnational community, which is the basis of human relationships.

Under the scorching sun of this God–refusing and human–infused narrative of secularism, the once fertile garden of the love of God in our hearts—which funded our benevolence, philanthropy, and generosity—has started to wither in the deserts of consumerism, entertainment, and isolation.

With these external, cultural wounds to our perception—the autocracy of reason, scientism, and secularism (all of which are interwoven)—we're sorely disadvantaged in our reading of reality. We suffer from a kind of cultural macular degeneration, which leaves us blind to the center of identity,

25. Ross Douthat, "A Gentler Christendom," *First Things* (June/July 2022), 31–32.

26. Its important to note that true gender dysphoria is a condition which requires love and compassion, not criticism and condemnation by the church. It should be viewed as yet another evidence of the disruption of the Fall to which we are all subject. People, after all are enfleshed and "ensexed" beings, but they are more than that as well. They bear the image of God, which must be remembered for all of us beyond our sexual confusions and struggles.

meaning, and purpose. All we're left with is a peripheral vision that can glimpse only non-essentials. The truth is that without a revelation from beyond we can have no confidence whatsoever in who we are and what we're to be about in the world. Wandering around in Chesterton's "maze with no center," we might as well just roll the dice to find our way out.

But if there has been a disclosure from the Author, if he has written a script and told us his story, and if, as Christianity proclaims, he himself has appeared to tell and live that story, then everything changes. Now we can no longer use confusion as our excuse. We must look squarely in the face of love incarnate and say either "yes" or "no" to him.

## OUR INTERNAL WOUNDS OF EXPERIENCE

As if these external wounds our culture imposes on us were not enough, we must also face the internal wounds that hinder our capacity to believe in the love of God for us.

### Father Wounds

For some of us, the very notion of God as Father makes it hard to trust God's love, because our own fathers were unloving. One of my sisters has talked with me about this problem in her own life. Our father was an alcoholic, and when he drank, he often became mean and sometimes violent. The very idea of God as a father figure is abhorrent to her. I've experienced this not only in conversation with her, but with a number of women who've experienced disrespect, abandonment, abuse, and other forms of misogyny from their own fathers and other men.

Not surprisingly, they project all that on God when he's referred to as Father. By the way, I've also known my share of men who've experienced their own forms of a lack of love from fathers, which creates a parallel set of problems for them. One of my ministry mentors in the first church I served once said to me. "Tom, I've never met an atheist who had a good relationship with his father." So far, I haven't either.

Despite all the associated pain and anguish here, I do think the way home is found in the biblical truth that God is our true Father. I must add that he is also our mother, and that there are passages in the script that reveal this. God is beyond sex. God is neither male nor female. God is Spirit. Nevertheless, I think that God's primary self-revelation in his role of Father is both telling and important. In the ancient world of the patriarchal Middle

East, men had control of the power. When God images himself as male, he's saying to them, "I am the all–powerful one, and you are accountable to me."

To accommodate himself into that world in his revelation, it was necessary that God be revealed as the Powerful One. Like parents with small children, they must first set boundaries as to who's in charge. "The *fear* of the Lord is the beginning of wisdom." I also believe that the *love* of the Lord is the end (the goal and perfection) of wisdom, because perfect love casts our fear. The nature of the relationship will mature over time, but in Israel's infancy the only effective cultural image available to communicate God's role in their lives was that of the father—a good, providing, protecting father of great power, love, and compassion. God the Father is the one by whom all other fathers (and all men) are to be measured.

Specifically, this meant that God would bless the Israelites by protecting and providing for them as his adopted children, and that they would obey him as the one true source of their well-being. One of the greatest temptations in Israel's heart, according to her prophets, was the temptation to idolatry. Her leaders were constantly going down this path, and the only one imagined strong enough to correct them and discipline them within their culture would have been imaged as a father. We may or may not like that image in our time, but I believe it was of divine necessity in theirs, and remains so today.

The role of Father is a male image, but God is not (and was not) a man. Fatherhood is a role, a set of responsibilities one embraces for the good of each child. How often have we heard the term, "He was like a father to me." It's about a lot more than biology, and often (in the case of adoption, for example) is not about biology at all.

Speaking of adoption, I have a friend who married a woman with three children. Her first husband abandoned them when they were young. When my friend married this woman, he adopted all her children, and now they have his last name. In fact, the oldest took the name of my friend's father as his own middle name. After the wedding, their first question was, "When do we get to change our name?" They wanted the name of their new father because they already knew his love for them.

The script says that when we believe in Christ, we become the adopted children of God. We're given his name. We become full inheritors of all that is his. We become family.

The core characteristic we see in the fatherhood of God is his love for Israel. God is their Father, and they know this by his love. If this love of God is manifested primarily in protecting and providing for his family, culminating at the cross, then we must return to the love of God as Father both to interpret our own father wounds and to find their healing.

All of us have a deep psychological need to be fathered well. We are made for this, and when our fathers (or mothers) model this poorly or not at all, it leaves a gaping hole in our souls. The remedy is not to repudiate our Father in heaven, but rather to engage with him and his love. Only in the light of experiencing God's true love—which he created us for—will we develop the resources to love those who've loved us poorly or not at all, and to forgive them. We then can move into spaces of healing where God can touch us in places beyond the reach of painful memory, repairing the wounds in our hearts.

My friend's children didn't know what the love of a father was until he became their father. Now they know, and that knowing brings healing and wholeness.

## Pride

Another internal wound that prevents us from experiencing the love of God is our pride. We tell ourselves that we don't need love, so we don't need God. We set ourselves up in the castle of self-sufficiency and pull up our defensive drawbridge. We've often been wounded by others, and we cover our fear of emotional risk-taking by telling ourselves that either we're above the need for love, or there's something about us that makes us unlovable in the first place. In either case, we withdraw from the love of God.

Rather than be attached to the powerline, we become our own generator, believing that this posture will carry us through life's storms. Eventually we realize that the generator itself has run out of fuel, and that we've left ourselves alone, shivering in an emotional winter of our own making.

At this juncture we have two options. The first is to double-down and continue headlong down the path of pride. We witness the cancer of this metastatic pride in William Ernest Henley's poem *Invictus,* which has become emblematic of the spirit of modern man. *Invictus* became the last words, written out in full, of Timothy McVeigh, the Oklahoma City bomber before his execution.

> Out of the night that covers me,
> Black as the Pit from pole to pole,
> I thank whatever gods may be
> For my unconquerable soul.
> In the fell clutch of circumstance
> I have not winced nor cried aloud.
> Under the bludgeonings of chance
> My head is bloody, but unbowed.

Beyond this place of wrath and tears
Looms but the Horror of the shade,
And yet the menace of the years
Finds, and shall find, me unafraid.
It matters not how strait the gate,
How charged with punishments the scroll,
I am the master of my fate:
I am the captain of my soul.[27]

*Invictus* was first published just twenty-five years or so after Macaulay's
Whig *History of England*. The poem reveals three key features of Enlightenment pride still on display among us today: despair masquerading as confidence, the denial of God, and total confidence in the self.

The other option—when we have isolated ourselves in the citadel of
pride—is to ask for God's help. To ask for help is to ask for love, because help
is love served straight up. To ask God for help is to recognize that God has
loved us the whole time. It's to turn, when we think we're alone, and discover
that he has been there all the while. I have a sign on my back patio which
reads *Vocatus atque non vocatus, Deus aderit*: "Bidden, or unbidden, God is
present." Pride poisons the human spirit, and the love of God is the antidote.

## Control

Another internal wound that prevents us from deeply knowing the love of
God is our need to control. Often in human relations between lovers there's
a wild sense of abandonment to one another. The ecstasy is in letting go. The
same must be true in our relationship with God. In his compelling book *The
Uncontrollability of the World*, Hartmut Rosa suggests that life at its best is
lived in the intersection of controllability and uncontrollability. When we
try to control everything, life becomes stale, flat, and predictable. But when
we relinquish our need to control and embrace our inability to control the
world, life is revivified.

What human beings long for, Rosa says, is resonance, because resonance transforms. Resonance is discovered at the intersection of control
and uncontrolability. A resonant experience makes us new and different
people. But we can never manufacture or control resonance; it comes upon
us. Resonance, by definition, is a surprise. It operates off the leash, comes as

---

27. Henley, Invictus, (1875).   https://www.poetryfoundation.org/poems/51642/
invictus.

a gift, and makes us feel alive.[28] Theologically speaking, resonance is a gift of grace.

There's a wildness in us which is suited for the wildness of God. God's love *is* wild. It can be shocking, raw, untamed, unfettered, overwhelming, unpredictable, unmeasured, startling. The love of God is like snow on Easter. It is standing on a ship's prow in a winter gale. It's the aurora borealis viewed from the Arctic Circle. It's falling in love. As Augustine said, "To fall in love with God is the greatest romance; to seek him the greatest adventure; to find him, the greatest human achievement."[29]

God's love is a pure gift freely given, while at the same time requiring our unconditional surrender. To surrender to love is to surrender to God, and to surrender to God is to surrender to love—because God is love. To love God, we must let go of our need to control. If resonance is an act of his grace, then surrender to that resonance becomes our act of faith.

Dissecting this contrast between our need to control and our need to surrender to God, David Benner has written,

> Surrender is the indispensable gateway to life, genuine freedom, and the fulfillment of humanity... The truth is that we must all surrender to something or someone. To refuse to find our place in relation to that which transcends the ego is to be in bondage to futile attempts to be in control... The egoic path of ascent is the way of control, willfulness, grasping and clutching. The spiritual path of descent is the way of surrender, willingness and letting go.[30]

But can we trust God if we really surrender? Doesn't God let people down? These questions lead us to the next internal wound that can prevent us from surrendering to his love.

## Suffering and Loss

In January of 1999, I took my oldest daughter to the Holocaust museum in St. Louis. We met a woman there whose name was Maria. She was a survivor from the Bergen-Belsen camp, and she graphically described her day of liberation to us. This is her testimony:

28. Rosa, *Uncontrollability of the World*, 34–39.

29. Augustine, https://kidadl.com/articles/st-augustine-quotes-from-the-philosopher-and-theologian-of-hippo.

30. Benner, *Surrender to Love*, 100.

300 girls, women, and I were in what was left of a barracks, most
of the wood of which had been stripped away by local peasants.
Because we had nothing to lean against, we leaned against each
other. We were starving to death, we had T.B., and many had
typhus, which is what Anne Frank died of in the same camp. I
was talking with my friend who was my "support" about what
her mother used to cook for dinner. I became angry with her
when she moved and I fell back. I moved her arm, and tried
to wake her up, saying, "Hey, what are you doing, talk to me." I
then realized that she was dead.

One of two twin girls next to her died shortly after, and when
I reached over to touch her, the other sister screamed, "Don't
touch her!" Only later did I realize that they were orthodox
Jews, and that they did not allow the dead to be touched. My
mother was close by, and was a skeleton. I told my mother my
friends were dead, and my mother said, "We are all going to
die." I said, "I don't want to die, I didn't do anything wrong." My
mother replied, "Maria, you're losing your mind, none of us did
anything wrong, but we're going to die." I told my mother, "I'm
going to get you something to eat." I stood up and almost fell
over from weakness, and struggled to the door.

I walked outside and smelled food cooking from the officer's
mess. When I looked in that direction, I saw a big white sheet
tied to the flagpole. I came inside and said to her mother, "We're
liberated." My mother said, "You're crazy, we're going to die." I
said, "I saw a white flag flying from the officer's kitchen." My
mother said, "You are hallucinating from the hunger." I walked
back over, and looked again. I saw the flag, and two German
soldiers walk by with white armbands on.

On the way back to my mother, I stepped over two more
girls I knew, who were now dead. "My eyes work fine, I'm not
hallucinating," I thought. I said again to my mother, "We are
liberated!" My mother said, "You are crazy." Another woman
spat on me and called me a liar. She threatened to hit me if I said
it again, and she was known as the "enforcer"; a blow from her,
in my condition could be fatal. But I insisted, "We're liberated!"
I saw the flag and the officers with the white armbands. Others
spat at me, and told me to shut up. Then the announcement was
made. The British army had liberated Bergen-Belsen.[31]

31. I included this quote from Maria in a sermon many years ago, but have long ago
lost its source, but I feel sure it was the St. Louis Holocaust Museum. I remember vividly
her story as she told it to us, the details of which are preserved in her written account.

Sometimes human beings, subjected to deep suffering over long periods of time, develop a debilitating sense of hopelessness. Psychiatrist Victor Frankel, who was also imprisoned in concentration camps during the Second World War, came to believe that it was simply a sense of hope which separated those who survived from those who didn't.[32] Sometimes we become vaccinated against good news by the sheer volume of bad news, the sheer weight of suffering. We, like Maria's and Frankl's fellow prisoners, are overcome by the darkness. We lose all hope, especially hope in God. When the good news comes, we simply cannot absorb it and will not trust it.

Probably the oldest biblical writing we have is the book of Job, which is fitting—because Job describes one of the oldest human experiences, the sense of having been forsaken by God. Having lost all that is dear to him, Job's pathos is palpable.

> Why is light given to those in misery,
>     and life to the bitter of soul,
> to those who long for death that does not come,
>     who search for it more than for hidden treasure,
> who are filled with gladness
>     and rejoice when they reach the grave?
> Why is life given to a man
>     whose way is hidden,
>     whom God has hedged in?
> For sighing has become my daily food;
>     my groans pour out like water.
> What I feared has come upon me;
>     what I dreaded has happened to me.
> I have no peace, no quietness;
>     I have no rest, but only turmoil.[33]

How can we love someone whom we believe has failed us, leaving us in the lurch? I've had many conversations with people over the years who felt forsaken by God—forsaken when their baby died, forsaken when their dreams exploded, forsaken when they were told they were terminal. One New Year's Eve, a man I know told me that he has a hard time with faith in God because he lost his mother to cancer at the age of seventeen. He not only felt his own loss acutely, he told me, but also the loss to his father, his brother, and others who knew his mother. He has not liked God, let alone loved him, ever since. Even after fifty-years, his sense of betrayal was palpable.

32. Frankl, *Man's Search for Meaning*, 112ff.

33. Job 3:20–26.

Some say that people in such circumstances should just "have more faith"; they should "trust God more." But faith and trust are not things you go to the spiritual gas station and fill up with. They're not commodities to be exchanged or bartered in an emotional bazaar. The feeling of suffering is hard enough to bear. But often with it comes something deeper: the sense that our suffering means that we've been abandoned by God. The feeling of God-forsakenness is as real as it is terrifying. Often the sense of abandonment is the afterbirth to the experience of deep loss and suffering. And the way through it is not the way of the spiritual alchemist, who attempts to conjure the gold of faith from the lead of suffering.

The way through loss and suffering is the way of Job and the way of Jesus. Job, for all his desolation, grabbed God even tighter. Rather than letting his suffering drive him away from God, it shoved him closer. Job grabbed hold of God's collar the way Jacob grabbed hold of the angel, unwilling to release him until the blessing came.

In Job's case, he gets in God's face with relentless questions. "Why did you let this happen? Why aren't you fair? Why am I being singled out for punishment? When are you going to do something about all this? Why aren't you listening? Why don't you jump in and fix this mess?" Verse after verse, chapter after chapter, Job's fusillade blasts the face of God. Job pulls God close with both hands to scream at him in agony. Job tenaciously, even virulently, maintains his innocence in this suffering. This isn't fair! This is unjust! It's undeserved!

His friends of course have reached the standard conclusion: Job is suffering because he deserves it! Obviously, he's done something wrong. People suffer because they screwed up—and of course the friends themselves are *not* suffering because they (so they suppose) have not screwed up. It's often our friends who don't understand who God is in relation to us. It's often our friends who abandon us in suffering, because it terrifies them: "If it happened to him, it could happen to me!" Because of this, such friends add deep insult to grave injury, becoming unwitting gas–lighters.

After all the counsel of Job's friends (chapter after chapter), it's absolutely striking that God finally and summarily dismisses all that they've said. God states his anger with them for misrepresenting him, and adds, " … you have not spoken the truth about me, as my servant Job has."[34] How are we to understand this?

I think the real answer is that although Job's *language* is that of forsakenness, his *behavior* is not. True forsakenness is followed by silence, not by argument. It has no one left to speak to. In arguing with God, Job is hanging

---

34. Job 42:7.

onto him. His arguing is, paradoxically, an expression of his faith. Like a child saying, "I hate you!" to her parents, so is Job with God. The opposite of love is apathy, not anger. Anger is often a barometer of broken love, but love, nonetheless.

The story of Job is remarkable in that he is healed neither by getting his questions answered (God never answers them), nor by the sudden restoration of what he'd lost (which God eventually brings about). Job is healed by neither answers nor goods, but by the very presence of God. God had been there all the time, and had never forsaken Job. God's appearance is the turning point. It's the moment of encounter that changes everything. Job says to him,

> My ears had heard of you
> but now my eyes have seen you.
> Therefore I despise myself
> and repent in dust and ashes.[35]

And even more so with Jesus, who is Job matured and perfected. He has read Job and has learned in the reading.[36] For all the truth to the fact that Jesus was God standing before man, it's equally true that Jesus was man standing before God. And like all men, he too struggled in that standing. If we lose his struggle, we lose his humanity, and with it the depth of our own.

During the searing hours before his scourging and death, we find Jesus struggling. He's in the garden of Gethsemane, the garden of the wine press, itself a symbol of the "pressing out"[37] which is facing him. He's alone, his disciples having fallen asleep. Alone, he cries out to God—who, as with Job, doesn't answer him. We're told that Jesus prayed so intensely that he sweated blood. This is not a literary device used by the evangelists, but a medical condition that can be brought on by extreme duress.[38] Jesus, like Job, is *in extremis.*

And Jesus, like Job, is persistent in prayer. We're told that three times he pleads with God to "let this cup pass by me." The cup Jesus refers to is the cup of God's wrath against all human sin alluded to in the prophets.[39]

---

35. Job 42:5–6.

36. Although Jesus neither mentions Job by name nor quotes him, Paul quotes Job twice and James mentions him by name, so clearly the book of Job was available to Jewish readers in Jesus's time.

37. Hebrew *gat shemanim*, "oil press."

38 "What Is Hematidrosis?" medically reviewed by Debra Jaliman, MD, January 26, 2022; https://www.webmd.com/a-to-z-guides/hematidrosis-hematohidrosis.

39. See, for example, Jeremiah 25:15–17, 49:12, 51:7; Psalm 75:8; Habakkuk 2:16; Zechariah 12:2–3; Revelation 14:10, 16:19, 18:6.

He knows that his mission as Israel's Messiah-King is to drink the cup of God's wrath against human sin, which he has taken upon himself passively in the incarnation, actively at his baptism, and now passionately at the cross in substitutionary atonement. Because of his death, freely given, others will live. Jesus has come for this unique purpose, yet he struggles as the horror of it all envelops him. Again, he, like Job in his suffering, receives no answer from God.

In his desperate prayer to the Father, Jesus utters perhaps the most important word in the Bible apart from the very name of God. Jesus says, "Nevertheless…." He prays, "Father, let this cup pass by me, *nevertheless*, not what I will, but your will be done."[40] And we would think that this would be the end of it. The cup would be snatched away from his lips just in time (just like in the movies).

But no. This isn't Hollywood. Having been arrested, flogged, crowned with thorns, stripped, then nailed to the cross, Jesus is lifted up to suffer the most excruciating death known in the ancient world. It was a death reserved especially for criminals, slaves, and traitors—a death that ancient authors preferred not to talk about in polite company. There on the cross, as Jesus is sagging in suffocation, he utters these words: "My God, my God, why have you forsaken me?"

Here it is. Jesus, as the representative man, faithful and true, the Holy One without sin now nailed, naked and crucified before God, asks why he has been forsaken. He is echoing the ancient cry of Job. He is echoing the ancient cry of every one of us. If we have cause to ask this question—and if Job had cause—then how much more did Jesus?

But there's a twist here. Jesus asks the question, but the question itself is a quote from the beginning of Psalm 22—a psalm that describes crucifixion in horrific detail. When we read the whole psalm, we come to the end and discover that it's a psalm of startling prophetic hope, which pours through the closing lines like bright sunlight through brooding black clouds. This is the setting of the whole of Psalm 22, from which Jesus quotes only the first verse—as an invitation to his hearers to reflect on the whole psalm.

A thousand years before the coming of Christ, David cried out "My God, my God, why have you forsaken me?" But standing between Job and Jesus, by the end of the psalm David was able to write, speaking of God:

> For he has not despised or scorned
> the suffering of the afflicted one;
> he has not hidden his face from him
> but has listened to his cry for help.

40. Luke 22:42.

From you comes the theme of my praise in the great assembly;
before those who fear you I will fulfill my vows.
The poor will eat and be satisfied;
those who seek the Lord will praise him—
may your hearts live forever!
All the ends of the earth
will remember and turn to the Lord,
and all the families of the nations
will bow down before him,
for dominion belongs to the Lord
and he rules over the nations.
All the rich of the earth will feast and worship;
all who go down to the dust will kneel before him—
those who cannot keep themselves alive.
Posterity will serve him;
future generations will be told about the Lord.
They will proclaim his righteousness,
declaring to a people yet unborn:
He has done it![41]

Then Jesus, having uttered his sense of forsakenness, addresses his last words to his loving Father: "Into your hands I commit my spirit." His last word is pure prayer—not a request for deliverance, but his declaration that he belongs to God. To commit one's spirit into another's hands is the ultimate act of surrender. Acute suffering and God-forsakenness need not be the last word. It wasn't for Job, it wasn't for David, and it wasn't for Jesus—and it need not be for us. God holds the power over all suffering and death to redeem them. In his Son Jesus, God has turned the tables on suffering and death and opened a new way forward into his new creation.

After retelling the story of Jesus's self-emptying in the incarnation and on the cross, Paul describes how it all turns out:

Therefore, God exalted him to the highest place
and gave him the name that is above every name,
that at the name of Jesus every knee should bow,
in heaven and on earth and under the earth,
and every tongue acknowledge that Jesus Christ is Lord,
to the glory of God the Father.[42]

As it was for Job, as it was for David, and as it was for Jesus, so shall it be for us. The presence of the living God will overcome even the torments

41. Psalm 22:24–30.
42. Philippians 2:9–11.

of suffering and the bitterness of God-forsakenness, and finally heal those wounds as well. Even those surviving prisoners in Auschwitz and Bergen-Belsen eventually realized that the unimaginable had happened. They'd been set free; their long night of suffering was over.

# 15

# The Way of Return

*Perhaps this is the time when, with anxious hearts and empty hands,*
*we are ready to receive the presence and the power of the One*
*who raised Jesus from the dead.*

—RUEBEN JOB

Now that we've navigated some of the outward and inward obstacles to receiving the love of God, how can we actually enter that love?

Earlier, we explored Jesus's parable of the prodigal son, which I suggested should really be called the parable of the prodigal father, because the father and his spendthrift love is really the center of the story. We saw in Jesus' ministry to sinners the Father's loving invitation to all who wanted to return home. We also witnessed in Jesus' story his invitation to the religious leaders to come to the banquet and celebrate the Father's grace.

Nevertheless, the story is also very much about that son who went into the far-off country, and we often read the story through his eyes, which isn't a bad thing at all. The parable is doubly instructive. It teaches us about God, and it teaches us about ourselves. Let's return to that story for a moment and ask ourselves what it can teach us about the way of return to the love of our Father.

## THE PRODIGAL SON REVISITED

Kenneth Bailey, who grew up in the Middle East and knew its culture well, has helped us understand this parable within its original context. He tells us that the younger son, in asking for his inheritance prior to his father's death, is saying to him, "Dad, I wish you were dead." No greater family insult would have been possible in a Middle Eastern village.

The astonishing thing, Bailey tells us, is that the father, rather than beating and banishing the boy, agrees to the son's terms, gives him his share, and lets him go on his way. Jesus tells us that the son did not invest his inheritance wisely, but blew (prodigalized) it on "wild living." The original term here connotes "an unusual and unhealthy lifestyle"; it carries with it the portrait of a party boy, "one who lives a wild and undisciplined life."[1]

As we remember, the upshot of all this is, of course, that he ends up broke and starving in pigsty. Ironically, here in the basement of his experience, he discovers a stairway back to the roof—or at least to the ground floor. The Greek text sums it up simply: "He came to himself." He was able to reframe his dreadful and dire situation based on a wider story—a fuller reality. We might simply say that he repented.

Repentance is one of the most important and misunderstood concepts among both believing and unbelieving people. It stands at the intersection of the relationship between God and every human being, and it involves a radical reorientation toward reality that brings with it salvation. Let me explain.

Here are Jesus's first words in the Gospel of Mark: "The time is fulfilled, the kingdom of God is at hand; *repent,* and believe in the good news." These words are the key to understanding the way of return, which comes only when we answer the call to repent. But what exactly does that word mean?

So often I've heard well-intentioned pastors teach and preach that repent means to turn around, to stop sinning and get right with God. Here, repentance is understood as a moral call to clean up your act and start behaving the right way. In this common teaching, repentance is something we do out of deep sorrow for sin. In fact, so deeply did the sense of sorrow become tied to repentance that the Greek *metanoia* was reduced to *poenitentia* (penance) in Jerome's fourth-century Latin translation of the Bible (known as the Vulgate). Jerome translated Jesus's call to repent in Matthew 4:17 (parallel to Mark 1:15) as *poenitentiam agite,* "do penitence."[2] Penance

1. Foerster, "ἄσωτος- ἀσωτία," Kittel and Friedrich, *Theological Dictionary of the New Testament,* Vol. 1, 507.

2. Muller, *Dictionary of Latin and Greek Theological Terms,* 229–30. It is interesting to note here that the Catholic Christian humanist Erasmus chose the verb *resipiscite*

as "sorrow for sin" became institutionalized in the Roman Catholic sacrament of confession and its prayers of contrition.

As a Catholic kid growing up, I would make my confession to the priest; I was then instructed, as my "penance," to say specified prayers a certain number of times so that the slate of my soul would be clean again. This was necessarily a process that had to be repeated regularly so that my soul wouldn't fall into spiritual jeopardy. But when the grape of biblical repentance shrivels into the raisin of ecclesiastical penance, it can never produce the wine of joy. We lose not only the meaning of the original word, but the essential spiritual juice that makes repentance not only possible, but desirable.

In Mark 1:15 (and in the New Testament in general), what the original word *metanoeite* means is not "turn around" but "think again." This is important. The word here is in imperative form—it's a command of Jesus. But the command is issued as a response to something. That something is the proclamation of the kingdom of God.

I always used to think that the most pressing question of the New Testament was Jesus's question to his disciples, "Who do you say that I am?" It is indeed a pressing and extremely important question. But these days I've begun to wonder if there's even a more pressing question to be answered first: "What time is it?"

In the gospel of Mark, Jesus begins his ministry by stating, "The time is fulfilled." The "time," as any first-century Jew would have known, was the time when God would fulfill his promises to Israel. The time when he would come to reign through his Messiah-King. The time when David's heir would be seated on the throne. The time when Israel's captivity would end, the time when God's justice and righteousness would find their home on the earth. The time when the long night of human suffering would finally be greeted by the sunrise of the forgiveness of sins, the redemption of Israel, the blessing to the nations, and the restoration of creation.

In this shortest of opening sermons, Jesus declares that the foundations of reality under the feet of his hearers (and of ours as well) are shifting. The time has come. The Messiah-King is among them—Emmanuel, "God with us."

It's this proclamation of the time shift into the Messianic age that becomes the basis for the call to *metanoia*. Jesus is calling his hearers to "again" (*meta*) "think" (*noeite*)—to literally *rethink* everything in light of the new time in which they now live. He's asking them if they know what time it

---

rather than *poenitentia* to translate *metanoeite* from Greek to Latin, as did the Reformers; see Muller, 264.

is. Everything hinges on this reconsideration (which, come to think of it, might not be a bad translation of the word *metanoia*).

Long before the consideration of what's to be done comes Jesus's statement of what is already happening. Indeed, the answer to "What's to be done?" flows out of our reconsideration of what is happening. If we are told that our house is on fire, our sense of what is to be done changes dramatically! If the reign of God has come upon the earth with the appearance of Jesus, then we're living in a new age. A new time has dawned. Proclamation of the new reality, *then* realization. *Metanoia* is realization. We realize in a moment that the ground underneath our feet has shifted. One of my professors, the late Gordon Fee, used to call it the "divine aha!" It's like when you are driving somewhere and become lost and disoriented. Suddenly you come upon a familiar sight and you know where you are, you *know*! Instant reorientation. That's metanoia.

Only with realization can then follow moral and ethical internalization. Proclamation, realization, internalization. The order is crucial, because the realization of the reality of the coming of the kingdom in Jesus becomes the only sufficient power for moral and ethical life change (internalization). The truth of the new reality changes us from the inside out. The new mind gives birth to the new heart, which gives way to a new way of life.[3]

The kingdom has its own ordering, which flows from its nature, and its nature reflects the personhood of the King. The kingdom is a perfect reflection of the character of the King, and it's this kingdom, *his* kingdom, which has now come upon the earth, causing us to reconsider and then reorder everything.

But let's not lose the appropriate emotional response to the proclamation. It's here that all the theologies which reduce repentance to penance run aground. Jesus says we're to rethink everything in light of the dawning of the kingdom of God; then he adds that we're to "believe the good news." The fruit of our repentance is not the raisin of a shriveled heart filled with heavy sorrow. Rather, it's the juicy grape yielding the luscious wine of trust and joy. Jesus illustrates this when he describes in two parables the fitting response to realizing what time it is, when we discover that the kingdom of God has come upon the earth.

First is Matthew 13:44, "The kingdom of heaven is like treasure hidden in a field. When a man found it, he hid it again, and then in his joy went and sold all he had and bought that field." Notice the response of the man in the story. He immediately "goes and sells everything he has," then "buys that field." The kingdom of God is of incalculable value compared to "everything

3. Romans 12:1–2.

that he has." Paul later refers to the "everything else" as human excrement by comparison.[4] The man in the parable hit the jackpot of the kingdom of God, and he's *overjoyed*. Indeed, it is his joy which propels him to acquire the treasure!

The second parable, which comes right after the first, trumpets the same celebratory notes. "Again, the kingdom of heaven is like a merchant seeking fine pearls, and upon finding one pearl of great value, he went and sold everything that he had and bought it."[5] Notice again that there was no calculation necessary, no weighing of the options, no tense deliberation. As soon as the merchant sees the pearl, he *knows*. And he responds immediately. One can only imagine the joy. He's won the pearl lottery!

For Jesus, the announcement of the kingdom reign of God brings with it a radical call to reconsider (*metanoia*) everything. It is sheer but startling, *good* news. When we realize—really realize—what time it is, we'll know what to do.

Jesus's startling proclamation— "The time is fulfilled, the kingdom of God is at hand"—accompanied by his extraordinary words and works situated in humanity's history, particularly the unique history of Israel, will now become the spiritual gestalt within which *metanoia* can occur. All the paper, kindling, and lighter fluid accumulating across the centuries of Israel's history now need only the match of his declaration. When the flame explodes, so does the old order of things, and a new creation is born into the world. The only appropriate response is commanded: "Rethink everything, and believe this incredibly good news!" And all of this is pure joy! That's the biblical meaning of repentance.

Returning to the prodigal son, we find him flabbergasted at his reception. He expects to return as one of his father's hired hands, but his father has had other plans all along. The ring, the sandals, and the robe—full reinstatement into the family! All this followed by a banquet, the richest symbol of reconciling joy in the ancient world.

I wonder what that young son was thinking when it dawned on him what was going on. He'd disgraced himself (and his entire family and village, according to Kenneth Bailey), and now this! This is what the kingdom of heaven is like. This is what the reign of God looks like upon the earth, according to Jesus. It's nothing less than the triumph of love.

But Jesus's tale of the prodigal is only a story, right? Aren't parables just stories?

4. Philippians 3:8. Gk. σκύβαλα.
5. Matthew 13:45–46.

## BECOMING THE SON

It *is* a story, but like all the parables, it is a subversive, explosive story. It is a verbal big bang that creates a new universe for us to inhabit. It's the story *of* humanity, *for* humanity. It's a story loaded with invitation. We're invited to see ourselves in the story. Jesus never told stories to entertain people. He told stories to invite people to discover God's kingdom and themselves along with it. The moment we realize, "This is *my* story," is the moment our destiny begins to shift. The pivot is when we realize, "I squandered *my* inheritance; *I* am starving to death—*I am the prodigal son!*" But that realization must be accompanied by another: understanding that I'm the son of the prodigal father, and a member of his household.

When I was teaching a few years ago, I had an African student named Joseph Byamukama. In a paper he turned in for the class, Joseph wrote, "In Africa, ancestral connections are essential, for to be human is to have a history. Without this history, one stands in the air, and he who is in the air has no identity."[6]

This is what it means when we enter the prodigal's story, shocked to find that we've stumbled into our own story and "come to ourselves," which means that we've come home to God. We need no longer to stand in the air. Because we belong to Jesus, the words spoken over him also belong to us: "This is my son, whom I love."

Just as the prodigal son had a choice to make, so do we. And we've encountered several obstacles that can make that choice difficult. The road of returning home can seem long, hard, and even frightening for some. I've known people who felt beyond the pale of love. I've known others who struggled with what God might ask of them should they surrender themselves to him. I've known others who seemed to drown in the deep questions and doubts that continued to wash over them like strong waves crashing relentlessly on the beach of their experience. Albert Camus and Jean Paul Sartre both fit the bill here. Apparently, in their later years, they too, like struggling salmon, were being drawn upstream in search of their source in God.[7] At the heart of all of it is whether we will believe God's words spoken personally to us. "You are my son." "You are my daughter." "You are my beloved child." These words spoken over Jesus, now, in him, belong to us too.

6. Joseph Byamukama, Unpublished "Integration Paper" for "Spiritual Formation for Ministry." Gordon-Conwell Theological Seminary, Spring 2018.

7. See Metaxas, *Is Atheism Dead?*, 289–99. These pages provide a fascinating look into the spiritual journey of these two French existentialists.

THE WAY OF RETURN

## ESCORTS INTO THE KINGDOM

What can help us when we stand on the doorstep of faith in Jesus Christ? Are there escorts into the palace of faith? Yes, there are many.

First is confidence in the script itself. The Scriptures of the Old and New Testaments have proven their trustworthiness across more than three thousand years.[8] No book on earth has been so thoroughly investigated, studied, and found resilient under analysis by friend and foe alike. No other ancient text has received the historical scrutiny, textual analysis, and archaeological corroboration as the Bible. I've rehearsed the strong evidence elsewhere, but will simply summarize it by saying that the script is trustworthy and founded on solid historical accounts of God's actions in Israel's history and in its historical accounts concerning the person and work of Jesus.[9]

Beyond the reliability of the Bible text is its message. Scripture's message of salvation and hope has undergirded Western civilization's highest achievements and brightest moments. The best of our art, architecture, music, and science is rooted in the biblical tradition. Likewise, the best of our educational, social, and scientific enterprises is rooted in Judeo-Christian thought and values.

By contrast, as our Western civilization continues its departure from biblical teaching and transcendent sources of value, we continue to experience the disintegration of our culture. If the "cult" in any civilization is their practice of belief and worship in their gods, and if the "culture" is an outgrowth of that cult, depending on it for life and vitality, then the culture will disintegrate if removed from its source in the cult.

Think of it as the cut flowers effect. If the cult is the garden where flowers grow, and they're cut and placed into a vase, they may look pretty for a while, but they've already started to wither. That's the way it is with cultures that attempt to sever themselves from their roots in transcendent sources. We have a front row seat to the withering of Western civilization as it abandons its worship of God. But it doesn't have to be that way. We'll get to that.

Not only is the Bible reliable in its text and message, it speaks volumes to the human heart. Its personal message of hope and forgiveness to the guilty and ashamed is unparalleled. Its message of healing and eternal life

---

8. I recognize that the dating of biblical books is a complex issue. I've never been talked out of the Mosaic authorship of the Torah, so I am settling on about 1,300 b.c. (when Moses lived) as the beginning of the biblical tradition.

9. Tom Pfizenmaier, *For My Daughters: A Father Reflects on Family, Faith and Friendship*, 213–18 in Pen2Paper edition. See pages 269–75 in the Outskirts Press edition. In addition to the references supplied in the footnotes there, see also Eric Metaxas, *Is Atheism Dead?*, Part II, 119–241; N.T. Wright, *History and Eschatology*, 41–69; and Craig Keener, *Christobiography: Memory, History, and the Reliability of the Gospels*.

to the suffering and dying are unsurpassed by any other philosophy or religion. Its message of inclusion and community to the alienated and lonely have offered renewed identity and support to billions. Confidence in the Bible as God's truth concerning the fundamentals of life is a great escort to help us in coming to faith.

Another escort can be found in the experience of human beings over time who've testified to the how the Bible has resourced their own journey of faith. Think of the church (the people of of God) as a protein that's cultured and grows in the petri dish of the Bible. The Judeo-Christian tradition is filled with stories of people (that great cloud of witnesses) whose lives were changed by trusting in the God of Israel and his Messiah-King.

From Augustine's *Confessions* to Thomas à Kempis's *Imitation of Christ*, from Teresa of Àvila's *Interior Castle* to Thomas Merton's *Seven Story Mountain*, the Western tradition is ladened with stories of lives changed because of faith in Jesus. When we read the likes of Mother Teresa, C. S. Lewis, G. K. Chesterton, Frederick Buechner, Henry Nouwen, Tim Keller, or Eugene Peterson, we realize that God is still at work in our lives and in the world, bringing Jesus's redemption and restoration to us and through us. (An excellent anthology in this regard is *Sources of the Christian Self*, edited by James Houston and Jens Zimmermann.)[10]  Reading the writing of these and many others, we are not only escorted on our journey, but fed by them along the way.

The Christian faith never wears out, and when we allow ourselves to be robed in it, we discover the living Christ who is calling to us today. That invitation is always fresh, always direct, always issued in love.

Jesus says, "Come, follow me." When we do that, when we finally say our yes to his, he comes to us in the midst of our lives and infuses them with new meaning, purpose, hope, and joy.

The polymath missionary Albert Schweitzer wrote,

> He comes to us as One unknown, without a name, as of old, by the lake-side. He came to those men who knew Him not. He speaks to us the same word: "Follow thou me!" and sets us to the tasks which He has to fulfill for our time. He commands. And to those who obey Him, whether they be wise or simple, He will reveal Himself in the toils, the conflicts, the sufferings which

---

10. Houston and Zimmerman, *Sources of the Christian Self*. The rich spiritual traditions of eastern orthodoxy is equally powerful here as a spiritual resource—see for an early example *The Philokalia*, and subsequent orthodox monastic literature. Russian Christian writers include Dostoyevsky, Tolstoy, Bulgakov and Pasternak, Solzhenitsyn and many, many others from Russia and other Slavic nations.

they shall pass through in His fellowship, and, as an ineffable mystery, they shall learn in their own experience Who He is.[11]

Often at the end of my Christmas Eve homily, after doing my best to explain what had happened on that night so long ago and what it meant for us now, I would simply say to the people there who were not yet Christ followers, "Just say yes—just say yes to the child whose birth we celebrate, the one who came, lived, died, and was raised for *you*. The one who loved you, and who loves you still, because he "loved you to the end." When we say "yes" to him, a whole new life begins. Just say yes to the God who is love.

11. Schweitzer, *Quest for the Historical Jesus*, 401.

# 16

# Recovering Love at the Center

*As the lily among thorns,*
*so is love among the sons of men.*
—CHARLES SPURGEON

Now I want to turn to where we are in this cultural moment, and propose what must be done to see love's renaissance. The church of Jesus Christ in the West is suffering atrophy, and our culture with it. The world is becoming colder and coarser as a result. Just this week my newsfeed has been full of stories about another tragic school shooting.

Sadly, this is not surprising news for anyone who sees the rising numbers of "nones" in our demographics. Some suggest that the remedy is to abandon the culture and just hunker down while it implodes, to survive and be here to pick up the pieces when it's all over. Others relish the twilight of "Christendom," as if the rising tide of neo-gnostic and Epicurean paganism is preferable in their varied technocratic, authoritarian, and materialistic epiphanies.

The truth is that we're falling short in our primary task of becoming salt, light, and leaven in our culture. We're failing to make disciples as Jesus defined them. We're failing to love well among ourselves, and to love well beyond ourselves. I don't say this lightly. As someone who pastored for thirty-two years, and who has watched (helped?) the bride of Christ become love–anorexic, I feel my own sad share of responsibility here. But we can, even now, encourage each other to pivot back to love. I don't believe it's too late, but I do believe the time has come for the church to make a resolute return to our first love, who is love. I believe we've lost our way, but we can find our way home again.

First, let me expand on the story I started in the preface and trace more clearly how I think we got lost.

## WHAT I LEARNED IN SEMINARY (THE LAST TIME)

As I mentioned, the realization that something was wrong started when I joined the theological faculty of an evangelical seminary a few years ago after my years of pastoral ministry. I thought this opportunity would be an exciting capstone project where I could take what I'd learned and pass it along to the next generation of rising church leaders. This would be the legacy season.

I came to the seminary in the fall of 2016 just in time for one of the most contentious presidential elections of my lifetime. I became aware of how our students were processing the election cycle on social media with deep anger expressed in bitter words reflecting strong hostilities. At first, I attributed their response to an overzealous youthful enthusiasm. They apparently believed the promises the politicians were making. They'd forgotten the wise words of the psalmist:

> Put not your trust in princes,
> in a son of man, in whom there is no salvation.
> When his breath departs, he returns to the earth;
> on that very day his plans perish.
> Blessed is he whose help is the God of Jacob,
> whose hope is in the Lord his God,
> who made heaven and earth,
> the sea, and all that is in them,
> who keeps faith forever;
> who executes justice for the oppressed,
> who gives food to the hungry.[1]

But it was deeper than that. Some of the students seemed to think of the State in almost messianic terms, as the author and giver of life. This, of course, is idolatry. One sees this sort of thing among people in general (sometimes even among Christians) who allow themselves no greater hope. Right after 9/11, a member of my congregation insisted that we immediately put an American flag in our sanctuary. When I asked why, he said strongly,

1. Psalm 146:3–7 (ESV).

"We need a sign of hope!" Had he somehow missed the massive stained glass triptych window at the front of the sanctuary presenting Jesus with open arms? Apparently, his pastor had work to do.

After that presidential election of 2016, we held our Student Association elections early the following year. One of the candidates was male, a person of color, who ran on a platform of social justice. The other was female, white, and running on a platform of deeper worship and holiness among the students. Again, there was vitriol, anger, and some character assassination—not from the candidates themselves, but from self-appointed social media surrogates.

These two incidents disquieted my spirit. I'd been called to a new position at the seminary to develop a program for discipleship. How could some of our students, future *leaders* of the church, be so spiritually immature as to respond to each other in these ways? How were we training them that they thought and acted so much like non-Christians when the pressure was on to think clearly and love well?

As I struggled to make sense of my experience, I began to reflect more deeply concerning Jesus' teaching on discipleship. Many of us are familiar with the Great Commission in Matthew 28—that we're to go into the world and make disciples of all nations. In John 13, Jesus also said that the world would recognize his disciples by their love for one another. What struck me for the first time was the connection between those statements. Between the New Commandment and the Great Commission.

If our task is to make disciples, and disciples are people known by their love, then could it be that Jesus was *commanding us to make lovers*? Could it be that simple—and that profound? Are disciples simply people who love like Jesus? (We'll come back to this). Perhaps teaching others to love as Jesus loves was, and remains, the content of his discipleship curriculum. If so, shouldn't it be the content of ours as well?

Disciples, as lovers, would be people who refract God's truth, goodness, justice, beauty, responsibility, and Spiritual tolerance into the world. They would be people capable of bearing, believing, hoping, and enduring all things. They would be women and men who live in his rhythms of submission, service, suffering, and sacrifice. Disciples would become people in whom love never ends. I'm embarrassed in having made this connection so late in my life and ministry. But there it was, clear as a bell. Better late than never.

Two years later, in the spring of 2019, I was asked to preach in chapel (this happens to faculty members occasionally). It was Holy Week, when we focus deeply on the last few days of Jesus's life, and especially on the meaning of his death and resurrection. When I mentioned to a colleague that I was going to preach on love, he was nonplussed. He expected that I would "preach on the cross." Another colleague responded to my choice of topic with a wry smile and said, "Ah, love..." Let's just say I was surprised by these responses.

Over time, if we aren't careful, we lose connection to the heart of God and substitute for it a knowledge of how he works. Knowing God becomes knowing *about* God. We forget the *why* and focus on the *how*.

Please understand me. This failure to put love at the center of discipleship was not particular to my beloved seminary to which I am very grateful for the gifts it gave me. I've studied or taught at five different Christian higher educational institutions, liberal and conservative. Love wasn't the primary focus of the curriculum or the teaching at any of them. There were no courses on how to love, no graduation awards that celebrated growth in love, no deep challenges to become people who love like Jesus loved. I'm a product of this kind of training—and my ministry reflected it. So I'm pleading with the church not as a critical outsider, but a total insider who loves the church deeply.

I've experienced a disconnect between love and our redemption, between God's deep passion for us and the study of redemption as a doctrine of the church. Full disclosure: I did my own doctoral work in Christian doctrine. I think orthodoxy (right worship, which arises from right belief) is essential to the life of the believer and the life of the church. But when it becomes detached from the love of God, we develop lifeless systems of theology, which can themselves become idols.

When we detach God's *mechanism* in our redemption from God's *motivation* in it, we're left with an artifact—interesting to turn around in our minds and examine, but no longer life-giving, no longer deeply personal.

Another part of the tragedy of the de–centering of love is that when we forget the "why" of Jesus's coming, we begin to disdain or caricature the word "love" itself. When this happens, we yield the high ground of love to a culture that trivializes and evacuates the word of its biblical content. This is a true tragedy for both the church and the world. Christians need to reclaim *agape*, and in its wake, the other loves of *eros, storge,* and *philos*. We need to scrape off *agape*'s cultural barnacles and make it once again the crown jewel, the centerpiece of Christian discipleship, which in fact is what Jesus did. "By *this* everyone will know that you are my disciples, if you *love* one another."

If this intuition is correct—that the center of Christian discipleship is developing lovers—how might it change the way we think about theological education, about disciple-making in the local church, and most especially about the meaning of our own lives? What would happen if we placed at the center of the church and all its institutions two simple questions: "Are we loving as Jesus loved?' and "Are we training others to do the same?"

The business guru Peter Drucker once said there are only two critical questions businesses must ask themselves. First, "What business are we in?" Second, "How's business?" If the church honestly assesses itself today, I think we must admit that "business" isn't good. It's not because we aren't trying. Perhaps it's because we've forgotten what business we're in.

If forming people who love like Jesus is our business, then a troubling question arises: How did we lose this focus? How did we get so far off-track that we're doing everything *except* making disciples as Jesus described them? I think the answer lies embedded in the past, and it's a past that still controls us.

## THE DE-CENTERING OF LOVE

I've tried to show that the love of God is the very center of reality, present eternally in the Holy Trinity, the driving force behind the creation, and the sole motivation in God's redemption and restoration in Jesus. Love is the golden thread that pierces and secures every pearl in the biblical narrative. If this is the case, how did love become marginalized? My own research has led me to the conclusion that this marginalization occurred as the result of three different waves of perception about how we should read and relate to the scriptures.

The first wave came with the shift from the monastic model of formation in the early centuries to the scholastic model of information in the middle-ages. The second wave came with the Protestant reformation, which privileged faith over love. The third wave came with the rise of the modern research university which privileged reason over faith, and professional expertise over a holy life. Let me explain.

In the first centuries after Jesus, Christians read the Bible in a particular way. We read it, as I've tried to do above, as a story into which we're invited. It was a story God was writing, it became the oven in which those early Christians' lives were baked.

This way of reading the Bible shifted in the Middle Ages because of something called scholasticism, which saw its golden age in the twelfth and thirteenth centuries. Up until that time, the primary spiritual formational institution of discipleship was the monastery. In the monasteries, the Scriptures, the teaching of the church fathers, and the liturgy formed the crucible within which souls were shaped for holiness to reflect the glory of God. From these monastic volcanoes flowed the magma of high medieval culture.

Scripture was the spiritual vat within which one's life was marinated. The point was to be changed by what you read.

With the rise of the middle-ages, the scholastics (the "school men"— those who trained in the new medieval universities) approached the Scriptures differently. Rather than immersing themselves in the biblical world with the goal of *formation*, they read the Bible for *information*, which they could debate through *quaestio* and *disputatio*. This was a fundamentally different approach to the Bible, not only as to their method of reading, but ultimately for how they understood the nature and purpose of Scripture itself.

Francois Vandenbroucke describes the scholastic approach this way:

> Theology henceforward claimed to be a science, and according to the Aristotelian ideal took on a speculative and even deductive character. Like all sciences, it was disinterested; it was no longer concerned with nourishing the spiritual life, as the monastic theologians would have it do. The Scriptures were read, studied, and taught with the view of the mind rather than the heart acquiring knowledge, and theological activity assumed a more purely intellectual character, less contemplative, less dependent on the atmosphere created by the liturgy.[2]

For the scholastics, the integration of the Bible, theology, and Greek philosophy into a wholistic system—a comprehensive framework and account of human understanding concerning God and the world—was paramount. The most famous of these theological systems was Thomas Aquinas's *Summa Theologica*. Etienne Gilson, the French philosopher of history, referred to these systems as "cathedrals of the mind."[3] The distinction between the two ways of approaching the text are well summarized by the Jean Leclercq,

> The scholastic lectio takes the direction of the quaestio and the disputatio. The reader puts questions to the text and then questions himself on the subject matter... The monastic lectio is oriented toward the meditation and oratio [prayer]. The objective of the first is science and knowledge; of the second, wisdom and appreciation. In the monastery, the lectio divina, this activity which begins with grammar, terminates in compunction, in desire of heaven.[4]

2. Vandenbroucke, "New Milieux, New Problems: From the Twelfth to the Sixteenth Century," in Leclercq, Vandenbroucke, and Bouyer, *Spirituality of the Middle Ages*, Vol. II, 225.

3. McGrath, *Christian Theology*, 50, 182–83.

4. Leclercq, *Love of Learning and Desire for God*, especially 89, 238ff., 243–49, 278.

For the monks, Scripture enabled an encounter with God when they read his word. Origen, one of the early church fathers, said this: "We encounter the Word when we read the word"—affirming that we encounter Christ when we read Scripture. Not quite a portal perhaps, but something having a similar effect. For the scholastics, the goal was extraction of theological truth (not a bad thing), which over time became the *primary* (a bad thing) use of Scripture. The result was that the Bible became instrumentalized, even weaponized, as a tool that experts manipulated to yield desired results for doctrinal and moral teaching.

The scholastics read for knowledge (*scientia*) and the monks read for wisdom (*sapientia*). The scholastics sat "over" the Scriptures dissecting them with the various literary tools available at the time. The monastics sat "under" the Scriptures, seeking wisdom for living a holy life. These are fundamentally different spiritual postures.

Starting in the Middle Ages, the scholastic model for education came to dominate Europe. Having been instantiated in the great universities, the scholastic approach became the standard method of theological education.

The rise of scholastic theology, with its focus on theological texts—for example, Peter Lombard's, The *Four Books of Sentences*—carried with it a shift from Scripture to theological questions. Lombard's *Sentences* became the standard theological textbook for several centuries. In summing up the impact of scholasticism, Vandenbroucke writes,

> The new methods of scholarship—the use of Aristotle, the arrangement of the "sentences" of the Fathers and theologians around each "question" put by the "master"—were thus the means of a remarkable intellectual flowering. But it is not clear that the result was always happy from the point of view of the spiritual life… Did it occur to the men of the time that the new methods might wither men's hearts? … There was real danger that the word of God would no longer be given to souls who longed to hear and live by it.[5]

Perhaps we can summarize the contrast in two quotes from the Middle Ages, one from the theologian Anselm (who was also a monk), and one from a central monastic figure, Bernard of Clairvaux. Anselm said, "I believe that I might understand"—*Credo ut intelligum*. Bernard said, "I believe that I might experience [the reality of God's presence]"—*Credo ut experiar.*[6]

5. Vandenbroucke, "The Schoolmen of the Twelfth Century," in LeClercq, Vandnbroucke and Bouyer, *Spirituality of the Middle Ages*, Vol. II, *History of Christian Spirituality*, 228.

6. From Houston's Introduction to Bernard of Clairvaux's *Love of God*, xxvii.

The monastic approach is known as *lectio divina*, which can be translated as "sacred reading" or "divine reading." It was a meditative approach centered in prayer and contemplation. When I was being trained in seminary, we were taught to avoid this approach to the Scriptures because it yielded strange interpretations through the use of an allegorical method of interpretation. That is true. There were some weird interpretations as a result of the allegorical method used by the monks.

But *lectio* need not be tied to the allegorical method. By disregarding *lectio* because of some strange interpretations when interpreted allegorically, the baby was hurled out with the bathwater. It would be like saying that because you'd once been served a piece of bad meat, you should therefore become a vegetarian. Aside from this, *lectio* had been the primary method encountering Scripture for a thousand years in the church. Its tradition was (and is) deep and rich.

The best integrative approach I've found for how to read the Bible spiritually is the late Eugene Peterson's little book entitled *Eat This Book: A Conversation in the Art of Spiritual Reading.* Peterson, who was trained as an Old Testament scholar, is a stickler for the value of understanding the meaning of the text in its original context. Nevertheless, the Bible is more than a source book we raid when we need ammo for a lesson or sermon. It is a deeply personal revelation of the heart of God for his people—for *us.* As such, it invites us to live our part of the story, and to be formed by it in the living.

Commenting on his approach to the Bible, and the title of his work, Peterson writes,

> The act of eating the book means that reading is not a merely objective act, looking at the words and ascertaining their meaning. Eating the book is in contrast with how most of us are trained to read books—develop a cool objectivity that attempts to preserve scientific or theological truth by eliminating as far as possible any personal participation that might contaminate the meaning...
>
> Eating a book takes it all in, assimilating it into the tissues of our lives. Readers become what they read. If Holy Scripture is to be something other than mere gossip about God, it must be internalized...
>
> Words—spoken and listened to, written and read—are intended to do something *in* us, give health and wholeness, vitality and holiness, wisdom and hope. Yes, *eat* this book.[7]

7. Peterson, *Eat This Book*, 20–21. His Emphasis.

The second wave powering our de-centering of love occurred as a re-sult of the Protestant Reformation. The struggles in the late medieval period with the corruption of the church are well known. The church had posi-tioned itself as a brokerage house for salvation. Its currency was the sacra-mental system. So much emphasis was placed on the role of good works and of merit—instead of the grace of God in Jesus Christ and his sacrifice—that a crisis ensued.

Martin Luther, himself an Augustinian monk, insisted upon a return to the gospel of salvation by grace through faith in Jesus Christ. But an un-intended consequence of the Reformation's necessary return to salvation through faith alone was the marginalization of love. The problem was simple. How do we know when we've loved enough to go to heaven—to be saved? For the spiritual accountants of the late medieval church, they were happy to tell you how many holy days of obligation, feasts, fasts, indulgences, masses, and drafts against the treasury of the merits of the saints would make that possible. For the reformers, the very asking of this question opened the back door into spiritual slavery to a gospel of works. For them, faith was to be the new basis and center of our relationship with God, not love.

In 2017, Protestants celebrated the five-hundredth anniversary of the Reformation. At our seminary, we held a conference where papers were presented on various aspects of the Reformation. These papers were sub-sequently published in a book entitled *Reformation Celebration: The Signifi-cance of Scripture, Grace, Faith, and Christ*. In recounting the history of the Reformation, the editors noted the shift in the roles of love and faith at the time of the Reformation.

> "But perhaps what is not so well known is that Christian salva-tion of the Middle Ages, at least since the twelfth century, had emphasized love instead of faith as the key element... The fact that we are saved by grace through faith moved Luther to the place where he could, along with Scripture, grant faith that new defining content that allowed it to supersede the medieval cen-trality of love (*caritas*) and its works (*opera*)."[8]

8. Isaac and Schnabel, *Reformation Celebration: The Significance of Scripture, Grace, Faith, and Christ*, viii. In a related article, one of our faculty members celebrated one of the seminary's founder's repudiation of the primacy of love. The Scottish evangelist Henry Drummond (1851–1897) had written a little book entitled *Love: The Greatest Thing in the World*, in which he made the case—following the apostle Paul in 1 Corin-thians 13—that love represents the apex and goal of the Christian life. In response, our faculty member quoted favorably A. J. Gordon's response to Drummond. Speaking of faith, hope, and love, Gordon wrote,

"Therefore, let there be no rivalry of strife for preeminence among these three. Yet we can but observe that Faith stands in her old place at the head of the line. And why

There's a problem here. To say that in Scripture faith supersedes love is flatly contradicted by 1 Corinthians 13:13. Beyond that, the prioritization of faith over love is defective for at least five reasons.[9]

this persistent priority? Only because we are justified by Faith; and justification is the first and initial transaction of the Christian life."

Our professor then added his own conviction, writing, "This chapter [on preaching] argues that *sola fide*, faith alone, is the foundation and the driving force of the ministry of preaching."

9. First, to say that "justification is the first and initial transaction of the Christian life" is incorrect, and particularly incorrect in Reformed theology. As Drummond noted—and every Reformed theologian affirms—regeneration (that gracious work by which the Holy Spirit enlivens a person so that they can receive the gospel of grace) precedes justification by faith.

Second, to think of justification as a "transaction" radically depersonalizes the whole Trinitarian grounding of the cross. Indeed, this kind of de-personalization is what often leads to the kind of dead Christianity so many people experience. I am not saying that our standing before God doesn't change, that we are not first guilty and then acquitted. Indeed, I believe those things to be essential and true. My point is that the *cause* of that change—the *reason* for it, the *ground* of it—is the love of God. To go back to something I said earlier, it is not enough to know that the judge acquitted the boy in courtroom. One must know why, and the why was because he loved the boy, and he loved him precisely because he was his father. It is the love of the Father that both initiates the regeneration and provides the justification.

Third, if faith holds the primacy, then why did Charles Spurgeon—that "prince of [Reformed] preachers"—write, "Love is the highest, the pinnacle... Just as a rose in full bloom is greater than the stem that bears it, so, while faith is most needful, and hope most cheering, love is the most beautiful and brightest of the three." The reason for this is obvious. Faith is itself a response to something prior, namely the love of God proclaimed in the gospel of his Son. It is love, via grace, which creates faith. And it is love which is faith's fruit and goal. In this sense faith is neither primal nor final. Faith is the conduit through which God's love flows into us and through us into his world.

Fourth, our professor appealed to Luther in a footnote to his work. But Luther's context was quite different from ours. As I noted above, in the late medieval period (in which Luther lived), the church was trying to determine salvation by measuring acts of love. This was disastrous on two counts. The first was that this attempt inverted the relationship between the root of faith and the fruit of faith. Biblical Christianity teaches that we are saved by grace through faith, not by works. The second problem was that the measuring stick they used had everything to do with promoting the Church, and not brotherly love. Luther identifies these works as "indulgences, vigils, offerings, the building of churches, the establishing of altars, memorials, anniversaries, and all the other things of this kind that serve gain more than love."

Finally, giving the primacy to faith rather than love contradicts the Scriptures and the whole narrative arc of the Bible itself. As we noted in the beginning, the whole Bible is the narrative of the God who is love creating and then redeeming and eventually restoring all of what he loves. In speaking of faith, hope and love, Paul wrote that the greatest of these is love. We are reminded that faith is the "evidence of things yet unseen," and we are taught to "walk by faith and not by sight" in this world, but it is clear from the context that this is a *temporary* arrangement. In other words, faith is *until* sight, when we will know just as we are fully known. On the other hand, "Love *never*

Finally, the third wave which powered the decentering of love was the birth of the modern university in Europe. Previously, universities were entrusted with the preservation and passing on of classical learning. By the end of the eighteenth century many felt that this was no longer an acceptable brief. Universities, rather than becoming repositories of learning, would become its innovators. The keyword here was research. The purpose of the modern university would be to expand the human knowledge base through research, rather than pass along what was already known and venerated.

Concurrently, theology, which had remained the "queen of the sciences" in the middle ages, with its deductive (Aristotelian) methods of reasoning, was supplanted by the modern period's reliance upon the inductive (experimentally driven) method of the scientific revolution.   As we've already seen, the enlightenment, with its singular emphasis on power of reason, coupled with the autonomy of the individual and his quest for freedom, resulted in the displacement of the *ancient régime* in French revolution. The revolution showed the authorities of church and monarchy to the door. With humanity, rather than God, placed at the center of the quest for knowledge, and faith banished as an unreliable partner in that quest, the modern quest for knowledge could advance.

Under the leadership of Friedrich Wilhelm von Humboldt, the University of Berlin was founded in 1809-10. Berlin became the epicenter of the new model of the research university which would come to dominate Europe and America.[10]

By the end of the nineteenth century the "scientific" study of the Bible was normative among the dominant (German) Scripture scholars. Scripture was just one historical text among others, to be read the same way with the same historical-critical tools and method. Once the "queen of the sciences," because it provided the "frame" or foundation and integration of all other fields of knowledge, theology became the ugly stepchild, marginalized in the universities as the modern model was exported across Europe. While the shift to a research focus opened up many lines of fresh inquiry for theologians who now felt liberated from dogmatic oppression, a number of unintended consequences ensued.[11]

---

ends." For now, faith, hope and love remain, but faith and hope will one day reach their goal who is God himself. At that point they will be eclipsed by love, which is eternal.

10. https://plato.stanford.edu/entries/wilhelm-humboldt/#RetuGerm PublEducPoli (accessed 2/28/23).

11. One can trace from this period the rise of profound skepticism, starting with the German "Higher Critics" concerning the historical foundations of both Christianity and Judaism. This skepticism became the dominant academic posture toward the Bible, Christian dogmatics, and Jesus himself for the next 175 years or so, well into the

First, was the alienation of the professional theologians from the Church. Even through the middle ages and Reformation periods, theology had always developed in the womb of the church. Linda Cannell writes that with the rise of the modern research university, "Theologians identified more closely with their academic guilds than with the church or practical departments. In time, theology became the realm of the schools and ministry the realm of the church."[12] The standing pun among some theological types that one's choice is "publish or parish" reflects the opinion many theological professors hold to this day of "church work." I knew Ph.D. students who, upon graduating, were worried that they would "wind up in the church" rather than the academy.

The current canyon between the modern university in America, and theological study still reverberates with this reality. Most colleges and universities have long ago substituted "religious studies" for "biblical" and "theological" studies. Seminaries are, for the most part, an archipelago of ministry training centers detached from the wider bodies of learning that universities provide. Universities are, by and large, secular institutions and even those with biblical and theological departments have been disengaged from the churches and the doctrinal concerns of the church for generations. The seminaries and the universities have each become their own intellectual ghettos as a result.

Coupled with the haute theology of the academy is the often-insinuated idea that the church should conform to the latest fashionable theological opinions. I experienced this in one of the seminaries I attended in the eighties when we were exposed to "Process Theology," "Liberation Theology," "Feminist Theology" and the like. The implication was that without being conversant with our professors' latest schools of thought, we could not be relevant pastors.

Returning to our historical trajectory, when the German research university model was first transmitted to America, it was marinated in the earlier English educational model's emphasis on character, "A desire that piety and learning should be united was characteristic of English schools."[13] This emphasis protected (at least initially) American schools from von Humboldt's experience. "His dream of an intellectual elite that would enlighten and humanize the state foundered on the realization that a well-stocked

---

1980's and beyond, with the work of the Jesus Seminar and the writings of John Shelby Spong, Marcus Borg, and John Dominic Crossan. This tide has been turned through the detailed historical research of N.T. Wright, William Lane Craig, Craig Blomberg, Craig Keener, Richard Bauckham, D.A. Carson and many others.

12. Cannell, *Theological Education Matters*, 141.

13. Cannell, *Theological Education Matters*, 141.

and well-trained mind is no guarantee of virtue, wisdom, or the capacity to reach beyond oneself into service."[14]

Today, the standard degree for ministers in many denominations is called a "Master of Divinity." The stories are legion of people who, while "mastering" their faith, lose it in the process. Therefore, an old joke never quite goes away—the one which says that students who want to be pastors go off to theological "cemetery." It would be funny if it weren't so tragically true.

So, love has been de-centered in three ways—first in the way we understand and use the Bible which occurred in the shift from monasticism to scholasticism. We've chosen the way of *scientia*, and have lost our love of *sapientia*. We've chosen information over formation, knowledge over wisdom. We've forgotten that the call to make disciples is, at the core, a call to enter God's formative work of shaping people who love like Jesus.

Second, love has been de-centered in our attempt (with good original intention) to reclaim the importance of salvation by grace through faith alone. The problem is that we—we Protestants at least—have severely overcorrected. Here we have lost the biblical view of discipleship, based in the words of Jesus, that makes love the central concern of discipleship. Disciples are known, according to Jesus, by their love, specifically by their capacity to love as he has loved us. To make disciples is to make lovers.

Third, we have reduced discipleship to theological education. This is the lingering effect of the enlightenment which celebrated reason, autonomy, individuality, and professional theology over personal holiness, tradition, Christian community, and practical theology. The resultant damage from this history is a cascading sterility of our seminaries, spiritual immaturity among our ministry leaders, impotence among our churches, and coldness in our culture.

I know this appears to be a bleak picture. Can anything be done about it? That's the theme of our final section.

14. Cannell, *Theological Education Matters*, 140.

# PART FIVE

Tikkun Olam

# 17

# Close Repair

*Plough deep in me, great Lord,*
*heavenly Husbandman,*
*that my being may be a tilled field,*
*the roots of grace spreading far and wide,*
*until thou alone are seen in me,*
*thy beauty golden like summer harvest,*
*thy fruitfulness as autumn plenty...*
*Quarry me deep, dear Lord,*
*and then fill me to overflowing*
*with living water.*

—"THE DEEPS," FROM *THE VALLEY OF VISION*[1]

So far, we've seen the story God is writing in terms of creation, collapse, and redemption. Now we enter into the final phase of that story, which is still being written. This is the fourth act of our drama—the story we're in. This is the phase of restoration, in which God uses redeemed people (and unredeemed ones) to set about putting his world back in order.

The wonderful Jewish term *tikkun olam* can be translated as "repair of the world," and it's fitting here. In Jewish thought, its meaning ranges from

---

1. If you are not familiar with *The Valley of Vision*, it is a beautiful compendium of Puritan prayers.

overcoming idolatry to working for social justice.[2] At its core it has the sense of entering God's work of putting the world back in working order. Jesus himself spoke of the restoration of all things envisioning a time when all things would be put to rights.[3]

In Christian thought, this repair of the world takes on a decidedly eschatological hue, with the repair having been inaugurated in the life, death, and resurrection of Jesus, to be consummated in his return. For example, in the Middle Ages, Hugh of St. Victor divided biblical history into two periods. The first, leading up to Christ, he calls the *opus conditionis* (conditional work—setting the conditions for what's to come); he called the second period the *opus reparationis* (work of repair), which is carried out in Christ and through the church.[4]

In Christian thought, the *tikkun olam* is heaven coming upon the earth, which inaugurates the work of repair that flows directly out of Jesus's work of redemption. Jesus stands not only at the center of the work of the world's redemption, but also its repair. And he asks us to join him there. It's in the fourth act of the drama of God that we're invited to take up our script and play our part in the divine play of life.

## HONESTLY FACING THE PROBLEM

Of course, to believe in the work of repair, one must believe that something is broken. It's apparent that believers and nonbelievers of goodwill are starting to realize that something just isn't right. It's like the moment between when your steering wheel starts to shudder, and you realize you have a flat tire. You just know something's seriously wrong. Looking out over the landscape of our culture, there's much wreckage to behold. People are beginning to question the road most traveled, and whether we've come to the end of a civilizational cul-de-sac.

As noted above, over the past three hundred years or so, we've pursued the path of autonomous (self-ruling) progress promised in the Enlightenment. While we've made great progress in scientific advances, we're realizing that our scientific and technological achievements have now far outstripped the moral maturity necessary to manage them. Concerns which were once limited to issues of nuclear war and genetic modification are now being

2. Wikipedia article, "Tikkun Olam," https://en.wikipedia.org/wiki/Tikkun_olam.

3. Matthew 19:28, see also Acts 3:21, where Peter picks up the theme, and then Revelation 21:5 for the fulfillment.

4. Vandenbroucke, "New Milieux, New Problems: From the Twelfth to the Sixteenth Century," Leclercq, Vandenbroucke, and Bouyer, *Spirituality of the Middle Ages*, 231.

voiced with the rise of artificial intelligence (AI) and our ability to control it.[5] Like children playing in the hayloft who've discovered matches, we're becoming more and more dangerous to ourselves and others.

Our capacity has only grown for war, for the destruction of innocent human life, and for ignoring our mandate to care for creation. We're divided from one another by an endless litany of "diversities," which themselves can be comprehensible only within the context of a more fundamental unity we've jettisoned. Technology has become an idol we've come to worship, entering the Faustian bargain that if we give it free rein, it will eventually remove our human limitations we've been taught to resent. We shall become like God, not only naming good and evil, but now creating alternative realities, metaverses, in which to live out those fantasies. We're invited to export our fallenness into outer space without even wondering whether it's wise, based upon the current state of our own planet.

While we aggressively pursue progress on the outside, we're becoming more insecure on the inside. Terms like "stress" and "anxiety," while once on the periphery of our social vocabulary, now stand at its center. As our confidence in a well-ordered world collapses, we desperately turn to governments, to leaders, and to institutions to deliver us. We substitute government agency for personal agency in the hopes that someone will take responsibility for our lives. Yet sadly, those institutions too are floundering, sailing in the fog with us without benefit of GPS. We sense that something's wrong, but we don't know where to turn, and we don't know what to do.

The more desperate our inner angst becomes, the more we palliate it with outer activity. Like all palliative care, it just postpones the inevitable. Our drugs of choice are all endorphins. We seek one high after another, and we've become serial experience junkies. Busyness is everything. Busyness has become our savior. Salvation by screen. Salvation by calendar. Salvation by relationship. Salvation by sex. Salvation by portfolio. Like hummingbirds flitting from flower to flower to support their extreme metabolism, we're constantly on the go—which means, of course, we're actually on the run.

On the run from what? From our fear and anxiety, and more particularly from their prophets, solitude and silence who are trying to get our attention. We've grown to see silence and solitude as aliens, odd, suspect—and

5. See, for example, the recent concerns over ChatGPT in Kissinger, Schmidt, and Huttenlocher, "ChatGPT Heralds an Intellectual Revolution," *The Wall Street Journal*, Saturday/Sunday Feb. 25–26, 2023, A-13. Also, Kevin Roose, "A Conversation With Bing's Chatbot Left Me Deeply Unsettled: A very strange conversation with the chatbot built into Microsoft's search engine led to it declaring its love for me." *The New York Times*, February 16, 2023, https://www.nytimes.com/2023/02/16/technology/bing-chatbot-microsoft-chatgpt.html.

even dangerous. But like the prophets of old who prepared the way of the Lord, if we would take the time to sit quietly in their presence and hear their message, these feet of our souls would guide us home to the father's house.

But we don't. So, we let the media, those haberdashers of stress and anxiety, clothe us in fear. The thing we now fear most is not "fear itself" but facing our fear. If love is the fuel that makes human life possible, perhaps our deepest fear is that our tank is nearly empty. Somehow, we know inside that when love runs out, everything that matters dies. That fear paralyzes us, and we simply refuse to face reality. Like those in dance marathons in years gone by, we'll keep dancing until we collapse or until the music runs out.

Staring at the clock of history we find ourselves at a *metanoia* moment. We need to rethink everything, including and especially God. We're at a real come–to–Jesus moment, not in the sense of clever cultural aesthetes issuing a throwaway line, but in the decided sense of a true spiritual crisis. Again, we're back to the meaning of *metanoia* as a renewed understanding of what is real and true. In the *metanoia* moment, we both realize and are realized. As we awaken from the cultural trance and come home to reality as God has given it to us, we're also awakened and come home to ourselves. We must discover, or rediscover, the pearl of great price—the kingdom of God, which is a reality of love refracted in all the ways we encountered in part three.

The repair of the world will come primarily through people who themselves have chosen to enter the way of repair. And the way of repair begins by acknowledging that God is God, and we are not. We must depart the cultural choir that would have us sing our own praises, and choose instead to "Amen" God. How might this happen?

## REPAIRING INDIVIDUALS

G. K. Chesterton once pondered the question, "What's wrong with the world?" His only answer was, "I am wrong."[6] He went on to add, "Until a man can give that answer, his idealism is only a hobby. But this original sin belongs to all ages, and is the business of religion."

If we're to see a renaissance of love in our time, it must begin with an honest assessment of the state of our own hearts as measured by the heart of Jesus. I've suggested that love is the core competency of discipleship. It isn't biblical or theological knowledge, it isn't interpersonal skills, it isn't our passion, it isn't determination, it isn't spiritual giftedness. It isn't our cache of faith, our expression of generosity, or our spiritual discipline.

6. Chesterton, *The Daily News*, August 16, 1905. https://www.jordanmposs.com/blog/2019/2/27/whats-wrong-chesterton.

All these are important and helpful aids in the spiritual life. But without love, they—and you and I—are nothing. Love is the core of discipleship, and whether we're growing in love (in all its forms—rooted in *agape*) is what matters in the end. This is what it means to become Christlike. By this is God glorified. This is Paul's message in his paean to love in 1 Corinthians that we visited earlier, which is read so often and lived so little.

This love is both the root and fruit of our salvation; his love is the root; our love is the fruit, but it is one and the same love which begins and ends in God. Since the fruit in us is in fact the fruit of the Holy Spirit, then it is all, finally, the work of God. Any fruit of love we bear—the supernatural, necessary, evidentiary fruit of the One who lives within us—is *his* fruit. Our salvation is not based upon our fruitfulness, but his—his fruit budded in the incarnation, bloomed on the cross, and burst forth in the resurrection. Our capacity to love is contingent upon the depth of his abiding in us and our abiding in him:

> I am the true vine, and my Father is the gardener. He cuts off every branch in me that bears no fruit, while every branch that does bear fruit, he prunes so that it will be even more fruitful. You are already clean because of the word I have spoken to you. Remain in me, as I also remain in you. No branch can bear fruit by itself; it must remain in the vine. Neither can you bear fruit unless you remain in me.[7]

The fruit Jesus is talking about is the fruit of his love within us as manifested in our love for the Father and our love for others. To be a disciple is to become an open floodgate of God's love pouring into the world, by which the world is redeemed and healed and restored.

I have a little valve at the head of my garden hose. When it's turned across the hose, it stops the water from flowing. Only when I turn the valve to align with the hose does the water gush forth. To be a disciple of Jesus is to open the valve of our hearts, aligning ourselves with the powerful flow of his love.

To be a disciple of Jesus is to live the fullness of a contra-indicated life, a life oriented around submission, service, suffering, and sacrifice. It's to take a point of view exactly opposite to that of our cultural clerisy. It's to bow before a different altar, to worship and serve a different God. To follow Jesus is to choose his towel, his crown of thorns, and his cross—not as an occasional hobby, but as our intentional way of life.

One of the fundamental ironies of the repair of people—which is the Christian life—is that it is pure gift. We cannot repair ourselves. Yet,

7 John 15:1–4.

paradoxically, this realization is the beginning of the repair. It turns us from ourselves to him.

So rather than start with "you" or "they," those who seek the repair of the world must start with Chesterton's "I." If I want the world to change, *I* must change. I must *be* changed. If we were to take all the moral rectitude we insist on from others, and ask it of ourselves, that would be a good start. We can't change the world, but we can be changed. For the Christian, the *tikkun olam* always starts in the microcosm of an individual's encounter with the living God. It's profoundly personal. Nothing changes without changed people, and it's the encounter with God, the I-Thou encounter, which changes us.

Institutions, governments, churches, businesses, schools, and families are all inhabited by people. They'll rise or fall according to the quality of the lives of those who inhabit them, and especially those who lead them. We should expect little of others, and much of ourselves, rather than the other way around. It's spiritually healthy to use a telescope when looking at the lives of others, and a microscope when looking at your own. I think this is what Jesus was getting at in the Sermon on the Mount when he said,

> Why do you look at the speck of sawdust in your brother's eye and pay no attention to the plank in your own eye? How can you say to your brother, "Let me take the speck out of your eye," when all the time there is a plank in your own eye? You hypocrite, first take the plank out of your own eye, and then you will see clearly to remove the speck from your brother's eye.[8]

If I'm honest with myself, I have the life of a forester ahead of me when I take Jesus's words to heart. It's much simpler to criticize the lives of others (especially those we've never met) than to be involved in the painful work of sorting your own soul. It isn't as simple as "be the change." Rather, it requires the infinitely harder work of "being changed." It's a humble, modest, beginning, but when that work is underway—person by person, surrendered heart by surrendered heart, conversion to the heart of God by conversion to the heart of God—then you may be sure that the *tikkun olam* is present.

## REPAIRING DISCIPLESHIP

If the intuition is correct that we've lost the core competency of discipleship, which is love, then it's time to reevaluate how we train disciples, both in

---

8. Matthew 7:3–5.

our leadership systems and in the local churches (for a growing number of churches the leadership systems *are* the local churches).

As I mentioned earlier, modern seminaries have inherited a university model that privileges knowledge over wisdom, information over formation, and data over experience, among other things. They've also inherited a "pull model" of how to do theological education. This is the expectation that those who want to train for ministry should leave their faith communities (local churches) where they're already being formed, and go off to seminary.

After studying for three or more years in an artificial environment, which at best is only a temporary community, they're then sent to pastor people they don't even know. The entire process is disorienting and dislocating. Jeffrey Bullock, a Presbyterian and president of the University of Dubuque and its Theological Seminary, has written,

> Though there are exceptions, healthy pastors are not formed by theological faculties or the Presbytery's Committee on Vocation. Healthy pastors are formed and nurtured best within healthy worshiping communities.[9]

The idea in the inherited university model is that seminary becomes the primary formative community. There are, to be sure, some positive aspects to this—intensive late-night conversations about theology and ministry, close contact with teachers, a sense of camaraderie among people all undergoing the same kind of training. Nevertheless, I think this traditional seminary model inhibits genuine discipleship development.

First, the whole process is very disruptive, both to single students and to the family life of married ones—not to mention very expensive. When seminarians graduate, many are in debt and their financial prospects are modest. This places great added emotional strain on those who are already laboring with intense study loads.

Second, the model is not integrative. A person leaves to study for three years or more, mostly with people a lot like them, people who have the same dreams and calling. Students are educated by highly trained academics, many of whom have never worked in full-time vocational ministry—imagine flight instructors without a pilot's license. These students are taught a whole new vocabulary and way to speak about God, one that's utterly foreign to those they'll serve. One of my former colleagues, who served for decades as a pastor, used to say that it would take him about two years with a new associate pastor to relieve him or her of "seminary speak."

---

9. Bullock, "Six Observations about Presbyterian Theological Education: The View from My Window," *Theology Matters* (Vol. 28, No.1, Winter 2022), 3.

Third, most seminaries don't see their role as being involved in the spiritual formation of their students. They're artificial incubators rather than organic soil. Seminaries say, "Our job is to teach them Bible, theology, and basic ministry skills. It's the church's job to shape their soul." I cannot describe how deep the disconnect is here. Students generally have a weak relationship with a local church while they're in seminary, often interrupted by their field education requirements at another church. Local pastors know that seminarians are just passing through, and so are unwilling to invest much time in them. Seminaries blame the churches and churches blame the seminaries for the spiritual immaturity of the graduates, but nothing changes. I've watched this go on for forty years.

Often seminary students' heads swell while their hearts shrink, and without a faith community in which they can be deeply embedded and process what they're learning as they go, the goal slowly morphs from becoming a disciple of Jesus to becoming a "Master of Divinity." These values are reflected in what is celebrated by the institutions—prizes at graduation for best preacher, counselor, interpreter of the Scriptures, etc. Competition for excellent grades becomes the path to the prize. Marriages and families get sacrificed on the altar of "success."

I once heard a seminary president say to the new students, "You can succeed in seminary but fail in life." He was right. But the training model and seminary gestalt set that good counsel up to become prophecy. Many of our seminaries are inadvertently designed to make biblical discipleship (becoming people who love like Jesus loves) difficult. The values, practices, and reward systems reflect more "the kingdom of this world" than "the kingdom of our Lord and of his Christ." How does one create disciples as lovers, when the seminary systems are built around competition and "academic rigor." I remember sitting in a faculty division meeting one day discussing the "value add" of coming to our seminary rather than attending another. One professor said the value we added was "prestige" while another opined that it was "us"—the faculty itself. Can we be surprised, then, that students themselves aspire to prestige and many decide to ditch the church for the reputation of being an academic? To quote C. S. Lewis, "We castrate, and bid the geldings be fruitful."[10]

Even those schools which have programs and centers for discipleship speak of them as being "co-curricular." That's academic speak for "not really important."

The good news is that this is starting to change. The pandemic has accelerated the rate of change, but others have noticed the need for substantive

10. Lewis, "Men Without Chests," *Abolition of Man*, 35.

change in leadership for the church to fulfill the Great Commission. Again, Jeffrey Bullock of Dubuque Seminary:

> Forming disciples to exercise leadership within a Great Commissioning movement requires a different kind of theological education than that which has been in existence in our mainline and PC(USA) seminaries for the last 100+ years.[11]

Some people and organizations who are exploring new options for ministry training are moving away from those that are obsolete.[12] Some pioneers are exploring "push" models where those seeking training remain in their local churches as the proper gardens of the soul. The seminary training is pushed out to them via various technological platforms, and they can put what they're learning to use right away. This allows them to reflect on its value (or lack of value) with a seasoned pastor in their home church. In this way the world of congregations can become the seminary classroom, but without the limitations of having to "attend" seminary.

Some of these innovators are also challenging the old imperialism of head over the heart (*scientia* over *sapientia*) in formational training. Some are now explicitly valuing and evaluating not only theological and biblical competencies and ministry skill, but also things like emotional and spiritual maturity, as well as leadership competency. The focus on the *integration* of biblical and theological truth into the local setting is taking priority. Pastoral ministry requires more than just intellectual acuity; it requires substantial human agility.

My own denomination, the *Covenant Order of Evangelical Presbyterians (ECO)*, is developing its "Flourish Institute of Theology" along the lines of thinking about the formation of pastors and ministry leaders the way we prepare medical doctors, with a strong dose of medical knowledge taking root in an equally strong clinical context of hospital experience. Flourish is being designed for twenty first century ministry.

After affirming the foundations of the Christian faith, Mark Patterson, the president of Flourish Institute for Theology, says in the overview video,

> The way we train church leaders and do ministry must adapt to modern times... Let's be honest, the traditional pathways for seminary education are time and cost prohibitive... Many of their training techniques have not adapted to meet the needs of twentieth century life and ministry... All of our online programs are designed around industry leading adult education

11. Bullock, "Six Observations," 4.

12. See, for example, Shaw, *Transforming Theological Education*.

techniques combining spiritual formation, theological integration, and mentored application. Our M.Div., M.A., and Lay
Leader certificate are integrated into the ministry you're currently doing. They provide rigorous theological training at your
pace and have practical real-life application.[13]

A renewed focus on the importance of peer groups and ministry mentors attentive to the growth of soul for those in their care is accelerating
a wholistic discipleship culture among those being trained to lead. This is
a long-overdue rebalancing, and will help churches become healthier and
stronger as their leaders do the same.

Still, the question must be asked whether all this isn't rearranging the
deck furniture on our sinking ship of church if the centrality of love is not
reasserted. Better delivery systems, personal interactions, and focus on
discipleship in local centers, without resetting the *target* of all of this, still
misses the point. If making disciples is about forming people who love like
Jesus loved (Jesus's stated hallmark of a disciple), then the *content* of our
message needs a reset, and not just our methods and platforms for delivery.

What would a Love Quotient (LQ) curriculum look like? How would
our evaluation processes of candidates for ministry be changed if the stated
outcome was for people to mature in their capacity to love? How would
hands-on ministry learning opportunities be shaped in our local churches
if their goal was to strengthen the learner's LQ? What if the capacity to love
like Jesus loves became the ultimate learning outcome? Taking these con-
siderations seriously will require a revolution in both content and focus of
theological education, if it's to become genuinely discipleship centered. As
Gaylord Ens has said so clearly in his *Love Revolution,*

> "For *rediscovery* to occur, seminaries and schools of biblical
> studies will need to feature the Command in their course of
> study...We must go beyond both personal and church *discovery.*
> Jesus' Command must not simply become a museum piece for
> curious fingers to touch. Rather, it must be fully restored to its
> place as a core commandment of authentic Christian faith and
> practice. That is when *discovery* becomes *recovery.*"[14]

Is it time for the church to ask ourselves Drucker's questions afresh:
"What business, are we in?" and "How's business?" The symptoms of decay
pointed out in the social surveys in Europe, and now America, indicate that
we've forgotten what business we're in, and that's why business isn't good.

13. Patterson, Flourish Institute of Theology (ECO), https://vimeo.com/703005349.

14. Ens, *Love Revolution, 182.* I am grateful to Gaylord for his generous gift of time
as we've discussed this project and his wonderful insights into the topic of love.

Perhaps the reason we often fail in carrying out the Great Commission is that it requires becoming New Commandment people. When we forsake the commandment, we forfeit the commission.

The early church, on the other hand, was exceptional in making disciples of all the nations because they lived in white-hot Jesus love. Jesus isn't looking for converts and students; he's looking for disciples who will choose a life of deep, radical, sacrificial, life-changing love, just as he did. He's looking for people he can inhabit with his love so that they in turn will draw others to him for the same purpose. That's the meaning of the Great Commission. Making disciples is multiplying lovers. But this can be accomplished only by people who are themselves lovers, in whom the first and original Lover dwells. Making disciples is about making lovers—people who love like Jesus loves.

## REPAIRING CHURCHES

Once church leaders are changed, once they begin to remember that we're in the discipleship business of forming people who love like Jesus loves, and once we begin to align all of our training for that purpose—then, and only then, will the spiritual temperature of our churches and ministries start to rise. Busyness is not a measure of spiritual fire.

The reason survey after survey of non-Christian people finds Christianity so unattractive is that Christians so often are. Getting to the heart of the matter, the root problem is not that Christians aren't reading the Bible enough, or that we don't contextualize the Bible well, or that we don't attend church enough, or that we lack evangelistic zeal, or that we don't go on enough mission trips. Those are problems, but not the *real* problem.

The real problem is not what we're doing so much as *why* and *how* we're doing it. If we continue to treat the Bible as a tool, if we continue to read it only for information, if we continue to mark the health of our churches and our success in ministry by the three B's—bucks, butts, and buildings (finances, worship attendance, and building campaigns)—all the while believing the myth that we've done discipleship when someone can articulate good theology or has memorized copious amounts of Scripture—then we're deluding ourselves. One of the most destructive Christians I ever met assured me that he had read through the Bible seven times.

I've looked at a lot of discipleship material over the last few years, and none of it has zeroed in on the goal of helping people grow in love. In knowledge—yes. In giving—yes. In service—yes. In evangelism—yes. In spiritual disciplines—yes. But when these are untethered from the primary thing—from love—they become empty, as Paul reminds us in 1 Corinthians 13. I worked in program–driven churches my whole career, and I never questioned the operating premise that if we develop enough fine programs and get enough people to attend them, then we're doing discipleship. I no longer believe that.

None of the things above are bad things. But we've become like golfers frantically trying club after club, chasing all over the course, but forgetting where the green is. If everything we do in the church doesn't make us better disciples, better lovers, then it's a distraction—a waste of time. Are we developing the heart of Jesus in our people? That's the question.

Dana Allin, synod executive of ECO, puts it this way in his book *Simple Discipleship*:

> I wonder, however, if at times this richness of resources has actually muddied the waters of discipleship. Do we sometimes miss the ultimate purpose of the great commission: helping people become more in love with Jesus and more reflective of His character in the world? Have we made discipleship more complicated than it needs to be?[15]

My answer to Dana's question is yes, we have—and until we stop making discipleship complicated and start making it compelling, we'll inhibit our churches' kingdom impact. We must rethink discipleship from the ground up in terms like Dana describes. Spiritual growth cannot be anything other than a deepening capacity to love God and love others. The rest is commentary.[16]

I mentioned above that the early church was enormously effective in its fulfillment of the Great Commission. Various historians have ascribed this to a variety of reasons, but I think the pagan emperor Julian the Apostate had it right in the fourth century. Sometimes outsiders see more clearly than insiders. Seeing the connection between the evangelistic success of the Christians he hated, and the love they expressed for their neighbors, Julian observed (with a deep sense of exasperation) that the Church's phenomenal growth

15. Allin, *Simple Discipleship*, xiv.

16. This saying that 'the rest is commentary' is generally attributed to the rabbinic sage Hillel, who was challenged by a cocky young man who said that he would convert to Judaism if Hillel could explain the law to him while he stood on one foot. The more conservative Rabbi Shammai derisively dismissed the young man, but Hillel gently responded saying: "What is hateful to you, do not do to your fellow: this is the whole Torah; the rest is commentary; go and learn." Babylonian Talmud, Shabbat 31a. According to the Talmud, the man did convert!

has been specially advanced through the loving service rendered to strangers, and through their care for the burial of the dead. It is a scandal that there is not a single Jew who is a beggar, and that the godless Galileans care not only for their own poor but for ours as well; while those who belong to us look in vain for the help that we should render them.[17]

My purpose here is not to recommend approaches to discipleship, but only to observe that those charged with this responsibility will do well seeing to it that at the center of the approach they take is the explicit and constant promotion of love, what Gaylord Ens calls *featured* love.[18] Does this approach to discipleship have growth in love as its core concern? And do its strategies support that concern by producing loving disciples of Jesus?

Churches are by nature disciple incubators. Some churches lean heavily on programs, others on small groups for discipling vehicles. My own thinking is that this should be a both-and proposition rather than either-or. Everything the church does should be about discipleship, which is to say about developing lovers of God and others. There are several "platforms" that should always be discipleship-centered. Worship should be an arena where our love for God is expressed through exercise. Songs, prayers, sermons, liturgies should all foster a deep and abiding expression of our love for God. Worship is the hothouse of discipleship when it's a hothouse of our love for God.

Classes have a strong place as a discipleship platform, but they can denigrate into information-only encounters that leave people unchanged. Unfortunately, I've seen (and created) some of these in my own experience. But if we constantly take our discipleship bearings from the desire to grow lovers, then classes can move beyond information centers to formation laboratories.

Service is also a great platform for practicing our love in the lives of others through sacrificial giving of time, ability, and finance. But if we do this out of anything other than love, these acts of service can quickly decay into Christian virtue-signaling.

This complementary approach in "making disciples" recognizes the value of people meeting one-on-one in dyads and triads, which will afford more life-on-life sharing and shaping. This is a necessary practice in

17. Julian the Apostate, "Letter to Arsacius," based in part on the translation of Edward J. Chinnock, *A Few Notes on Julian and a Translation of His Public Letters* (London: David Nutt, 1901), 75–78; as quoted in Nagle and Burstein, *The Ancient World: Readings in Social and Cultural History*, 314–15; http://www.thenagain.info/Classes/Sources/Julian.html.

18. Ens, *Love Revolution*, 182.

a disciple-making church, and should be done alongside the things mentioned above. But once again, at the heart of it all needs to be the conscious, featured, stated goal of growing in love for God and others. Change, growth, and maturation in love—these should be goals of both the larger platforms and smaller groups of people who are being discipled in our churches.

Currently I'm spending time each week with a young man named Tim. He and I have been meeting one-on-one for over a year now. We've just been joined by a man named Lew. We read the Bible together and ask questions about who Jesus is and what it means to follow him. In case you haven't guessed it yet, love has *a lot* to do with both those questions. I've also been meeting online with a group of four young pastors just starting out in ministry. These are rich conversations about challenges they face, but it's also an opportunity to constantly return to the center of Jesus and his love for us, and our desire to grow in our love for him and others.

The *tikkun olam*, when applied to the church, will require a return to biblical discipleship, which in turn requires us to learn to love like Jesus loves. This is a lifelong journey. When churches start to produce disciples who love like Jesus, others will notice. People in our world are hungry for love. You can tell by some of the things they do to try and get it. We who belong to Jesus carry a message no others on the face of the earth are privileged to share. That message is that we're loved by the God of the universe, the God who is love. We do best when we not only carry the message but become part of it, being lovers ourselves who love like Jesus. This is Christian discipleship.

Now imagine a church across the world, filled with disciples who live and breathe the love of God for others. Imagine a church on fire with the kind of submitting, serving, suffering, sacrificial love we find in the Gospels when they tell us who Jesus is. We know Jesus' followers were first called Christians at Antioch in Syria. That name was issued as an insult by their enemies. But those who belonged to the Way turned that label into an honorific. I wonder if that description of "little Christs" might not again become the goal of discipleship—to be little Christs who love like Jesus loves. What would happen if people like that, people on fire with the love of God, spread out across the world? Perhaps the whole world would warm again.

# 18

# Broad Repair

*Finally, let us not forget the religious character of our origin.*
*Our fathers were brought hither by their high veneration for the*
*Christian religion. They journeyed by its light, and labored in its hope.*
*They sought to incorporate its principles with the elements of their society*
*which partakes in the highest degree of the mild and peaceful spirit of*
*Christianity, and to diffuse its influence through all their institutions,*
*civil, political, or literary. Let us cherish these sentiments, and extend*
*this influence still more widely; in full conviction that that is the happiest*
*society which partakes in the highest degree of the mild and peaceful*
*spirit of Christianity.*

—DANIEL WEBSTER

Christianity was never meant to be a private religion or a personal affair. It has always been about following a public King and living in a new kingdom. The apostle Paul tells us that "our citizenship is in heaven, and we eagerly await a Savior from there."[1] Most Christian writers have presumed that this means we bide our time here in holy living, and then either at our death or his second coming, we're whisked away from earth to heaven. No one has done more in our time to disabuse us of this notion than N. T. Wright.

A few years ago, I was at Fuller Seminary and heard him lecture on the theology of Paul. One of the things he said dramatically changed my

1. Philippians 3:20.

understanding of our situation. It transposed the way I understand my relation to, and purpose in, this world.

Wright reminded us that Philippians was written to colonists.[2] Philippi was one of the premier Roman colonies of the ancient world. Wright's main point was that as colonists, these Roman citizens were never expected to "go home" to live in Rome. Precisely the opposite. Their job was to serve the empire by bringing Graeco-Roman culture and law to the city of Philippi—to incorporate it into the empire and make it Roman.

Wright's point was that the role of the Christian is the same. Our citizenship is in heaven (the place where God is), and our job is to eagerly share in Jesus's ongoing work to bring heaven down upon the earth until he returns. We're ambassadors on permanent assignment.[3] I've read that Cyrus Vance, Ronald Reagan's secretary of state, upon sending a new ambassador oversees would hold a going-away party. He would put a globe in front of the ambassador, and ask them to point out their country, which they did. He would then point to America and say, "No, *that's* your country. Don't forget it!"

Taken seriously, our ambassadorships means that we have work to do *in this world* to help ready it for its final destiny under the reign of God when Christ returns. This is *not* about political power, but about a renewed creation. This is a Christian way of understanding the *tikkun olam*. The repair of the world is Jesus's work, begun and finished by him. And we're called to put our shoulders to the kingdom wheel to forward it in the power of his Spirit. We must remember that since it is his work, it must be done as he would do it. The work of the Lamb cannot be done in the way of the dragon.[4]

## REPAIRING CITIZENS

Christians in the West hold a kind of dual citizenship. We're citizens of the ultimate kingdom of God, and provisional citizens of the kingdoms of this world, working in love until "the kingdom of this world has become the

2. I realize that I write these words in a decidedly post-colonial atmosphere. It might be more helpful to think of Paul's point as "re-colonizing" in the sense that the earth was God's to start with until the "ruler of this world" came to have dominion over what had been given to Adam and Eve. Thus the "re-colonization" is actually the restoration of earth's "indigenous" people, the holy ones of God. This is one of the central features of the coming of the kingdom of heaven as it overshadows and interlocks with the earth.

3. Wright, *Paul for Everyone: Philippians*, 126–27.

4. See Goggin and Strobel, *The Way of the Dragon, or The Way of the Lamb*.

kingdom of our Lord and of his Christ."[5] Our role is to use our heavenly citizenship to leaven our earthly citizenship so that our King's will is done on earth as it is in heaven. We're to work to bring the earth into congruity with heaven.

Of course, this has already begun in Christ, and will be completed at his return—and not until then. This is not a repair rooted in human dreams, fantasies, and visions of progress. It's not funded by the idols of state, power, technology, and wealth. It's a repair in which all things are made new by the same love that made all things in the first place. The repair is accomplished in and by Trinitarian love from beginning to end.

Practically speaking, this repair necessitates Christians listening, speaking, and acting in this world for the sake of God's very good creation. We live and act in order for this world to fully glorify God, as it did in the beginning. We love what God loves, and we act accordingly. It means that we work for the restoration of truth, goodness, justice, beauty, responsibility, and Spiritual tolerance in this world as refractions of the love of God and his lordship.

All of this will be opposed of course. Expect it. We love the world for the sake of the God who loves the world, and when that love grows costly in submission, service, suffering, and sacrifice, we'll find ourselves in good company, and know that we've entered the narrow way of Jesus.

I think the most helpful thing believers can do in our time is to restart the public conversation about Jesus. We should help people think through whether our world is better off with or without him. Has our sophisticated setting aside of his way of life helped us or hurt us? Has laying aside his teaching made us finer or coarser people? I'm not talking about proselytizing and indoctrination, but exposure, what Daniel Webster called "diffused influence." It seems to me that we've deprived ourselves of the richest nourishment a civilization can have by divorcing ourselves from the Judeo-Christian tradition.

By ripping our culture out of its rootedness in God, Christ, and the Bible, we cut ourselves off from the very transcendent sources of renewal that have sustained and renewed us through our history. It's the history of Israel and Israel's Messiah that provided our values concerning the dignity and equality of every person, the moral agency of individuals, love and care for the poor, universal human rights, and the dignity of work. It's the Judeo-Christian worldview that laid the foundations of modern science and fostered the cultivation of knowledge and the arts. This tradition was able

5. Revelation 11:15 (ASV).

to purify, refine, and amplify the ancient Greek and Roman contributions to philosophy and law.[6]

The secular desire to cast off these foundations is also untrue to our history as Americans. I don't desire to open the question of whether America is a Christian nation. I don't think that question can be answered, because of definitional problems.[7]

However we may try to answer that question, it's clear historically that Judeo-Christian belief rocked the cradle of America's infancy. Alexis de Tocqueville noted something similar to what Daniel Webster said in his quote above. In Europe, and especially his native France, religion and republican (representative) government had been at each other's throats (and necks). Not in America. Tocqueville noted the difference. He perceived that American settlers

> brought with them…a form of Christianity, which I cannot better describe, than by styling it a democratic and republican religion… From the earliest settlement of the emigrants, politics and religion contracted an alliance which has never been dissolved.[8]

Regarding these dynamics in early American religion, esteemed historian Mark Noll has written,

> This synthesis was a compound of evangelical Protestant religion, republican political ideology, and common sense moral reasoning. Through the time of the Civil War, that synthesis defined the boundaries for a vast quantity of American thought, while also providing an ethical framework, a moral compass, and a vocabulary of suasion for much of the nation's public life.[9]

Throughout our history our leaders have understood the organic connection among Judeo-Christian religious belief, political liberty, economic prosperity, personal morality, and civic stability. I'm writing this section on

6. Holland, *Dominion*, 343, 385–86, 478, 524, see also Maier's Foreword to Schmidt, *How Christianity Changed the World*, 8–9. For further reading see Stark, *For the Glory of God*, D'Souza, *What's So Great about Christianity?*, Carroll and Shiflett, *Christianity on Trial*, Hill, *What Has Christianity Ever Done for Us*, Russell, *Exposing Myths about Christianity*, and McLaughlin, *Confronting Christianity*.

7. Does it mean a nation of individual Christians? Does it mean a nation of Christian values? Does it mean both? Does it mean something altogether different?

8. de Tocqueville, Henry Reeves, trans., *The Republic of the United States and Its Political Institutions Reviewed and Examined*, Vol. I, 328.

9. Noll, *America's God*, 9.

George Washington's birthday. Speaking of the health of infant America upon the occasion of his entering the "shade of retirement," Washington wrote,

> Of all the dispositions and habits which lead to political pros-
> perity, religion and morality are indispensable supports. In vain
> would that man claim the tribute of patriotism, who should
> labor to subvert these great pillars of human happiness, these
> firmest props of the duties of men and citizens. The mere politi-
> cian, equally with the pious man, ought to respect and to cher-
> ish them. A volume could not trace all their connections with
> private and public felicity... And let us with caution indulge the
> supposition that morality can be maintained without religion.
> Whatever may be conceded to the influence of refined educa-
> tion on minds of peculiar structure, reason and experience both
> forbid us to expect that national morality can prevail in exclu-
> sion of religious principle.[10]

Maybe Washington's words could offer a jumping-off spot for conversations among today's "politicians" and "pious." When people of goodwill
stand side by side, silently looking out over what we've become, maybe there
will come a *metanoia* moment, a time to rethink everything, a time to see
things freshly. Perhaps we can, as new citizens living in an old world, inhabit
it with the kind of love and grace, patience, and virtue, which will breathe
fresh air into our lives. Together, perhaps we can begin again to think in
terms of the commonweal.[11]

This alliance (observed by de Tocqueville), this synthesis (seen by
Noll), these connections (urged by Washington) have broken down, and
they need our heartfelt attention and repair. It reminds me of the situation
we saw earlier with religion and science. Historically they were allies, and
indeed, as we've seen, the Judeo-Christian understanding of God served as
the incubator for modern science. The same is true here regarding our public life. Judeo-Christian understandings of human dignity and fallenness,
equal rights, and the rule of law were foundational for the way our Declaration of Independence and our Constitution were written.

10  Washington, "Farewell Address," 1796. https://www.ourdocuments.gov/doc.php
?flash=false&doc=15&page=tranScript.

11.  Four of our "states" were not founded as "states," but as "commonwealths"—
Massachusetts, Virginia, Pennsylvania, and Kentucky. The name communicates the
notion that those who founded those entities were concerned with the preservation of
the common good—the "common weal" or "common wellbeing." The body politic is
not merely concerned with preserving personal liberty, but also with "ordered liberty"
which holds in view the wellbeing of the public as a whole.

Jonathan Sacks has said that of the four great revolutions of the modern period, two enhanced liberty, and two undermined it. The two that enhanced it were the Glorious Revolution in England and the American Revolution. The two that undermined it were the French Revolution and the Russian Revolution. The Anglo-American revolutions were based upon a biblical understanding of freedom—what is known as "ordered liberty." This was a liberty rooted in personal responsibility which balanced its freedom with a societal need for order and the wellbeing of others. The other revolutions were based upon atheism and secular notions of unrestrained (autonomous) liberty. One set of revolutions established our rights in our Creator, the other established them in the state. This is why what has happened in France recently would be unthinkable in America. Rabbi Sacks writes,

> The French formula, where rights are simply brought about by the generosity of the state tells us, if you want more rights, then you need more government. It is the formula for maximal government. And that, frankly—it can step in, as the French recently did, and ban Christians from wearing a crucifix, ban Jews from wearing a Yarmulke, and ban Muslims from wearing a Hijab in public places. Now does that make France a more tolerant society than America or less tolerant?[12]

As with the religion and science situation, we've been handed a "warfare thesis" by academia and the media. For reasons of power and money, this face-off pits republican government against the Judeo-Christian values that gave birth to it and upon which its future depends. It is a revisionist history, and we need to reject it. Today secularists are told to fear a Christian theocracy. Christians are told to fear a secularist totalitarianism. But this warfare thesis belies our historic national understanding. It is alien to American thinking.

To deny the connections between the Judeo-Christian faith, our form of government, and "political prosperity" (Washington's term) serves none of us well—neither the Christian nor the secularist. And it isn't true to our history. The American paradigm has historically seen republican (representative) government and religious faith as mutually supportive pillars of our culture. Remembering this simple truth may serve as a basis for a renewed

---

12. Rabbi Lord Jonathan Sacks' Speech at The Becket Fund's 19th Annual Canterbury Medal Dinner, May 16, 2014; https://www.youtube.com/watch?v=ocXAqbVy908. The transcript of this speech can be found at https://www.becketlaw.org/wp-content/uploads/2017/02/Rabbi-Sacks-Speech-Transcript.pdf.

conversation about our national interest between the "mere politician" and "the pious man."

From the confessing Christian perspective, we might take hope from the prophet Ezekiel. When all was lost, or so it seemed, Ezekiel—in a time more desperate than our own—was asked by God, "Son of man, can these bones live?"

> I said, "O Sovereign Lord, you alone know." Then he said to me, "Prophesy to these bones and say to them, 'Dry bones, hear the word of the Lord!' This is what the Sovereign Lord says to these bones: I will make breath enter you, and you will come to life."[13]

My scholar friends will remind me that America is not Israel, nor the Church. Granted. But as much as I believe that the promise to Abraham envisioned the blessing of the whole world through his seed Jesus, so I believe that anyone, and all people, who are willing to hear the word of the Lord in its fullness, and to live it out in their shared life, can come back to life. It is a word given to Israel, and through Israel, to the whole world.

The core of this word is the Word, who is Jesus, the incarnation of the love of God. When we follow him, becoming lovers as we go, as citizens of heaven living out that citizenship on the earth, then all things become possible: heaven permeating the earth until all things are permanently restored in the new creation. For Christians, it's a matter not of power but of becoming what Jesus said we should be in our culture—light, leaven, and salt. These words hold in common the notion of influence—they change things by being in direct contact with them.

As Christians, we have a lot to answer for. The litany of the church's sins long. For our critics, it's like shooting ducks in the baptismal barrel. What we need to remember is that all the items in the litany of the church's sins (and there are plenty) were the result of our *failures* to follow Jesus. G. K. Chesterton once said the problem with Christianity isn't that it has been tried and found wanting; the problem is that it has been found difficult and left untried. Despite his hyperbole, there is truth in Chesterton's words. The Christian life is always, to some degree, aspirational. Yet our failures in walking with Jesus in the past shouldn't prevent us from rejoining him in the present and letting him escort us into his future.

From the side of those who choose not to share the Christian faith but are troubled by the same picture of our deteriorating culture, the question is this: Can you look into the mirror of our history and remember that when we acknowledged and engaged with one another as allies in the common

---

13. Ezekiel 37:3–5.

cause of building a healthy culture—and not as enemies taught to distrust each other—our partnered achievement became a republic uniquely remarkable in human history?

What's needed is for us to start a serious conversation about the benefits for all of us of a renewed alliance between the pious and the politician—for the benefit of believers and nonbelievers alike—all who are gravely concerned about our culture. We need to find a way to recreate the alliance, the synthesis, and connections mentioned above, which formed the sinews of a sound America. Are we better off in a Christless culture? Is a Christ-haunted culture preferable to a Christ-hallowed one? What does the teaching of the Judeo-Christian tradition contribute to our national character, dignity, and form of government? Is our republican experiment sustainable without its religious foundations? How can we draw on that teaching in ways that acknowledge and respect our differences regarding personal faith, while finding common ground to rebuild what we treasure?

Yoram Hazony has recently advocated for America to establish Christianity as its national religion, along the lines of Britain's established church. Hazony, who is a practicing Jew, laments that the founders were not more explicit about this in the Constitution, while recognizing that they left the question of religious establishments to the states, many of which continued to have them well into the nineteenth century.[14] Hazony sees this establishment of religion as a necessary pillar for a renewed conservatism based in the empirical Anglo-American conservative tradition, and not the conservatism that shares Enlightenment rationalist presuppositions.

While there's much to consider in Hazony's work, I'm twitchy about the church getting too cozy with the state. Too often history teaches that the state will use the church for its own purposes, then kick it to the curb. Hitler did this with the establishment of the German Christians, which became a propaganda arm of the Nazi Party. Vladimir Putin is doing it now, using the Orthodox Church and its leader, Patriarch Kirill of Moscow, to bless his Tsarist imperial ambitions. Kirill has called Putin "a miracle from God."[15]

I'm also skeptical of the power of established religion to produce moral individuals. Less than two percent of Britain's citizens attend church, and the Anglican Church seems to have had little impact on the morality and ethics of its citizens.[16] Indeed, this was acknowledged and lamented by many in the media when Queen Elizabeth II died.

14. Hazony, *Conservativism*, 249.

15. Archbishop Kirell, https://en.wikipedia.org/wiki/Patriarch_Kirill_of_Moscow.

16. Rich, "Anglican Churches in the UK Are Shrinking in Size but Not Impact," *Christianity Today* (November 24, 2020). https://www.christianitytoday.com/ct/2020/november-web-only/church-of-england-decline-theos-growing-good-social-action.

Finally, I fear for the church in the temptation of such an arrangement. The temptation to use the levers of state power to impose faith on the consciences of others is all too real to contemplate a formal alliance. I think there needs to be a separation of church and state, but I understand it not as a wall (Jefferson), nor even as a hedge (Roger Williams). Recall that the phrase itself appears nowhere in our Constitution. It's worth noting that in original context, the setting of a hedge or wall was to protect the *church from the state*, not the other way around.[17] The image has been falsely reversed in our time (part of the revisionism I mentioned), as though the people need to be protected from the church. This is ahistorical secular jujitsu of the first order.

We need a separation of functions, but not a separation of vision. Think of it like a medieval cathedral. Those cathedrals contained both interior pillars and external buttresses. Both had the same purpose, viz. to uphold the cathedral. In American history the resources of both church and state served the purpose of sustaining our republic. What is needed now is a renewed and robust alliance along the historical lines that have served us well in the past. That alliance was a soft partnership of mutual support. The contours of that alliance would include—at a minimum—an honest historical recounting of the founders' understanding of the partnership, the welcoming, even soliciting, of religious voices in the public square, strong support in our laws for religious conscience and exemption, and the welcoming of the Bible back into the classroom as a source of study, conversation, and learning. Even an atheist of the conviction of Richard Dawkins has written about the centrality of the Bible in the Western literary canon and culture. Dawkins wrote in *The God Delusion*, "But the main reason the English Bible needs to be a part of our education is that it is a major source book for literary culture. The same applies to the legends of the Greek and Roman gods, and we learn about them without being asked to believe in them."[18]

Laying aside for the moment Jesus's claims as Savior and Lord (claims I very much believe), we need to ask ourselves if we wouldn't we be better off at least studying the moral teaching of the New Testament, as well as the Mosaic law, the Hebrew prophets, and the wisdom literature of the Hebrew scriptures?[19] Historically, Americans have always drawn from the well of

---

html.

17. The phrase first appears in Roger Williams and then again in Thomas Jefferson. Eidsmoe, *Christianity and the Constitution,* 242–45, and Barton, *Myth of Separation,* 41–46.

18. Dawkins, *God Delusion,* 341. See 341–43 for his fuller treatment.

19. The wisdom literature includes Psalms, Proverbs, the Song of Solomon,

scripture's rich and illustrious stories—good, bad, and ugly stories—as food for thought about how to build ethical and virtuous lives. The Bible has been uniquely foundational in the training of our citizens in this regard for all but the last sixty years.[20]  Mark Noll wasn't wrong to title his book on the role of the Bible in American history as *America's Book*.

Again, I'm not for proselytizing in the classroom, but if we lament the lack of virtue in the rising generations we can't help but see George Washington's voice in his Farewell address as prophetic in this regard—that virtue is impossible in exclusion of religious principle. Perhaps a little civil religion in our educational system is better than none. Students rightly perceive in America today that since prayer and the Bible have been removed for our public institutions, that secularism has become our religion.

I remember learning Psalm 23 in my third–grade public school class, and it neither damaged nor made a convert of me.  But it did at least acquaint me with some of the most beautiful poetry in the western literary canon. A recent Pew survey states, "that 8% of teens in public school have never seen a teacher lead the class in prayer," and the same share have never had a teacher read to the class from the Bible as an example of literature.[21] One can be assured, based upon other data, that this eight percent are outliers, far from the elite centers of our culture.[22]

In truth, we've followed our own lights far too long, and our culture, country and civilization are worse off for it. In forfeiting access to transcendent truths about love, we are left in a cultural pantheon worshipping the idols of power, money, and sex. All around us the signs are that our batteries are running low, and the darkness is growing. Raw secularism unleavened by biblical wisdom isn't serving anyone well. It's time to renew America's soul and end our love affair with an all too strident form of secularism that has become our abuser. That old piece of teaching known as the *Didache*

---

Ecclesiastes, and Job.

20. I also have no objection to studying other religions as well.  I have personally found such study beneficial.  But education without the study of religion and religious moral principle creates cardboard citizens who have lost the transcendent resources necessary to build a government and a culture which will endure. And our concept of government is *uniquely* informed by Judeo-Christian presuppositions (even when they are denied as such as Tom Holland has so persuasively argued in *Dominion*).

21. "Religion in the Public Schools" Pew Research Center. October 3, 2019.
https://www.pewresearch.org/religion/2019/10/03/religion-in-the-public -schools-2019-update/.

22. Diamant, "Teens in the South more likely than other U.S. teens to experience religion in public school."
https://www.pewresearch.org/fact-tank/2019/12/10/teens-in-the-south-more-likely-than-other-u-s-teens-to-experience-religion-in-public-school/.

rightly says, "There are two ways, one of life and one of death, and there's a great difference between the two."[23] It's time to rethink our choices and repair the fabric of our relationships and our understanding of our own history.

## REPAIRING INSTITUTIONS

Repaired disciples give birth to repaired churches, which can develop repaired citizens (influencing believers and nonbelievers alike) who can repair our institutions. And don't they need it? According to a recent Gallup poll Americans' overall average confidence in fourteen of our major public institutions hasn't risen above 36 percent in the last fifteen years.[24] Highest confidence remains in small businesses (70 percent), the military (69 percent), and police (51 percent). Our lowest confidence is in Congress (12 percent), television news (16 percent), big business (18 percent), and newspapers (21 percent).

In his book *Institutional Intelligence*, Gordon Smith defines institutions this way:

> An institution is a social structure that leverages wisdom, talent and resources toward a common cause or purpose. More specifically, it is a means, an architecture—specifically a social architecture—by which we can pursue a shared and greater good together.[25]

While the popularity of institutions ebbs and flows in the Western social imaginary,[26] and especially the American mind, the truth is this: No society will long endure without institutions that represent, instantiate, cultivate, and propagate its values. Institutions are civilizational ballast to stabilize us in tumultuous times. Sometimes they prove themselves to be a necessary evil or a necessary good, but they're always necessary. Some must be torn down and replaced by revolution or renewed through evolution, but institutions are always present in any society, organization, or nation with proven staying power.

23. Gould and Lake, "The Didache," *Apostolic Fathers*, Loeb Classical Library, Vol. I., 309.

24. Brennan, "Americans' Confidence in Major U.S. Institutions Dips."
https://news.gallup.com/poll/352316/americans-confidence-major-institutions-dips.aspx.

25. Smith, *Institutional Intelligence*, 4.

26. Taylor has coined this term in *Secular Age*. See pages 171–76 for its meaning.

Movements, even great ones, will explode with uncontrollable centrifugal force unless they're counter-balanced with the centripetal force of sound institutions. Movements are sexy; institutions are sturdy.

Smith identifies seven distinctive features of effective institutions:

1. mission clarity

2. appropriate governance

3. quality personnel

4. a vibrant institutional culture

5. financial resilience

6. generative built spaces

7. strategic alliances and collaborative partnerships

In my own experience of working in two kinds of institutions—the church and the academy—this resonates. For the sake of our discussion around a renaissance of love, I'd like to reflect for a moment on just two of these: quality personnel and a vibrant institutional culture.

On the question of personnel, there's much to be said for expertise in the skill sets required for one's work. I'm reminded of the story of the ship's captain and chief engineering officer who were arguing about whose role was most important:

> To prove their point to each other, they decided to swap places. The chief engineer ascended to the bridge, and the captain went to the engine room. Several hours later, the captain suddenly appeared on deck covered with oil and dirt. "Chief!" he yelled, waving aloft a monkey wrench. "You have to get down there: I can't make her go!" "Of course you can't," replied the chief. "She's aground!"[27]

Certainly, there's much to be said for the emotional maturity that would never have allowed such an immature, pride-driven predicament to come about. There's more to the life of healthy institutions than IQ. In fact, we know through the extensive research on EQ (emotional intelligence) done by Daniel Goleman and his team that "EQ contributes 80 to 90 percent of the competencies that distinguish outstanding from average leaders—and sometimes more."[28] I believe this is true not only of leaders, but of effective people at every level.

27. Story of the sea captain and the engineer can be found in *Leadership*, Vol. 12, no. 4.

28. Goleman, Boyatzis, and McKee, *Primal Leadership*, 5.

Is it any surprise that we see such a low level of confidence in the institutions in our countries when we look at the quality of their personnel, and especially their leaders? Most of us read the papers and just shake our heads as we hear the stories about what goes on in Congress, the White House, governor's mansions, corporate board rooms, and the salons of Hollywood. (I'm making a bipartisan statement here.) We're being led by many (certainly not all) who are morally hollowed out, and committed only to the preservation of their own power and prestige. Few of us trust the sources who give us our news to be honest with what they're telling us. Scandal after scandal flows down from our institutional leaders to the point where the bar of expectation has become so low that we think of politics as just an iterative limbo dance, while the populace wonders, "How low can you go?"

If our institutions are to be renewed, we'll need to have a different type of people serve in, and lead them. The hallmarks of these individuals will be clear moral values resting on transcendent beliefs. Charles Taylor believes that the most hopeful of these transcendent beliefs can be found in the Judeo-Christian tradition. Considering the question of our hope of finding a transcendent grounding for the modern self, Taylor writes,

> There is a large element of hope. It is a hope that I see that implicit in Judeo-Christian theism (however terrible the record of its adherents in history), and in its central promise of a divine affirmation of the human, more total than humans can ever attain unaided.[29]

That hope—of God's primal affirmation of humanity in creating them as his image-bearers—flows from the fountain of God's *agape* love. Precisely because of his transcendence, God provides a surer grounding for the self than the stripped down, secular moral sources (goods) of the Enlightenment, which Taylor identifies as reason, nature, and benevolence."[30]

When our self finds its way home in God, then our character is reshaped according to our remembered identity as his son or daughter. Specifically, as we abide in Christ, we bear his fruit in the world. This rediscovery of our true self in a transcendent source is the difference between virtue, which is always a human achievement funded by human sources and achieved by human means, and holiness, which takes its funding from God.

When our institutions are labored in and led by people grounded in God's love, they begin to flourish. These are people who think and act differently. As new men and new women they steward the institutions they serve

29. Taylor, *Sources of the Self*, 521.
30. Taylor, *Sources of the Self*, 520, 351, 408.

rather than use them. They keep their eyes on the final goal of the glory of God manifesting his *tikkun olam* in their little corner of his kingdom. They're more concerned with the commonweal of their institution than the commonwield of their own power for personal gain.

These leaders are marked by the transcendent values of their transcendent God and his descending kingdom. Because they live to love, they enter the work of serving, suffering, and sacrificing for the good of others.

Like darkness, bread and meat, all who are around them are affected by their light, leaven and salt, and made the better for it. Their spiritual stability makes them an un-anxious presence in anxious times. Their personal humility opens a space for others' vulnerability. Their mature wisdom permeates the minds and hearts of those around them. Over time, who they are changes who others become and the cultures of the institutions they lead.

People that are a host for love naturally become hosts for others because love is hospitable. People are drawn to them, often unknowingly, intuitively sensing there's life in them. When organizations and institutions are possessed of such people, the institutions themselves begin to change and become life-giving rather than life-sapping.

What would it be like if our institutions were filled with people who were humble, transparent, honest, and spiritually and emotionally mature? What would it be like if our institutions were led by people who were preoccupied with selflessness rather than selfies? Imagine our institutions staffed and led by men and women of strong character, deep determination, and clear vision. Imagine institutions where people disagreed fervently, but respected one another graciously—where people valued each other's counsel, even if it wasn't always followed. Imagine institutions where people trusted each other deeply, and always made generous assumptions concerning one another's motives.

When we begin to love one another as Christ has loved, to forgive one another as he has forgiven us, to regard one another as he regards us, then our institutions can be reformed, renewed, and repaired. But we must understand that this is first and foremost a *spiritual* project, and we must commit to it as such. There can be no renaissance of institutions without a renaissance of us.

## REPAIRING CULTURES

Since cultures are derivative of the "cult," the frames or worldviews they provide as moral sources are critical for how our culture is shaped. Historically, Western civilization was built on a three-legged stool. One leg is the Judeo-Christian religions, another is Greek philosophy, and the third is Roman law (as restructured under the Christian Emperor Justinian). What we've witnessed gradually over the last three hundred years or so has been the sawing-off of the first leg. So now our culture is wobbling. The details of how this occurred need not detain us here. I've sketched a little of it earlier in my remarks about modernism, postmodernism, and secularization. What's important to recognize is the shift. Let me suggest an illustration.

On October 17, 1989, an earthquake in San Francisco caused the Bay Bridge to Oakland to collapse. My sister and her husband lived just north of Berkeley in the town of Kensington, and their house was damaged in that earthquake. They discovered cracks running along their indoor fireplace, separating the wall and the chimney. Wanting to get it fixed, they called engineers to assess the damage. They were concerned about having to rebuild the fireplace.

The engineers told them that the fireplace wasn't the problem. The fireplace was securely anchored to the foundation. The problem was that the whole house had shifted on the foundation! This turned out to be very bad and expensive news for them.

My point is that our Western house has shifted on its foundation and stands in need of repair. The third leg needs to be reset for the stool to stop wobbling. Not only is the Judeo-Christian faith necessary in and of itself (as the third leg) for a cultural renaissance, but it also is necessary to interpret the meaning and purpose of the other two legs. Revealed religion undergirds both the best philosophy and the best law. Philosophy, which is based upon reason, needs the light of faith to make sense of itself. We remember Anselm's maxim: "I believe in order that I might understand." Faith and reason are complements, not enemies. Revelation is also needed to purify reason. Since our rational faculty was damaged in the fall, it too stands in need of the *tikkun olam*. It, too, requires redemption and repair.

While Greek philosophy has a deep and rich tradition from which we've drunk deeply, it doesn't possess the depth of moral-sourcing that Christian virtue and lived holiness deliver. At the end of the day, you can "choose" your philosophy, and it becomes your source for virtue. You can be a Stoic or an Epicurean and construct your life and world according to their principles, as you try to live them out by your own effort. At the end of the day, these are designer philosophies, because they're of human origin.[31]

Revealed religions are another matter. Rightly or wrongly, they claim truth from beyond, grounded in a personal source or transcendent authority.

---

31. Much the same can be said for eastern religions/philosophies as well. Even those who believe in sacred Scriptures—Hindus, for example—must face the problem of authority when those Scriptures point to multiple gods.

From this angle, whether a person believes or disbelieves in a revealed religion is immaterial. Its truth rises and falls on its own authority (God, gods, or Ideals), and not man.

The Judeo-Christian faith, as revealed religion, is also fundamental to our western understanding and ordering of the law. Of the eighteen figures in the "Great Lawgivers of History" frieze on the north and south walls of the Supreme Court, ten descend from the legal tradition grounded in Mosaic law. [32] Justice Stevens commented on this blending of secular and religious figures on the building:

> A carving of Moses holding the Ten Commandments, if that is the only adornment on a courtroom wall, conveys an equivocal message, perhaps of respect for Judaism, for religion in general or for law, the addition of carvings depicting Confucius and Muhammad may honor religion, or particular religions, to an extent that the First Amendment does not tolerate. Placement of secular figures such as Caesar Augustus, William Blackstone, Napoleon Bonaparte and John Marshall alongside these three religious leaders, however, signals respect not for great proselytizers but for great lawgivers. [33]

While Confucius and Muhammed are in the frieze, and rightly acknowledged as famous lawgivers, the West has never lived under either Confucianism or Sharia law. It has lived by the law of Moses and its lawgiving descendants. It's no accident that Moses—and not Confucius or the Greek legalist Solon—sits at the center of another frieze above the east pediment of the court.

So, when the West loses its first leg, it loses the transcendental part of its foundation. With this, the West loses its strongest support for its philosophy and law. This is also the part that secures our most important political commitments and values: Without a Guarantor, there are no guarantees.

For example, the "self-evident" notion that "all men are created equal" is an Enlightenment conceit. When Jefferson wrote those words, he was cashing that check at the Bible's bank, on the Creator's account. If the equality and intrinsic value of all humanity were self-evident, then we would never have had slavery, sex trafficking, the ghetto, the gulag, or the gas chamber.

---

32. "Courtroom Friezes: South and North Walls," https://www.supremecourt.gov/about/northandsouthwalls.pdf.

33. Biskupic, "Lawgivers: From Two Friezes, Great Figures of Legal History Gaze upon the Supreme Court Bench," March 11, 1998; https://www.washingtonpost.com/archive/1998/03/11/lawgivers-from-two-friezes-great-figures-of-legal-history-gaze-upon-the-supreme-court-bench/b9372b89-5b94-4fa2-81d9-300ee24913db/.

There's nothing in the charnel house of human history that remotely leads us to believe that such a truth as "all men are created equal" was ever "self-evident" to the world. It was the word of God, revealed to human beings, that evidenced these things.

It is God alone who is the guarantor of human life, equality, dignity, and ordered liberty, because those things are grounded in his love and revealed by his will. Remove the love of the Revealer as well as his revelation, and all else becomes subjective, debatable, and finally optional. As Rabbi Sacks keenly observed, the state then becomes the guarantor of our liberties, and what the state gives, the state can take away. Totalitarianism requires the elimination of revelation. This explains why communism and fascism alike have sought to eliminate biblical Christianity and its Jewish roots.

When we cease to worship the God of the Bible in our religious practice, we quickly lose the culture He underwrites in His love, will, and commandments. As we saw above, what we're left with is a cultural bouquet of flowers cut from the cult of faith and left to wither and die before our eyes. We can be good without God—but not for long. This is our present situation; our flowers are wilting.

If we're to participate in a cultural renaissance in the West, we need to wrestle again with the question of God. We must face the question of the existence of God and understand the implications of how we answer that question. Likewise, we must face the question of the identity of Christ and the implications of how we answer that question for doing the work of the *tikkun olam*.

Several recently published books are an intriguing invitation to just such a re-wrestling. Yoram Harzony's *Conservatism: A Rediscovery* calls for a reappraisal of faith in the God of the Bible as an essential feature of historical conservativism's effort to sustain Western culture. Stephen Meyer's *The Return of the God Hypothesis* investigates the role of science as a support for classical theism. *Is Atheism Dead?* by Eric Metaxas is an attempt to upend the "God is dead" inheritance of the 1960s. Tom Holland's *Dominion: The Making of the Western Mind* reminds us of just how powerful the Christian revolution has been. Carl Truman's *The Triumph of the Modern Self* explores the roots of who we've become and how we got here, particularly our revisionist notions of human sexuality.[34]

---

34. Meyer's title is a riff off Laplace's response to Napoleon which we saw earlier. When Napoleon asked why Laplace had not mentioned God in his new book on the workings of the universe, Laplace said, "Sir, I have no need of that hypothesis." Meyer argues that what we now know about the origins, fine-tuning, and information complexity of our universe—in other words, what we now know from *science* since Laplace's time, read without religious animus, makes a compelling case for belief in an intelligent

Western culture is at an inflection point where people of good will who are deeply concerned about the direction we're headed are beginning to reappraise the importance of the first leg of the stool, realizing that our culture isn't sustainable without it.

For the repair to extend to the culture of the West, we need an honest accounting of the ideas, forces, and events that pushed or drew us down this increasingly secular road. I'm not a historical determinist; I think the idea of there being an arc of history—normally portrayed as an impersonal inevitability—is nonsense. It's simply a hangover from that cocktail political party known as the Whig interpretation of history discussed earlier.

Real history is simply the recording of facts and events along with their interpretation. History doesn't create itself. I don't believe in an impersonal inevitability to history, but I believe that God is active in shaping history. The intersection of human choice and divine sovereignty can be evaluated only after the fact, if at all, before all things are finally revealed. I like to think of it as God waving to us in the rearview mirror.

At any rate, I think a society-wide prayer of examen is in order. If you're unfamiliar with it, the prayer of examen is a spiritual exercise of looking over the past day in the evening, or over the past year at its end, and examining in a deep way one's thoughts and actions. It requires a robust humility and a willingness to hear the voices of others—most especially God's. We simply can't proceed with our Western arrogance and not ask some hard questions about who we're becoming. These are first and foremost spiritual questions that go to the heart of our identity, how it's discerned, and how we live it out at all levels.

We need to assess not only our "sources of the self" but the state of the self who's selecting the sources. What's needed is deep repentance in the biblical sense of *metanoia*, a rethinking of everything, beginning with ourselves and our place in the world. As a culture, the West is running on

---

agent behind creation.

Metaxas's title is a riff off the front cover of Time Magazine in 1966 which read, "Is God Dead?" Like Meyer, his title calls for a reappraisal of the evidence. Metaxas argument for the death of atheism arises from his review (like Meyer's) of science, but also new textual and archeological data pointing toward the historical reliability of the biblical text, and the exploration of a host of questions around the issue of truth and how it is discerned.

Holland's *Dominion* retells the monumental impact the gospel of Jesus has had in the shaping of the western imaginary, even of those secularists who believe they have escaped it. He quotes the Jewish scholar Daniel Boyarin, who wrote that Christianity was "the most powerful of hegemonic cultural systems in the history of the world."

Truman's *The Rise and Triumph of the Modern Self* examines the thinking of Charles Taylor, Alasdair MacIntyre, and Philip Rieff in helping us map the migration of modern and post-modern man from our biblical foundations to today.

vapors. Trying to run faster in the wrong direction isn't helping. We're simply becoming more manic and frantic. Like our story of the prodigal son, it's time for a cultural pivot. It's time to come home to the Father's house. It's time to recognize that we need to be freed from our conjured "freedoms," which have served only to enslave us, and finally become free indeed. This can happen only when we return to the source of love, who is God himself.

It's time.

# Conclusion

*The vocation of a Christian disciple is to feed the soul as well as the mind; to offer the world a vision of men and women made whole by the love of God, the knowledge of creation, and the reality of things unseen; to see the beauty of the world in the light of eternity; to recapture the nobility of the human story and the dignity of the human person. This is the work that sets fire to the human heart. It starts the only kind of revolution that really changes anything: a revolution of love. Jesus said, "I came to cast fire upon the earth, and would that it were already kindled." Our task is to kindle that blaze, and then use all our strength to help it grow.*

—CHARLES J. CHAPUT

I wrote this book to fuel a conversation about the *centrality* of love for the church and the world. When the church loses sight of love, it loses sight of Jesus. When the church marginalizes love, it marginalizes God, for God is love. When that happens, the world is also in trouble. That's because the church is God's unique witness to what love truly is.

When the world cannot find God's love in and through the church, it will seek it in impostors. I think the time is upon us for a deep, intentional conversation about love. We live in a world full of problems. At the core, all these problems result from a failure of people to love as Christ has loved us. We must learn to love well again, and to love well means to love as Jesus loves.

I began by talking about our longing to be part of a story that's greater than we are, a story which, unlike Camelot, ends in eucatastrophe—the ultimate happy ending. That story is the story of God's love, which unfolded like a play in four acts.

Act one began in the Trinity as a community of love among the Father, the Son, and the Holy Spirit. Love, by its very nature spreads in self-sharing. The creation itself is an act of God's love and the arena for its glory. Love produces image-bearers in the likeness of God who are made to receive and reflect his love and extend its hegemony across the creation. Act two took us down the dark road of the collapse where the creature turned on the Creator and brought sin, suffering, and death into the world. This was followed by act three—in which God, in pursuing humanity, becomes man. In Jesus Christ, God bears away the sin of the world on the cross. In Jesus' resurrection from the dead, God opens the way to a new creation. This was the climax of the drama.

We explored deeply the dynamism of God's love for Israel, and the appearance of God in Jesus, Israel's Messiah-King. We examined the implications of his coming in love and its impact on his followers. We then explored an anatomy of the love of Jesus with a deep dive into Paul's paean to love in 1 Corinthians 13. From there we beheld the splendor of God's love as we saw this love refracted through the light spectrum in wavelengths of truth, goodness, justice, beauty, responsibility, and Spiritual tolerance.

Then we rounded the corner into act four. Here we headed into our own time as we reflected on God's invitation for us to live his love today, and the challenges we meet in accepting that invitation. Finally, we talked about God's *tikkun olam*, his repair of the world, and how we might join in that work at many levels.

Much more needs to be said, but not here—not now. I hope this has given you a place to begin your own thinking about love. I hope it will prompt a public conversation among you, your families and your friends and colleagues about how to become better lovers as modeled in Jesus' love. I hope this will be read by Christian people, Christian leaders, and especially by those of you who may not share the Christian faith, but share deeply its concern for the world. Let's talk to each other. Love beckons us to move beyond frustration and anger to engagement and understanding. We need to work together and help each other in God's *tikkun olam*, his repair of the world. "Dear friends, let us love one another, for love comes from God."[1]

1. 1 John 4:7.

# Bibliography

Allin, Dana. *Simple Discipleship: Grow Your Faith, Transform Your Community*. Colorado Spring, CO: NavPress, 2018.

Anselm, St. "Anselm: Proslogion." Open Philosophy Texts. https://www. openphilosophytexts.com/anselm-proslogion.

Arendt, Hannah. *Eichmann in Jerusalem: A Report on the Banality of Evil*. London: Penguin, 2022.

Augustinus, Aurelius. Confessions. Translated by Henry Chadwick. Oxford: Oxford Univ. Press, 1991.

Augustine, St. "Saint Augustine Quotes about Love: A-Z Quotes." AZquotes. https://www.azquotes.com/author/663-Saint_Augustine/tag/love.

Augustine, St. and Daniel Day Williams. "The Spirit and the Forms of Love." Religion Online. https://www.religion-online.org/book/the-spirit-and-the-forms-of-love.

Bailey, Kenneth E. *The Cross and the Prodigal*. Saint Louis: Concordia Pub. House, 1973.

Barth, Karl. *Church Dogmatics*. G.W. Bromiley, T.F. Torrance eds. London: T & T Clark, 1975.

Barton, David. *The Myth of Separation: What Is the Correct Relationship between Church and State?: An Examination of the Supreme Court's Own Decisions*. Aledo, TX: WallBuilder Press, 1992.

Bauerschmidt, Frederick Christian. *The Love That Is God: An Invitation to Christian Faith*. Grand Rapids: Eerdmans, 2020.

Benner, David G. *Desiring God's Will: Aligning Our Hearts with the Heart of God*. Downers Grove: IVP Books, 2015.

Biskupic, Joan. "Lawgivers: From Two Friezes, Great Figures of Legal History Gaze upon the Supreme Court Bench." The Washington Post. WP Company, March 11, 1998. https://www.washingtonpost.com/archive/1998/03/11/lawgivers-from-two-friezes-great-figures-of-legal-history-gaze-upon-the-supreme-court-bench/b9372b89-5b94-4fa2-81d9-300ee24913db/.

Bonhoeffer, Dietrich, *Life Together*. Translated with Introduction by John Doberstein. San Francisco: Harper and Row, 1978.

Boorstin, Daniel J. *The Discoverers: A History of Man's Search to Know His World and Himself*. N.Y.: Vintage, Random House, 1985.

Brenan, Megan. "Americans' Confidence in Major U.S. Institutions Dips." Gallup.com. Gallup, September 21, 2022. https://news.gallup.com/poll/352316/americans-confidence-major-institutions-dips.aspx.

Buechner, Frederick, and George Connor. *Listening to Your Life: Daily Meditations with Frederick Buechner*. San Francisco: HarperSanFrancisco, 1992.

Bullock, Jeffrey. "Six Observations about Presbyterian Theological Education: The View from My Window." *Theology Matters* (Vol. 28, No.1, Winter 2022).

Cahoone, Lawrence E. *From Modernism to Postmodernism*. Oxford, U.K.: Blackwell, 1996.

Cannell, Linda. *Theological Education Matters: Leadership Education for the Church*. Newburgh, IN: EDCOT for MorgenBooks, 2006.

Carroll, Vincent, and Dave Shiflett. *Christianity on Trial: Arguments against Anti-Religious Bigotry*. San Francisco: Encounter Books, 2002.

Charlesworth, James H. The Old Testament Pseudepigrapha. Vol. 1. Garden City, N.Y.: Doubleday, 1983.

Chesterton, G. K. *The Complete Father Brown*. Oxford: Benediction Classics, 2012.

Clairvaux, Bernard of. *The Love of God*. Edited by James M. Houston. Classics of Faith and Devotion. Portland: Multnomah, 1983.

Cohen, Norman M., "Love Your Enemy? No Way! Treat Him Fairly. Way!" Reform Judaism. https://reformjudaism.org/learning/torah-study/torah-commentary/love-your-enemy-no-way-treat-him-fairly-way.

"Courtroom Friezes: South and North Walls - Supreme Court of the United ..." https://www.supremecourt.gov/about/northandsouthwalls.pdf.

Cox, A. Cleveland, Alexander Roberts, and James Donaldson, eds. *The Ante-Nicene Fathers*. Grand Rapids: Eerdmans, 1981.

Cranfield, CEB. *A Critical and Exegetical Commentary on the Epistle to the Romans*, Vol. I. Edinburgh: T. & T. Clark, 1979.

Davies, Paul. *God and the New Physics*. N.Y.: Simon & Schuster, 1983.

Dawkins, Richard. *The Blind Watchmaker*. N.Y.: Norton, 1996.

———. *The God Delusion*. Boston, N.Y.: Houghton Mifflin, 2006.

Delling, Gerhard, "τέλειος" Kittel, Gerhard and Gerhard Friedrich, eds., *Theological Dictionary of the New Testament*, Vol. 8,

Dembski, William A., ed. *Mere Creation: Science, Faith and Intelligent Design*. Downers Grove: InterVarsity Press, 1998.

Denton, Michael. *The Wonder of Water: Water's Profound Fitness for Life on Earth and Mankind*. Seattle: Discovery Institute, 2017.

Diamant, Jeff. "Teens in the South More Likely than Other U.S. teens to Experience Religion in Public School." https://www.pewresearch.org/fact-tank/2019/12/10/teens-in-the-south-more-likely-than-other-u-s-teens-to-experience-religion-in-public-school/.

Dockery, David S. *The Challenge of Postmodernism: An Evangelical Engagement*. Grand Rapids: Baker Academic, 2001.

Donne, John, Charles M. Coffin, and Denis Donoghue. The Complete Poetry and Selected Prose of John Donne. New York: Modern Library, 2001.

Douthit, Ross. "A Gentler Christendom." *First Things* (June/July 2022).

Duckworth, Angela. *Grit: The Power of Passion and Perseverance*. N.Y.: Scribner, 2016.

Ecklund, Elaine Howard, David R. Johnson, and Brandon Vaidyanathan. *Secularity and Science: What Scientists around the World Really Think about Religion*. New York: Oxford University Press, 2019.

Eidsmoe, John. *Christianity and the Constitution: The Faith of Our Founding Fathers*. Grand Rapids, MI: Baker Book House, 1987.

Elizaga, Carmen. "What Is the Difference between Post-Modernism and Marxism?" - Quora. https://www.quora.com/What-is-the-difference-between-post-modernism-and-Marxism.

Ens, Gaylord. *Love Revolution: Rediscovering the Lost Command of Jesus.* 2nd ed. Chico: Love Revolution Press, 2011.

"Eucatastrophe." Wikipedia. Wikimedia Foundation, February 2, 2023. https://en.wikipedia.org/wiki/Eucatastrophe.

Flew, Antony, and Roy Abraham Varghese. *There Is a God: How the World's Most Notorious Atheist Changed His Mind.* New York, N.Y.: HarperOne, an imprint of HarperCollinsPublishers, 2007.

Foerster, Werner, "ἄσωτος-ἀσωτία," Kittel, Gerhard and Gerhard Friedrich, eds. *Theological Dictionary of the New Testament,* Vol. 1.

Foerster, Werner, "διάβολος," Kittel, Gerhard and Gerhard Friedrich, eds. *Theological Dictionary of the New Testament,* Vol. 2.

Frankl, Viktor E. *Man's Search for Meaning: The Classic Tribute to Hope: From the Holocaust.* N.Y.: Simon and Schuster, 1963.

Fromm, Erich. *The Art of Loving.* New York: HarperPerennial, 1956.

Fusselman, Midge. "What Blaise Pascal Saw in a November Night of Fire." The Federalist, November 29, 2017. https://thefederalist.com/2017/11/23/blaise-pascal-saw-november-night-fire-inaugurated-year-grace/.

Gates, Bill. "A Quote from The Road Ahead." Goodreads. https://www.goodreads.com/quotes/336336-dna-is-like-a-computer-program-but-far-far-more.

Geri Walton. "Festival of Reason during the French Revolution." November 3, 2019. https://www.geriwalton.com/festival-of-reason/.

Ghorayshi, Azeen, and Roni Caryn Rabin. "Teen Girls Report Record Levels of Sadness, C.D.C. Finds." The New York Times. The New York Times, February 13, 2023. https://www.nytimes.com/2023/02/13/health/teen-girls-sadness-suicide-violence.html.

Gibran, Kahlil. *Jesus the Son of Man: His Words and His Deeds as Told and Recorded.* New York: Knopf, 1928.

Goggin, Jamin, and Kyle Strobel. *The Way of the Dragon or the Way of the Lamb: Searching for Jesus' Path of Power in a Church that Has Abandoned It.* N.Y.: Thomas Nelson, 2021.

Goleman, Daniel. "Empathy" (HBR Emotional Intelligence Series). Google Books. Google. https://books.google.com/books?hl=en&lr=&id=qGofDgAAQBAJ&oi=fnd&pg=PT7&dq=daniel%2Bgoleman%2Bon%2Bempathy&ots=zDMOunlS25&sig=eZuyD1dPeDL-iJuSAkid1JxUmoc#v=onepage&q=daniel%20goleman%20on%20empathy&f=false.

Goleman, Daniel, Richard E. Boyatzis, and Annie McKee. *Primal Leadership: Learning to Lead with Emotional Intelligence.* Boston: Harvard Business School Press, 2004.

Graham, Ruth. "Funeral Service Transcript." Billy Graham Memorial, September 11, 2019. https://memorial.billygraham.org/funeral-service-transcript/.

Hankins, James. "Imprudent Expertise." *First Things* (June/July 2020), 25.

Hazony, Yoram. *Conservativism: A Rediscovery.* Washington, D.C.: Regnery Gateway, 2022.

Heeren, Fred. *Show Me God: What the Message from Space Is Telling Us about God.* Olathe, KS: Day Star Publications, 2004.

Henley, William Ernest. "Invictus by William Ernest Henley." Poetry Foundation. https://www.poetryfoundation.org/poems/51642/invictus.

Hill, Jonathan. *What Has Christianity Ever Done for Us?: How It Shaped the Modern World.* Downers Grove: InterVarsity Press, 2005.

Holland, Tom. *Dominion: The Making of the Western Mind.* London: Little Brown, 2019.

Houston, J. M., and Jens Zimmermann. *Sources of the Christian Self: A Cultural History of Christian Identity.* Grand Rapids, MI: William B. Eerdmans, 2018.

Hysolli, Eriona. "A DNA Synthesis and Decoding Strategy Tailored for Storing and Retrieving Digital Information." Wyss Institute, August 6, 2019. https://wyss.harvard.edu/news/save-it-in-.

Isaac, Gordon L., and Eckhard J. Schnabel, eds. *Reformation Celebration: The Significance of Scripture, Grace, Faith, and Christ.* Peabody, MA: Hendrickson, 2019.

Jenson, Robert W., and Adam Eitel. A Theology in Outline: Can These Bones Live? New York, NY: Oxford University Press, 2016.

Kaufmann, Walter Arnold, and Friedrich Wilhelm Nietzsche. *The Portable Nietzsche.* New York: Viking Press, 1982.

Keener, Craig S. *Christobiography: Memory, History, and the Reliability of the Gospels.* Grand Rapids: Eerdmans, 2019.

Kerrigan, Mike. "Opinion | Sports Movies That Continue to Inspire." *The Wall Street Journal.* Dow Jones & Company, April 16, 2023. https://www.wsj.com/articles/sports-movies-that-continue-to-inspire-eighties-beauty-transcendent-friends-texting-5f77c0e7.

Kimbrell, Andrew. *The Human Body Shop: The Engineering and Marketing of Life.* San Francisco, CA: HarperSanFrancisco, 1994.

King, Martin Luther. https://christiananimalethics.com/martin-luther-king-jr-quotes/?gclid=CjwKCAjw9LSSBhBsEiwAKtfonxYSUY3PwAX_Gwm_j4XrlsQYXTrUWSlWF2WOHBXCkqIxA35-6_h6vxoCRToQAvD_BwE

King, Martin Luther, and Coretta Scott King. *Strength to Love.* 2nd ed. Philadelphia: Fortress, 1982.

Kissinger, Henry, Eric Schmidt, and Daniel Huttenlocher, "ChatGPT Heralds an Intellectual Revolution," *The Wall Street Journal,* Saturday/Sunday Feb. 25–26, 2023, A-13.

Kittel, Gerhard, Gerhard Friedrich, Geoffrey W. Bromiley, and Ronald E. Pitkin, eds. *Theological Dictionary of the New Testament.* 10 Volumes. Translated by Geoffrey W. Bromiley. Grand Rapids: Eerdmans, 1964.

Kline, Meredith G. The Structure of Biblical Authority. Eugene, OR: Wipf and Stock Publishers, 1997.

Lake, Kirsopp, trans. *The Apostolic Fathers: Vol I.* Loeb Classical Library. Cambridge, MA: Harvard University Press, 1977.

Leclercq, Jean. *The Love of Learning and the Desire for God. A Study of Monastic Culture.* Translated by Catharine Misrahi. 2nd ed. New York: Fordham University Press, 1974.

Lerner, Alan, and Frederick Lowe. "Camelot Script." Scribd. Scribd. https://www.scribd.com/doc/81524205/Camelot-Script#.

Lewis, C.S., *The Abolition of Man.* N.Y.: Macmillan, 1965.

———. *The Four Loves.* London: Harcourt, Brace, Jovanovich, 1960.

———. *Mere Christianity.* N.Y.: Macmillan, 1960.

———. *Surprised by Joy.* N.Y.: Harcourt, Brace & Co, 1955.

———. *The Weight of Glory and Other Addresses*. San Francisco: HarperSanFrancisco, 2001.

Lewis, William. "The Spirit and the Forms of Love." Religion Online. https://www.religion-online.org/book/the-spirit-and-the-forms-of-love/.

"Love Has a Name." Wikipedia. Wikimedia Foundation, December 15, 2022. https://en.wikipedia.org/wiki/Love_Has_a_Name.

Luther, Martin. *Martin Luther's Basic Theological Writings:* Edited by Timothy Frank Lull. Minneapolis: Fortress, 1989.

Margenau, Henry, and Roy Abraham Varghese. *Cosmos, BIOS, Theos: Scientists Reflect on Science, God, and the Origins of the Universe, Life, and Homo Sapiens*. La Salle, IL: Open Court, 1992.

Martin, Regis. *The Last Things: Death, Judgment, Heaven, Hell*. San Francisco: Ignatius, 1998.

McGrath, Alister E. *Christian Theology: An Introduction*. Chichester, West Sussex: Blackwell, 1994.

McLaughlin, Rebecca. *Confronting Christianity: 12 Hard Questions for the World's Largest Religion*. Wheaton: Crossway, 2019.

Merton, Thomas. *The New Man*. N.Y.: Farrar, Straus & Cudahy, 1961.

Meslier, Jean. "Jean Meslier." Wikipedia. Wikimedia Foundation. https://en.wikipedia.org/wiki/Jean_Meslier#cite_ref-13.

Metaxas, Eric. *Is Atheism Dead?* N.Y.: Regnery, 2021.

Meyer, Stephen C. *Return of the God Hypothesis: Three Scientific Discoveries Revealing the Mind behind the Universe*. N.Y.: HarperCollins, 2021.

"Milestone Documents." National Archives. https://www.ourdocuments.gov/doc.php?flash=false&doc=15&page=tranScript.

Miller, Calvin. *The Singer Trilogy: The Mythic Retelling of the Story of the New Testament*. Vol. 3 *The Finale*. Downers Grove, Ill: InterVarsity Press, 1990.

Miller, Donald. *Blue like Jazz: Nonreligious Thoughts on Christian Spirituality*. Nashville: Thomas Nelson, 2003.

Mueller-Vollmer, Kurt, and Markus Messling. "Wilhelm Von Humboldt." Stanford Encyclopedia of Philosophy. Stanford University, May 24, 2022. https://plato.stanford.edu/entries/wilhelm-humboldt/#RetuGermPublEducPoli.

Muller, Richard. *Dictionary of Latin and Greek Theological Terms: Drawn Principally from Protestant Scholastic Theology*. Grand Rapids: Baker Book House, 1985.

Nagle, D. Brendan and Stanley M. Burstein, The Ancient World: Readings in Social and Cultural History. "Julian the Apostate." Then Again. http://www.thenagain.info/Classes/Sources/Julian.html.

Nash, Robert J. *Answering the "Virtuecrats": A Moral Conversation on Character Education*. New York: Teachers College Press, 1997.

Niebuhr, Helmut Richard. *The Kingdom of God in America*. Middletown, CT: Wesleyan University Press, 1988.

Noll, Mark A. *America's Book: The Rise and Decline of a Bible Civilization, 1794-1911*. N.Y.: Oxford University Press, 2022.

———. *America's God: From Jonathan Edwards to Abraham Lincoln*. Oxford: Oxford University Press, 2005.

Ortlund, Dane Calvin. *Gentle and Lowly: The Heart of Christ for Sinners and Sufferers*. Wheaton: Crossway, 2020.

"Patriarch Kirill of Moscow." Wikipedia. Wikimedia Foundation, March 6, 2023. https://en.wikipedia.org/wiki/Patriarch_Kirill_of_Moscow.

Patterson, Mark. "Flourish Institute of Theology." Vimeo, March 22, 2023. https://vimeo.com/703005349.

Peterson, Eugene H. *Eat This Book: A Conversation in the Art of Spiritual Reading.* Grand Rapids: Eerdmans, 2006.

"Religion in the Public Schools" Pew Research Center. October 3, 2019. https://www.pewresearch.org/religion/2019/10/03/religion-in-the-public-schools-2019-update/.

Pfizenmaier, Tom. *For My Daughters: A Father Reflects on Family, Friendship, and Faith.* Cheyenne, WY: Pen2Paper Press, 2023.

Pickard, Michael. *Rediscover the Bible: Or Discover It for the First Time.* Kitsap Publishing, 2017.

Poss, Jordan. "What's Wrong, Chesterton?" Jordan M. Poss. Jordan M. Poss, February 28, 2019. https://www.jordanmposs.com/blog/2019/2/27/whats-wrong-chesterton.

"Preamble." European Union Agency for Fundamental Rights, December 17, 2019. https://fra.europa.eu/en/eu-charter/article/0-preamble#:~:text=EU%20Charter%20of%20Fundamental%20Rights,-Previous%20title&text=Conscious%20of%20its%20spiritual%20and,and%20the%20orule%20of%20law.

Putnam, Robert D., David E. Campbell, and Shaylyn Romney Garrett. *American Grace: How Religion Divides and Unites Us.* New York: Simon & Schuster Paperbacks, 2012.

Rathore, Devangana. "50+ St Augustine Quotes from the Philosopher and Theologian of Hippo." Kidadl. Kidadl, February 13, 2023. https://kidadl.com/articles/st-augustine-quotes-from-the-philosopher-and-theologian-of-hippo.

Ratzinger, Joseph Cardinal. *Truth and Tolerance: Christian Belief and World Religions.* San Francisco: Ignatius Press, 2004.

"Religious Landscape Study." Pew Research Center's Religion & Public Life Project. Pew Research Center, June 13, 2022. https://www.pewresearch.org/religion/religious-landscape-study/belief-in-absolute-standards-for-right-and-wrong/.

Renn, Aaron M. "The Three Worlds of Evangelicalism." *First Things*, February 1, 2022. https://www.firstthings.com/article/2022/02/the-three-worlds-of-evangelicalism.

Rich, Hannah. "Anglican Churches in the UK Are Shrinking in Size but Not Impact." ChristianityToday.com. Christianity Today, November 24, 2020. https://www.christianitytoday.com/ct/2020/november-web-only/church-of-england-decline-theos-growing-good-social-action.html.

Roman, Ancient. "Aureus (Coin) Portraying Emperor Tiberius." The Art Institute of Chicago. Arts of the Ancient Mediterranean and Byzantium. https://www.artic.edu/artworks/5602/aureus-coin-portraying-emperor-tiberius.

Roose, Kevin. "A Conversation with Bing's Chatbot Left Me Deeply Unsettled." *The New York Times.* The New York Times, February 16, 2023. https://www.nytimes.com/2023/02/16/technology/bing-chatbot-microsoft-chatgpt.html.

Rosa, Hartmut. *The Uncontrollability of the World.* Translated by James C. Wagner. Cambridge, UK: Polity Press, 2020.

Rose, Steve. "Alain De Botton's 'Temples for Atheists' Have a Foundational Flaw." *The Guardian.* Guardian News and Media, January 26, 2012. https://www.theguardian.com/artanddesign/2012/jan/26/alain-de-botton-temple-atheists.

Russell, Jeffrey Burton. *Exposing Myths about Christianity: A Guide to Answering 145 Viral Lies and Legends*. Downers Grove, IL: IVP Books, 2012.

Sacks, Jonathan. "Covenant & Conversation: Mishpatim: Helping an Enemy: Rabbi Sacks." The Rabbi Sacks Legacy, January 11, 2022. https://rabbisacks.org/covenant-conversation-5769-mishpatim-helping-an-enemy/.

———. "Rabbi Jonathan Sacks' Speech on Religious Freedom at Becket Canterbury Dinner." YouTube. YouTube, May 16, 2014. https://www.youtube.com/watch?v=ocXAqbVy9o8.

Saint-Exupéry Antoine de. *Wind, Sand and Stars*. New York: Harcourt, Brace & World, 1967.

Schaff, Philip, Henry Wace, eds. *A Select Library of the Nicene and Post-Nicene Fathers of the Christian Church*. Grand Rapids, MI: Eerdmans, 1979.

Schmidt, Alvin J. *How Christianity Changed the World*. Grand Rapids: Zondervan, 2004.

Schweitzer, Albert. *Quest for the Historical Jesus: A Critical Study of Its Progress from Reimarus to Wrede*. New York: Macmillan Co., 1968.

"Scribes and Scripture (Part One): Digging for Truth Episode 196." Home - Associates for Biblical Research. https://biblearchaeology.org/research/the-daniel-9-24-27-project/4364-john-2-12-21-and-herodian-chronology.

Shaw, Perry. *Transforming Theological Education: A Practical Handbook for Integrated Learning*. Carlisle, UK: Langham Global Library, 2022.

Singer, Peter. *Rethinking Life and Death: The Construction of a New Ethic*. New York: St. Martin's Press, 1995.

Smith, Christian, and Melinda Lundquist Denton. *Soul Searching: The Religious and Spiritual Lives of American Teenagers*. Oxford: Oxford University Press, 2011.

Smith, Gordon. *Institutional Intelligence: How to Build an Effective Organization*. Downers Grove: IVP Academic, 2017.

Stählin, Gustav, "ἁμαρτάνω," Kittel, Gerhard and Gerhard Friedrich, eds., *Theological Dictionary of the New Testament*, Vol. 1.

Souza, Dinesh d'. *What's so Great about Christianity*. Washington, D.C: Regnery, 2007.

Stark, Rodney. *For the Glory of God: How Monotheism Led to Reformations, Science, Witch-Hunts, and the End of Slavery*. Princeton, NJ: Princeton University Press, 2003.

Taylor, Charles. *A Secular Age*. Cambridge: Belknap Press of Harvard University Press, 2018.

———. *Sources of the Self*. Cambridge: Harvard University Press, 1989.

"Tikkun Olam." Wikipedia. Wikimedia Foundation, March 25, 2023. https://en.wikipedia.org/wiki/Tikkun_olam.

Tolkien, J.R.R. *The Lord of the Rings*. Boston: Houghton Mifflin Co., 1993.

———. "Eucatastrophe." Wikipedia. Wikimedia Foundation, February 2, 2023. https://en.wikipedia.org/wiki/Eucatastrophe.

Tocqueville, Alexis de, Henry Reeve, and John C. Spencer. *The Republic of the United States of America: And Its Political Institutions, Reviewed and Examined*. Memphis, TN: General Books, 2010.

Torrance, Thomas F. *Atonement: The Person and Work of Christ*. Robert T. Walker, ed. Downers Grove: InterVarsity Press Academic, 2009.

———. *Incarnation: The Person and Life of Christ*. Robert T. Walker, ed. Downers Grove: InterVarsity Press Academic, 2008.

Trevan, Tim. "Why Scientists Got the Covid Lab Leak Wrong." *The Wall Street Journal*, Tuesday, March 7, 2023, A15.

Truman, Carl R., and Rod Dreher. *The Rise and Triumph of the Modern Self: Cultural Amnesia, Expressive Individualism, and the Road to Sexual Revolution.* Wheaton: Crossway, 2020.

"Ukraine: Apparent War Crimes in Russia-Controlled Areas." *Human Rights Watch*, October 11, 2022. https://www.hrw.org/news/2022/04/03/ukraine-apparent-war-crimes-russia-controlled-areas.

Vandenbroucke François, Louis Bouyer, and Jean Leclercq. *The Spirituality of the Middle Ages.* N.Y.: Seabury Press, 1982.

Vine, W.E. *Vine's Complete Expository Dictionary of Old and New Testament Words.* Nashville: T. Nelson, 1984.

von, Balthasar, Hans Urs. *Love Alone Is Credible.* Translated by D. C. Schindler. San Francisco: Ignatius Press, 2004.

Washer, Paul. "'God Saved You for Himself; God Saved You by Himself; God Saved You from Himself." #Savedbyfaith #Gospel #Gospelofjesus Pic.twitter.com/oq5ic3bhhc." Twitter. Twitter, January 18, 2019. https://twitter.com/paulwasher/status/1086231884139499525?lang=en.

"Milestone Documents." National Archives, August 3, 2022. https://www.ourdocuments.gov/doc.php?flash=false&doc=15&page=tranScript.

"Webmd Common Health Topics A-Z - Find Reliable Health and Medical Information on Common Topics from A to Z." WebMD. WebMD. https://www.webmd.com/a-to-z-guides/hematidrosis-hematohidrosi.

Walton, Geri. "Festival of Reason during the French Revolution." Geri Walton, November 3, 2019. http://www.geriwalton.com/festival-of-reason/.

Wellman, Jack. "Top 25 Christian Quotes about Love." ChristianQuotes.info, December 4, 2019. https://www.christianquotes.info/top-quotes/top-25-christian-quotes-about-love/.

Wright, N.T., "Beginning to Think about the New Creation." N.T. Wright Online, January 29, 2020. https://www.ntwrightonline.org/beginning-to-think-about-the-new-creation/.

———. *Broken Signposts: How Christianity Makes Sense of the World.* New York: HarperOne, an imprint of HarperCollins Publishers, 2020.

———. *The Day the Revolution Began Reconsidering the Meaning of Jesus's Crucifixion.* New York: HarperOne, an imprint of HarperCollinsPublishers, 2018.

———. *History and Eschatology: Jesus and the Promise of Natural Theology.* Waco: Baylor University, 2018.

———. *Paul for Everyone. Ephesians, Philippians, Colossians and Philemon.* Louisville, KY: Westminster John Knox Press, 2015.

———. *Surprised by Hope: Rethinking Heaven, the Resurrection, and the Mission of the Church.* N.Y.: HarperOne, an imprint of HarperCollinsPublishers, 2008.

Zerwick, Max, and Mary Donald Grosvenor. *A Grammatical Analysis of the Greek New Testament.* Rome: Biblical Institute Press, 1974.

*Zondervan NASB Exhaustive Concordance.* Reuben A. Olson, Robert L. Thomas, Peter P. Ahn, W. Don Wilkins, eds. Grand Rapids: Zondervan, 2000.

# Subject Index

# Scripture Index

## Isaiah

| | |
|---|---|
| 4:2 | 91n8 |
| 5:20—21 | 75, 75n4 |
| 28:5 | 90n5 |
| 42:1 | 20n1 |
| 64:11 | 90n6 |
| 66:1 | 36n9 |

## Jeremiah

| | |
|---|---|
| 25:15—17 | 153n39 |
| 49:12 | 153n39 |
| 51:7 | 153n39 |

## Lamentations

| | |
|---|---|
| 2:1—5 | 91n8 |
| 2:5 | 91n8 |

## Ezekiel

| | |
|---|---|
| 16:14 | 91n8 |
| 16:15 | 91n8 |
| 37:3—5 | 201n13 |

## Amos

| | |
|---|---|
| 2:4—8 | 17n11 |
| 5:7—15 | 17n11 |

## Jonah

| | |
|---|---|
| 4:9—11 | 110n4 |

## Habakkuk

| | |
|---|---|
| 2:14 | 37n14, 137 |
| 2:16 | 153n39 |

## Zechariah

| | |
|---|---|
| 12:2—3 | 153n39 |

# NEW TESTAMENT

## Matthew

| | |
|---|---|
| 3:17 | 41n4 |
| 4:17 | 158 |
| 5:17 | 24n12 |
| 5:44—48 | 113n9 |
| 7:3—5 | 186n8 |
| 7:21—23 | 52n2 |
| 12:6 | 128n13 |
| 13:44 | 160–61 |
| 13:45—46 | 161n5 |
| 19:28 | 182n3 |
| 24:1—2 | 128n13 |
| 28 | 168 |

## Mark

| | |
|---|---|
| 1:15 | 158, 159 |
| 10:45 | 22n8, 124n4 |

## Luke

| | |
|---|---|
| 21:5 | 90n6 |
| 22:42 | 123n1, 154 |

## John

| | |
|---|---|
| 1 | 37 |
| 1:4—5 | 63 |
| 1:5 | 71n15 |
| 1:14 | 37n11, 92 |
| 2:12—21 | 36–37n10, 37 |
| 2:19—21 | 128n13 |
| 3:16—17 | 26:21 |
| 8:12 | 71n14 |
| 8:34 | 17n12 |
| 8:46 | 21n4 |
| 11:33 | 43n9 |
| 11:36 | 43n9 |
| 13 | 168 |
| 13:1 | 46n26 |
| 14:6 | 72n18 |
| 14:20 | 107n9 |
| 15:1—4 | 185n7 |
| 15:4 | 107n9 |
| 15:13 | 103n3 |
| 17:10 | 107n9 |
| 17:20—23 | 37n13 |
| 17:20—24 | 107n9 |
| 19:11 | 72n17 |

# Acts

| | |
|---|---|
| 2:23 | 126n8 |
| 3:21 | 182n3 |

# Romans

| | |
|---|---|
| 1:7 | 44n16 |
| 1:24—27 | 17n11 |
| 3:10—18 | 25n17 |
| 5:8 | 44n16 |
| 5:8—10 | 116n14 |
| 5:11 | 41n6 |
| 5:12 | 14n6 |
| 5:18—19 | 14n6, 26:20 |
| 6:23 | 14n6, 25n18 |
| 7:14—24 | 17n12 |
| 8:5—8 | 16n10 |
| 8:19—25 | 18n14 |
| 8:21 | 157 |
| 8:28 | 44n16 |
| 8:29 | 21n5, 41n5 |
| 8:30 | 138 |
| 8:31 | 34n5 |
| 8:35—39 | 44n16 |
| 11:15 | 41n6 |
| 12:1—2 | 160n3 |

# 1 Corinthians

| | |
|---|---|
| 1:21 | 16n10 |
| 2:9 | 108n10 |
| 3:16 | 92n10 |
| 3:16—17 | 37n13 |
| 6:19 | 92n10 |
| 6:19—20 | 37n13 |
| 13 | 50, 174n8, 192, 215 |
| 13:1—3 | 52n1 |
| 13:4—8 | 53n3 |
| 13:13 | 175 |
| 15:17 | 57n9 |
| 15:22 | 14n6 |
| 15:26 | 43n9 |
| 15:45—49 | 21n3 |

# 2 Corinthians

| | |
|---|---|
| 1:20 | 40n2 |
| 4:4 | 118n19 |
| 4:18 | 57n12 |
| 5:2 | 21n4 |
| 5:17—20 | 41n6 |
| 5:19 | 128n14 |
| 5:21 | 25n19, 83n5, 103n2, 130n20 |

# Galatians

| | |
|---|---|
| 2:20 | 45n19 |
| 3:13 | 23 |
| 4:4 | 127n12 |

# Ephesians

| | |
|---|---|
| 1 | 46n21 |
| 1:4 | 40n1 |
| 1:5—6 | 45n20 |
| 1:18 | 157 |
| 2:1 | 14n6 |
| 2:1—3 | 17n12 |
| 4:17 | 16n10 |
| 6:12 | 117n18 |

# Philippians

| | |
|---|---|
| 2:9—11 | 155n42 |
| 3:8 | 161n4 |
| 3:20 | 195n1 |

# Colossians

| | |
|---|---|
| 1:24 | 129n17 |
| 2:13—15 | 87n13 |

# 1 Thessalonians

| | |
|---|---|
| 1:4 | 46n22 |
| 3:12 | 46n22 |
| 4:9 | 46n22 |

# 2 Thessalonians

| | |
|---|---|
| 2:16 | 46n22 |
| 3:5 | 46n22 |

# 1 Timothy

| | |
|---|---|
| 1:14 | 46n22 |
| 6:10 | 17n11 |